ILLINOIS CENTRAL COLLEGE   2

A12901 316648

W9-BXQ-618

Educational Freedom for a Democratic Society

A Critique of National Goals, Standards, and Curriculum

Edited by Ron Miller

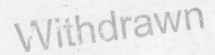
Withdrawn

I.C.C. LIBRARY

Resource Center for Redesigning Education
PO Box 298, Brandon, VT 05733-0298
1-800-639-4122

LC
84
.R1
1995

Books by Ron Miller

The Renewal of Meaning in Education: Responses to the Cultural and Ecological Crisis of Our Times. Brandon, VT: Holistic Education Press, 1993 (Editor)

What Are Schools For? Holistic Education in American Culture. Brandon, VT: Holistic Education Press, 1992

New Directions in Education: Selections from Holistic Education Review. Brandon, VT: Holistic Education Press, 1991 (Editor)

Educational freedom for a democratic society: a critique of national standards, goals, and curriculum / edited by Ron Miller

p. cm.

ISBN 1-885580-01-0

1. Miller, Ron 2. Education - Standards - United States 3. Education and state - United States 4. Education - United States - Aims and objectives 5. Educational planning - United States 6. Academic freedom - United States

LC89.F7 1995

© 1995 by Resource Center for Redesigning Education
(Box 298, Brandon, VT 05733-0298). All rights reserved.
ISBN 1-885580-01-0

Table of Contents

Introduction: The Case Against National Goals, Standards, and Curriculum

Ron Miller

How can the pluralism that we claim to value, the liberty that we prize, be reconciled with a "state pedagogy" designed to serve state purposes?
— *Charles Leslie Glenn* (1988, 12)

The educational literature and mass media of the 1990s are filled with repeated calls for national goals, high standards, and strict accountability in education. Presidents and corporate leaders insist that the very survival of our economy, indeed our nation, are at stake if tougher standards are not adopted and enforced; hearing little dissent, many educators and citizens complacently agree. But there are many reasons — many urgent and compelling reasons — that we as a nation should *not* embrace federally mandated goals and standards in education.

Most criticism of national standards has come not from highly visible politicians or powerful corporate executives but from professional educators and concerned citizens whose influence on educational policy is negligible. For example, James Moffett, a leading theorist of language arts education over the past 30 years, wrote a powerful, visionary book in 1994 — *The Universal Schoolhouse* — that presented a thorough and compelling case for educational freedom and analyzed the political and intellectual roots of the national standards agenda. (A portion of the book is reprinted in this volume.) Needless to say, the book did not receive the media attention given to the *Nation at Risk* report or the education "summit" between President Bush and the nation's governors. The present volume, *Educational Freedom for a Democratic Society*, will probably not receive such attention either, but we believe the issue of educational freedom is so vitally important that it must be offered for public discussion at every opportunity. This book invites other educators and citizens to examine the agenda of national goals and standards more critically; it is our aim to encourage the rise of a grassroots movement for educational freedom that would vigorously oppose the imposition of national educational goals, standards, and curricula.

President Clinton's "Goals 2000: Educate America Act" that was passed by Congress in March 1994 was the culmination of a determined campaign for national standards on the part of government officials, corporate leaders, commissions, foundations, and other policymakers. Educators and citizens concerned about educational freedom became deeply alarmed by the sweeping power and influence that Goals 2000 gave the federal government over American education, and many of the authors in this book focus their critiques on this historic legislation. Although the bill had been strongly supported by both major parties, the election later in 1994 of a Republican majority committed to reducing or dismantling federal programs may lead to at least a partial repeal of Goals 2000. Nevertheless, the philosophical assumptions and political agendas that produced Goals 2000 are still very much alive, and they still wield a powerful influence over the content, process, and management of education in this country. In this book, we are attempting to expose these assumptions and agendas and demonstrate why they are inappropriate for a truly democratic society. Even if Goals 2000 is junked (and let's hope it is!), the cultural forces that produced it are well positioned to crank out a Goals 2005 or Goals 2010 that could be even more threatening to educational freedom in a democratic society. It is therefore urgent to address these cultural forces now.

This volume attempts to develop a perspective that transcends the conventional polarization of "liberal" and "conservative" political views; we seek to examine the nature of modern schooling in light of a more penetrating critique of the moral and spiritual crisis of modern culture, as well as a more holistic understanding of human learning and development (see Purpel 1989; Bethel 1994; Miller 1993).

This perspective recognizes that the institution of schooling suffers from (as well as perpetuates) the moral, cultural, and epistemological faults of the modern era as a whole — faults that have led us to the brink of social disintegration and ecological catastrophe (Rifkin 1991; Mander 1991; Orr 1994; Sloan 1983). In traditional cultures that supported a sustainable relationship between human society and the natural world for many centuries, education took place organically in the daily interactions between youths and adults (Cajete 1994). But in modern societies, education is no longer a natural, organic relationship between generations, rooted in a sense of place and a spiritually nourishing traditional wisdom. Largely confined to the highly formal institution of schooling, which is ultimately controlled by the powerful political force of the state, education is thrust into a political context in which opposing values and ideologies contend for supremacy. The argument for educational freedom is, in large part, an effort to reclaim education as a nourishing, sustaining, organic relationship between generations.

As Sanford Reitman (1992) has shown, zealots of all ideological persuasions have sought to influence the course of history by taking control of schooling in the United States, and in the process, have sacrificed a genuinely *educational* relationship between adults and children. In this book, we are arguing that education should not be used as it has been used for the past 150 years — as an agency of intellectual, cultural, and moral uniformity, as a means of imposing one or another cultural perspective on the lives of young people and their families. In a sense, the argument for educational freedom can be said to reflect a "libertarian" philosophical outlook, but as will be made clear in the essays that follow, our argument is not a simple endorsement of free-market capitalism, nor is it remotely related to the violent antistatism manifested in the "militia" phenomenon of recent months. It is true that the case for genuine educational freedom shares with many conservatives a mistrust of state power, but it also embraces liberals' hopes for a just, fair, compassionate, and truly diverse multicultural community. This combination of libertarian and progressive ideals is extremely unusual, but we offer it here as a promising solution to the deeply troubling problems of contemporary education.

Charles Leslie Glenn, Jr., tracing the origins of state-controlled schooling in the United States, has defined the "common school agenda" as "the deliberate effort to create in the entire youth of a nation common attitudes, loyalties, and values, and to do so under central direction by the state" (1988, 4). Historically, as Rush Welter (1962) has argued, both conservatives and liberals supported this agenda. But over the last 50 years, the increasing secularization, professionalization, and dramatic growth of educational institutions have led many conservatives to take a harder look at the sociological and moral aspects of state schooling. The new right is suspicious of professional elitism, "political correctness," and an insatiable appetite for social engineering that it perceives in the education establishment. Libertarian conservatives emphasize that public schooling is essentially a servant of the state, which during the past century has grown into a dangerous concentration of political, economic, and cultural power.

Consequently, the conservative agenda in recent years has embraced ideas such as vouchers, school choice, free-market competition, and the dismantling of teachers' unions and the federal Department of Education. There is now a growing movement calling for the complete separation of school and state. The homeschooling movement — the quintessential grassroots rebellion in education — has found many (though certainly not all) of its most ardent supporters among conservatives, especially among the religious right. Those who take these positions claim to be defending democratic values against the encroachment on individual freedom by massive, oppressive bureaucratic institutions — and there is a great deal of truth to this claim.

Yet progressive educators assert that *they* are the real defenders of democratic education. They argue that conservatives' emphasis on individualism and the free market fails to address the economic, social, spiritual, and ecological devastation being wrought on a vast scale by corporate capitalism; not only does the right fail to confront the raging tide of greed in this society, it *endorses* the atomistic pursuit of self-interest as a positive social good. Progressive liberals argue that other moral and social values — such as compassion, community, emotional authenticity and wholeness, an appreciation for the richness of human and cultural diversity, and an understanding that the natural world is more than an economic resource — are essential for a healthy and humane democratic society.

Progressives point out that vast economic inequity, racial and ethnic animosity, and sheer greed have come to characterize American society, despite 150 years of "common" schooling ostensibly designed to head off such developments, because public education has been dominated by the agenda of corporate capitalism ever since the time of Horace Mann (e.g., see Nasaw 1979; Spring 1972; Callahan 1962). At present, they would argue, there is no cultural force stronger than the overwhelming influence that multinational corporations exercise over our economic system, communications and entertainment media, the food we eat, or even the air, water, forests, and soil upon which the entire ecosystem depends. From the left's perspective, the repudiation of public education does not represent an advancement of democratic values but an abdication of the struggle against powerful economic interests, which must take place in education as well as elsewhere in society.

Consequently, progressive educators wish to replace corporate domination of public schooling (the Goals 2000 legislation being only a recent manifestation of a much deeper ideological agenda) with a program they see as more just, humane, and democratic. Progressives today are waging a courageous effort to transform public schools into more genuine incubators of democratic community life, as they have since the time of John Dewey; they tirelessly call for fairness, equity, and inclusive public policies that welcome the multiracial and multicultural character of our society.[1]

Indeed, for millions of children in public schools, especially those in neglected, impoverished regions of this country, the progressive agenda offers important rays of hope and empowerment.

In calling the fight for educational freedom "libertarian," I do not mean to imply that all the authors in this volume oppose public schooling as such. The question remains, however, whether state schooling can truly become a reliable instrument for democracy and fairness. As a historian of American education with a particular interest in dissident, person-centered educational movements (Miller 1992), I do not share the left's enthusiasm for public schooling as a means of nurturing democratic community life. The "common school agenda," by its very nature, is inimical to genuine educational freedom, and the roots of this agenda run deep in American educational history. In the years following the War of Independence, leading intellectuals such as Thomas Jefferson, Noah Webster, and Benjamin Rush argued that a system of government schooling was vitally necessary to ensure that the American population would become competent and loyal citizens of the precariously new republic. It may well be that these architects of American democracy had nothing but the best intentions; however, now that we are reaping the results of 200 years of modernist thinking, we are able to look at the founding fathers' ideas more critically. We are able to see the implications of Rush's statement that individuals are "public property" who should be converted, through education, into "republican machines." Rush concluded that "this must be done if we expect them to perform their parts properly in the great machine of the government of the state" (quoted in Rudolph 1965, 17).

This pithy statement by the respected physician and Enlightenment thinker provides an important key to understanding the cultural foundation of state-controlled schooling. To view the democratic political process, and even more so the human being, as a *machine*, is to reveal the reductionistic, Cartesian worldview that firmly took root during the age of Enlightenment (see Berman 1981; Rifkin 1991). This reductionism is the epistemological basis of modern social institutions, particularly the bureaucratic

---

[1] Among these efforts are The National Coalition of Education Activists, the *Rethinking Schools* journal, the Institute for Democracy in Education, several important journals, books, and publishing enterprises dedicated to multicultural education, detracking and other democratic programs, and scholars developing the literature of "critical pedagogy."

state. Human and societal affairs are treated as mechanistic processes requiring management by experts and professionals. There really is no room for organic qualities such as spontaneity, creativity, insight, idiosyncracy, or passion in these affairs; all must be reduced to uniformity, conformity, and standardization in order to permit efficient technocratic management.

By the early twentieth century, educational leaders openly promoted "social efficiency" as the primary purpose of education. I have found no more naked statement of the common school agenda than this quotation from a 1908 textbook by efficiency advocate Colin Scott:

> It is not primarily for his own individual good that the child is taken from his free and wandering life of play. It is for what society can get out of him, whether of a material or a spiritual kind, that he is sent to school. (quoted in Spring 1972, 56–57)

This view was advanced by the major educational thinkers of the late nineteenth and early twentieth centuries (particularly William Torrey Harris) and echoed in other important elements of the culture. During these years, the reductionism of Enlightenment social philosophy reached its peak. The social sciences, especially psychology, turned to statistical measurement and behaviorism. Political theorists and industrial managers, obsessed with efficiency and control, embraced elitist and technocratic models of organization. Cultural uniformity was upheld by a determined campaign against immigrants, minorities, and the radical labor movement (see Miller 1992). Despite the articulate protests of John Dewey and the various progressive educators who followed, American education was deeply and lastingly influenced by this "cult of efficiency" (Callahan 1962): By the middle of the twentieth century, public schools had become solidly established as a political and ideological institution. As Douglas Sloan (1994) has put it,

> In our time, the most important part of what educators call the hidden curriculum in much of our schooling is the imparting of the values of the modern mindset: that the world is a great machine; that the human being is basically a higher animal; that all human problems are fundamentally technological problems and therefore have technological solutions. These are the assumptions undergirding a good deal of modern education. In fact, a good deal of modern education has, as its primary purpose, to make sure that these views of the human being are imparted and inculcated in the student.

Ultimately, in the reductionist Enlightenment view, it is the state's role to ensure this uniformity of culture, values, and beliefs. The modern state was formed in close partnership with the very interests — corporate capitalism, economic colonialism, militarism, and class privilege — that progressives today seek to overcome. Hence, it seems to me, the left's perennial vision of a genuinely liberating public education will require nothing less than a redefinition of the state itself. If this is possible at all, it will take decades of exhausting, unending political agitation and cultural struggle. As many of the contributors to this volume will argue, herein lies the fundamental antithesis to an education that is organic, rooted in traditional wisdom, or conducive to genuine human relationship.

Initiatives such as *A Nation at Risk* and Goals 2000 are especially dangerous because they are backed by the vast power of the modern state. Corporate interests strongly *influence* the public through their control of resources and the media, but it is the state that has prisons; only the state can *enforce* compulsory attendance laws and curriculum standards. If educational freedom and, indeed, democratic society itself are grounded in a vision of nonviolence, dialogue, and cooperation, then it would seem counterproductive to use political force to obtain desired social results — even if those results are intended to be benevolent. The call for educational freedom, then, asks us to question the concentration of cultural power in both the economic and political domains of society. In this view, a truly democratic, compassionate, spiritually nourishing society needs to reject both institutionalized greed and social engineering. It is a society that restrains all forms of ideological, political, and economic domination so that human diversity can truly flourish.

I would like to suggest a radical but intriguing hypothesis: perhaps the state — even a liberal state — is an incredibly blunt and inappropriate instrument for administering the delicate task of supervising children's moral, spiritual, and intellectual development. If this hypothesis contains any truth, then surely it is vitally important to wholly abandon the campaign for national educational goals, standards, and curricula. And then we must begin to build a free educational system based on principles other than economic competition or marketplace individualism. The contributors to this volume offer several possibilities as to how this might be done.

Educational freedom is not a romantic notion concerned only with idiosyncratic personal activity; we recognize that education is essentially a cultural endeavor. The education of each new generation is the means by which a society preserves and (hopefully) rejuvenates its core values and basic identity. But we would argue that it fulfills this role best in a climate that is free of political and ideological compulsion, a climate in which the intellectual and spiritual growth of the human being can thrive. In other words, if it is to embody truly humane and democratic values, the practice of a genuinely liberating education requires forms of social organization other than the coercive force of government and modern capitalism's obsession with competition and profit.

The most elaborate expression of this view was provided by the Austrian philosopher Rudolf Steiner (1861–1925), who initiated a multifaceted movement for cultural and spiritual renewal called "Anthroposophy," which includes the Waldorf education method. Steiner's conception of the "threefold" society holds that culture, economy, and politics each have their own appropriate activities and institutions and that a balanced relationship must be cultivated between them (Steiner 1977, 1985). Writing around 1920, he offered a critique of state schooling that applies directly to the agenda of *A Nation at Risk* and Goals 2000:

> At every level, schools mold human beings into the form the state requires for doing what the state deems necessary. Arrangements in the schools reflect the government's requirements. There is much talk, certainly, of striving to achieve an all-around development of the person, and so on; but the modern person unconsciously feels so completely a part of the whole order of the state that he does not even notice, when talking about the all-around development of the human being, that what is meant is molding the human being into a useful servant of the state. (1985, 70)

Throughout his prolific work, Steiner emphasized the development of creativity, insight, and spiritual maturity.through personal individuation. If personal identity is absorbed into the interests of the state and the economic system, as it surely is in the modern world, then the true sources of wisdom and human development are choked off. Hence, Steiner insisted that educational freedom is a vital necessity:

> The real need of the present is that the schools be totally grounded in a free spiritual and cultural life. What should be taught and cultivated in these schools must be drawn solely from a knowledge of the growing human being and of individual capacities. A genuine anthropology must form the basis of education and instruction. The question should not be:

"What does a human being need to know and be able to do for the social order that now exists?" but rather: "What capacities are latent in this human being, and what lies within that can be developed?" A healthy relation exists between school and society only when society is kept constantly supplied with the new and individual potentials of persons whose educations have allowed them to develop unhampered. This can be realized only if the schools and the whole educational system are placed on a footing of self-administration within the social organism. (1985, 71, 72)

Steiner's thinking presents an especially coherent and substantial basis for the case against national goals and standards. His message from 75 years ago directly addresses today's educational climate:

The government and the economy must receive people educated by the independent spiritual-cultural life; they must not, however, have the power to prescribe according to their own wants how these human beings are to be educated. What a person ought to know and be able to do at any particular stage of life must be decided by human nature itself. Both the state and economic life will have to conform to the demands of human nature. It is neither for the state nor the economic life to say: We need someone of this sort for a particular post; therefore *test* the people that we need and pay heed above all that they know and can do what we want. (1985, 72).

In the United States, Steiner's visionary work is virtually unknown outside the tiny Anthroposophy community and the approximately 100 Waldorf schools in this country. A handful of contemporary American thinkers have drawn upon his insights, including Joseph Chilton Pearce (author of *Magical Child* and *Evolution's End*), Douglas Sloan (author of *Insight-Imagination* and former editor of *Teachers College Record*), Jeffrey Kane (Dean of the School of Education at Adelphi University and editor of *Holistic Education Review*), Arthur Zajonc (professor of physics at Amherst College), and Robert McDermott (President of the California Institute for Integral Studies and author of several works on philosophy and religion). Whether or not one accepts every facet of Steiner's thought or every aspect of Waldorf education (and I do not; see my essay later in this volume), Steiner does offer a rare and valuable perspective in this technocratic age: the possibility of an education rooted in a profound moral vision and a holistic under-standing of human development rather than in the crude demands of the state and the marketplace.

This perspective is the starting point for any serious discussion of educational freedom. Indeed, the present book was first conceived in November 1994 at a conference on national goals and standards that was organized by Waldorf educators and others who are working today to interpret and apply Steiner's theory of the threefold society.[2]

I subsequently invited other contributors who have no connection to Steiner's work but whose views add complementary dimensions. These authors represent diverse perspectives, even diverse worldviews. They include college professors, parent activists, and a veteran public school principal. Some of them are progressive liberals, while others reflect a more libertarian point of view. They criticize different aspects of the movement for national standards, for different reasons, and offer various alternative proposals. In my mind, the primary message that emerges from this collection is the notion that if we are to maintain a truly democratic culture, we must possess genuine intellectual and spiritual freedom — and it is precisely this freedom that is threatened by the autocratic political control of education.

When we bring together the numerous and diverse arguments against national standards, we are presented, I believe, with a clear case for educational freedom. In view of these arguments, the agenda for nationalized education is surely a morally stunted, pedagogically stupid, and ultimately violent program for guiding young people into the adult world. The following overview does not treat each point in detail — many of these are discussed at greater length in the chapters that follow — but it does suggest that, taken together, the arguments against mandated goals and standards are convincing, if not overwhelming.

Pedagogical Arguments for Educational Freedom
Fashioning Education According to How Children Actually Learn

Politicians, corporate executives, and bureaucrats have little or no understanding of child development or pedagogy. The art and science of successful education rest upon a huge and complex body of experience, research, and theory, which is almost entirely foreign to the training or concerns of those who wish to dictate educational policy. (Further, as we will see later, the ideological agenda of leading policymakers is essentially opposed to the

[2]The conference was organized, in particular, by Gary Lamb of the Social Renewal Foundation, co-editor of *The Threefold Review*. (See the resource list at the end of this volume).

knowledge and concerns of actual educators.) This is an obvious and important point that is somehow always ignored when the "big boys" (as Gerald Porter calls them in his chapter) issue their demands for competition, accountability, or "excellence." In his chapter, David Purpel points out that the educational theory underlying the national standards agenda is incredibly limited and naive. James Moffett agrees, observing that politicians are "not conversant with the actual processes of education." This pedagogical ignorance is a root problem that produces egregious educational mistakes, as the next several points indicate.

The recognition of the learner's active role in education is totally missing in the standards and goals agenda. Developmental psychology shows us that children *construct* knowledge through their active engagement with the world; when intellectual content is simply poured in, it is not learned in meaningful or deep ways. Subject matter that appears logically coherent to some people may not make sense to a given individual's experience, and certainly, as Piaget has amply demonstrated, much that appears obvious to adults is simply not accessible to children until they have assimilated the knowledge through purposeful exploration. In this book, Nel Noddings, Pat Farenga, and Lynn Stoddard all address the need for "assent" or "interest" in any genuine learning. Lacking the student's collaboration, mandated education only succeeds to the extent that the student is bribed or coerced into learning — in a word, brainwashed.

Any possibility of innovative, student-centered, hands-on, integrated, cooperative, and other engaging ways of learning is destroyed by the ruthless demand for accountability. When teachers must gear instruction to rigid sets of standards and performance outcomes measured by standardized tests, they cannot become engaged with students' characteristics, personalities, experience, interests, or "domains of caring" as Noddings calls them. In *Schools that Work* (1992), George H. Wood describes actual public school classrooms in which students are genuinely challenged and inspired by an education that is personally meaningful and culturally relevant. He bluntly points out that such learning becomes impossible when teachers are forced to meet mandated standards:

> We are witnessing a 'legislated excellence' movement throughout America that, while perhaps well-intentioned, will make excellence in education even more difficult to attain.... The unfortunate consequence of this

campaign will be to simply swallow up the school day with drill-and-kill exercises designed to prepare students for the onslaught of tests. Already teachers are reporting that state-mandated curriculum requirements make projects that go beyond the textbooks more difficult. In fact, anything that doesn't come directly from a textbook, or appear on the state-mandated tests, is actively discouraged." (pp. xviii, xxi)

The goals and standards movement is similarly threatening to independent schools and homeschooling families. In their chapters, Pat Farenga and Linda Dobson explain why "unschooling" and the concept of community learning centers offer important alternatives to conventional schooling and point to learning models for the future. (Dobson's portrayal is similar to James Moffett's visionary proposal in *The Universal Schoolhouse*.) Yet such alternatives could well be stymied by federal and state mandates.

National standards enshrine the "curriculum," which in many ways is a lifeless abstraction of what there is to be learned about the world. As Gerald Porter writes in his chapter, "Curriculum decomposes real life experience into contextually meaningless facts that may be logically arranged but are not at all reminiscent of how a child would naturally learn." Natural, genuine learning is a search for relevance and meaning; as I describe more fully in my essay later in this book, learning is a living encounter between a purposeful, seeking human being and an enormously complex world (also see Palmer 1993; Sloan 1983; Doll 1993). At best, "curriculum" is a framework or scaffold — an auxiliary structure that helps us approach the vast richness of the world in a coherent way. To substitute the curriculum for the world is like mistaking a menu for the meal; there is no actual nourishment in a menu, and there is little or no meaningful engagement with the world in a curriculum that is determined and imposed by people who are not directly involved in the learning experience. In recent years, one of the few educators who has seen this clearly and had the courage to question the sacred cow of curriculum is Lynn Stoddard, a 40-year veteran of public school teaching and leadership. In this book, as in previous writings (Stoddard 1990, 1992, 1995), he points out the marked contrast between *curriculum* development and *human* development and argues why we need to be far more serious than we are about the latter. The establishment of content standards and performance goals works in precisely the opposite direction.

In this era of rapidly proliferating information, no single curriculum can possibly cover all the knowledge that students may need for future learning or careers. Furthermore, what is known, or assumed to be important to know, for today's world will likely be obsolete within a decade or two. The truest, most enduring measure of educational success in a rapidly changing world is not the volume of facts and trivia that are memorized ("what every fourth grader needs to know"), but the student's ability and willingness to continue inquiring, learning, interpreting, and evaluating new information and new situations as they constantly arise. Yet, national standards enshrine certain fields of knowledge (especially science, math, and computer literacy) because they are assumed to have greater value for economic success. This narrow, utilitarian measure of knowledge denies educators the freedom to draw upon a wide range of subject areas in order to achieve meaningful educational purposes — to evoke critical or metaphorical thinking, or to meet the particular learning style or developmental readiness of individual students, or to introduce students to concerns that may be especially relevant to them or to their communities, to name a few examples. Entire areas of human experience and achievement (such as the arts and humanities) are neglected in the narrow and pragmatic focus on economic success.

When the authorities dictate what must be learned and when, undue pressure is placed on children as well as teachers. Early childhood and other developmental educators, proponents of holistic teaching approaches such as Waldorf education, and leading psychologists including David Elkind all caution against pushing children into academic, overly cognitive activities before they are ready. Children acquire cognitive capacities in different ways (as learning style research and Howard Gardner's multiple intelligence theory tell us), and at different rates. One standard set of learning expectations will not promote academic "excellence" for all students but will indeed be counterproductive for many, producing another generation of learning disabilities and alienation. Teachers, with their creativity already diminished by having to conform to a standardized curriculum, will face increasing discouragement and burnout because they will be unable to churn out the learning "products" demanded of them.

Schools and teachers will be pressured by the demand to meet standards to label and isolate the many young children who are not ready to perform as expected. A perceptive critique by three educational policy researchers (Fulk, Mantzicopoulos, and Hirth 1994) argues that "the imposition of national standards may herald a new age of tracking, with children's academic futures being jeopardized faster and much earlier than ever before" (p. 367). The authors believe that more and more young children will be placed in "prekindergarten" programs or will be retained after kindergarten in "transitional first grade" classrooms for "slow" learners — practices that offer few academic benefits but serious social and emotional consequences for students. In addition, "vast numbers" of students who fail to meet the standards could be labeled as candidates for "special" education. In other words, many students will not receive the education they need but will, instead, be subjected to reductionistic labeling that may well mar their education and career record for life. Those who do not fit the mold are simply abandoned to their fate.

Standardized assessment reflects a drastically narrowed range of possible learning modes and educational goals. As James Moffett writes in this volume, assessment can only serve truly educational purposes when it is flexible, composite, and situational. An accurate portrayal of a student's achievements and potentials requires multiple samplings over long periods of time, not one-shot superficial tests. When the entire educational process is geared to standardized tests, the complexity, subtlety, and variety of meaningful learning is reduced to mere bits of data. This reductionism may serve the interests of politicians and administrators, but it does not help students learn.

Political and Cultural Arguments for Educational Freedom

What Kind of Society Do We Truly Want?

The call for national goals and standards is essentially a diversion, a political sleight-of-hand, to protect what David Purpel calls a "cruel and unjust cultural vision." The Goals 2000 agenda, like most educational policy over the past 150 years, fails to seriously address deep social issues such as poverty, racism, militarism, expanding corporate power, the widening gap between rich and poor, and other factors that are far more relevant to the economic and cultural health of the nation. As Henry J. Perkinson (1968), Sanford W. Reitman (1992), and other scholars have pointed out, American policymakers have repeatedly turned to school reform as a way of sidestepping these difficult issues. The drive for national standards is a classic expression of our deeply rooted cultural malady that Reitman calls "the educational messiah complex" — the inappropriate use of schooling to address issues that should be more directly confronted by the community as a whole. Several authors in this book observe that blaming American schools for the supposed lack of economic competitiveness neatly takes the spotlight off of government and corporate policies that are more directly implicated.

In the context of the modern economic system, educational attainment does not guarantee economic security. To emphasize the link between educational achievement and economic success is a false promise. Patrick Shannon points out in his chapter that even if we could turn out a generation of highly educated, highly skilled people, there are not enough jobs for them in the present corporate economy. As Nel Noddings has written elsewhere,

> What do we want for our children? What do they need from education, and what does our society need? The popular response today is that students need more academic training, that the country needs more people with greater mathematical and scientific competence, that a more adequate academic preparation will save people from poverty, crime, and other evils of current society. Most of these claims are either false or, at best, only partly true. For example, we do *not* need more physicists and mathematicians; many people highly trained in these fields are unable to find work.... And, clearly, more education will not save people from poverty unless a sufficient number of unfortunate people either reject that education or are squeezed out of it. Poverty is a *social* problem. No person who does honest, useful work — regardless of his or her educational attainments — should live in poverty. A society that permits this is not an educational failure, it is a moral failure. (1995, 365–366)

Uniform standards assume that students are equally prepared for educational achievement, yet this is clearly not the case. For millions of children in the United States, learning is difficult, if not unimaginable, because they attend dilapidated and violence-ridden schools, such as those Jonathan Kozol described in *Savage Inequalities*, or because they have grown up in homes — or on the streets — where they have experienced abuse and hunger. To suggest that higher standards offer any relief to these children smacks of callous elitism, as Harvey A. Daniels argues in an aptly titled essay in *Rethinking Schools*, "Let Them Eat Standards." He asks,

> Is it fair to promulgate academic standards before the opportunity for all to learn is guaranteed? Will having grade-level achievement targets challenge the existing social hierarchy? Will a national standardized test

upgrade instruction and materials in poor, neglected schools? Will bench-
marks deliver resources to inner city classrooms which lack them? And,
unless resources are added, won't poor, immigrant, or non-English-
speaking kids continue to score in the bottom quartile, stanine, or decile,
whatever the standard? (1994, 22)

*From a rich and complex range of possibilities, the agenda of national
standards arbitrarily and heavy-handedly determines which fields of knowledge,
which kinds of learning, and which moral visions of education shall be imposed on
all communities, all families, and all children.* In this Republican/corpo-
rate/fundamentalist era of cultural "restoration," as it has been called,
policymakers favor traditional subjects (including a patriotic reading of
history and an emphasis on the Eurocentric literary canon), "basic" skills,
technological literacy, and rugged classroom discipline over more progressive and holistic educational possibilities such as multicultural and antira-
cist education, ecological literacy, peace education, emotional literacy, creative and artistic expression, critical pedagogy, and constructivist,
interdisciplinary ways of teaching. But perhaps in another decade progressives will manage to eke out a slim majority in Congress and state legislatures; should they then have the authority to seize the educational helm and
impose holistic education on conservatives who find such ideas repugnant?
As Pat Farenga points out, this is precisely why Outcomes-Based Education
has stirred up the wrath of the religious right; Farenga and other authors in
this book believe that the attempt to impose *any* educational ideas on the
entire population should be disturbing to anyone who believes in a free
democratic society. Regardless of which agenda one prefers, should the
authority of the state be used to impose *any* educational program on *all*
people in a democratic society?

*Official national standards and curriculum establish a monocultural vision
of American society and act powerfully to close off the possibility of a truly
multicultural democracy.* Ethnic, racial, and cultural diversity has become a
highly charged issue in many parts of the world today, from Bosnia to
Rwanda, from France and Germany to American universities and the
streets of our cities. As Harold Berlak points out in his chapter, we have
entered a critical historical moment when centuries of racism and ethno-
centrism are being challenged, provoking a powerful backlash — and education is caught right in the middle of this conflict; today, as never before,
educators are being challenged to reconceive the school and the curriculum

in order to practice a democratic vision that embraces diverse human experiences (Nieto 1992; Perry and Fraser 1993; Renyi 1993), but when they do, they are severely criticized for injecting "political correctness" into the school. As Gerald Porter shows in his essay on "the white man's burden," the national standards agenda is closely tied to an elitist, monocultural view of society and would effectively clamp down on efforts to provide opportunities for multicultural learning.

National goals and standards establish the agenda of powerful, elite institutions, not the goals of educators, parents, or local communities. Leaving aside the conflicts over specific ideological *content*, as described in the previous two points, the national goals movement is a shift of power as such, from individuals and communities to institutions that already wield a disproportionate share. Kenneth S. Goodman has pinpointed this aspect of the goals agenda:

> I accuse the politicians and technicians of the standards movement of using standards as a cover for a well-orchestrated attempt to centralize power and thus control who will teach, who will learn, what will be taught in the nation's schools, and who will determine the curriculum for schools and for teacher education.... The standards movement promises the political power brokers that by controlling outcomes they can control schools while appearing to support local control, and they can avoid spending money to deal with the real needs of education. (1994, 39)

In the critique quoted earlier, Harvey A. Daniels distinguishes between two "profoundly opposing" reform movements at work in the United States today — the "top-down, business-driven, government-officiated, blue-ribbon-panel/skill-and-drill/E. D. Hirsch/William Bennett/-Chris Whittle/Back-to-Basics/Educational Testing Service approach," and the "bottom-up, progressive, democratic, curriculum-rooted, humanistic, developmental-minded" movement, which "is concerned less with national economic defense than with the personal and intellectual growth of children" (Daniels 1994, 22). Daniels suggests that mere teachers

> cannot collaborate with forces as powerful and partisan as the Educational Testing Service or the Department of Education and expect to have our voices genuinely heard or to materially affect their processes.... They disagree with us, they disrespect us, and they will not be brought around by us. These grown-ups will not allow us to sit at their big table unless we support their views or unless the outcome is a foregone conclusion — or both. (p. 25)

Later in this book, Seth Rockmuller and Katharine Houk make a very similar comment about the national goals movement's attitude toward parents.

Fundamentally, the question of national standards and curriculum causes us to ask what sort of political culture we wish to establish in the United States — a climate in which public discussion and compromise freely take place or one in which interest groups vie for control of schooling in order to enforce their views. The question of monocultural literacy versus multicultural democracy is one example of a crucial issue that ought to be settled through democratic dialogue rather than bureaucratic mandate. The argument for educational freedom, as Stephen Arons has articulated so well, holds that moral and ideological conflicts, which often rest on deep historical roots, cannot be solved through political force; that is precisely the response that leads, ultimately, to violence. Arons quotes the Supreme Court decision of *West Virginia v. Barnette* (1943):

> As government pressure toward unity becomes greater so strife becomes more bitter as to whose unity it shall be. Probably no deeper division of our people could proceed from any provocation than from finding it necessary to choose what doctrine and whose program public education officials shall compel youth to unite in embracing. Compulsory unification of opinion achieves only the unanimity of the graveyard.

Constitutional Arguments for Educational Freedom

National Goals and Standards Violate the American Model of Constitutional Democracy

The United States Constitution does not clearly authorize the federal government to control the form and content of education. To be sure, massive federal programs have been established in numerous domains over the past 50 years, though not specifically mentioned in the Constitution, because Congress is allowed to provide for the "general welfare of the United States" (Article I, Section 8). What qualifies under this vague heading has often been the subject of judicial interpretation or partisan debate (the contrast between the Great Society and the Contract With America being a prime example), so it is possible to make a case for federal involvement in education. However, to defend the notion of national educational standards requires a "loose" and highly statist interpretation of the Constitution. The fact that policymakers, educators, and the public have by and large assented to the steady increase of federal control over education during the past 40 years seems to confirm Steiner's comment that "the modern person unconsciously feels ... completely a part of the whole order of the state." It now seems normal to us that federal officials can determine how, what, and when our children must learn. But there are at least two specific and important reasons why this perception should be challenged:

Many of the founders of the American republic recognized that as political power becomes more centralized and concentrated, it also becomes more distant and unresponsive to the needs of individuals and local communities. For some areas of concern, such as international trade, national defense, and protection of civil rights, the concentration of power may be necessary and appropriate. But in areas that most intimately affect the daily lives of people and their communities, decrees and mandates by distant authorities are often irrelevant, insensitive, and destructive. Linda Dobson reminds us in her chapter that this is why such democratic theorists as Jefferson and Samuel Adams cautioned against the excessive growth of state power. As we saw earlier, there is in fact an inherent conflict between the agenda of the powerful institutions supporting national goals and those who would reform education from the bottom up. This is not just a specific policy issue but a broad and urgent constitutional question. According to David Purpel, the agenda of national goals "seriously erodes the vitality of grassroots, local involvement in the public schools, surely an extremely important dimension of a democratic society."

In a constitutional democracy, government policy must reflect a free, genuine public dialogue and exchange of ideas; government must not attempt to shape the form and content of those ideas. Stephen Arons emphasizes this point in his chapter in this book (also see Arons 1983). He argues that the First Amendment was intended to protect the formation, as well as the communication, of ideas. He quotes the Supreme Court's *West Virginia v. Barnette* (1943):

> We set up government by consent of the governed, and the Bill of Rights denies those in power any legal opportunity to coerce that consent. Authority here is to be controlled by public opinion, not public opinion by authority.

The Transcendentalist philosopher Orestes Brownson made this same argument when he criticized the formation of state boards of education in the 1830s. In autocratic societies, he said, it may be appropriate for teachers to be "the pliant tools of the government," but in a democratic nation,

> the people do not look to the government for light, for instruction, but the government looks to the people. The people give the law to the government. To entrust, then, the government with the power of determining the education which our children shall receive is entrusting our servant with the power to be our master. (quoted in Nasaw 1979, 64)

It is truly worth reflecting on the thought that Goals 2000 and similar efforts may well be giving government "the power to be our master."

Philosophical and Moral Arguments for Educational Freedom

The Crusade for Educational Standards in the Service of Economic Goals Represents a Destructively Reductionistic Worldview

Education should be about the nurturing, the calling forth ("ex ducere" or "educare") of our highest and best human possibilities, not the servant of crass economic interests. In his 1994 State of the Union message, President Clinton expressed the philosophical essence of the goals movement: Schools, he said, should be measured by "one high standard: Are our children learning what they need to know to compete and win in the global economy?" Is this what we most value as a culture? Is human existence truly no more than a competition for prestigious jobs and consumer goods? Have we utterly lost our sense of beauty, our sense of place and connection to the earth, our compassion and commitment to human community? Have we totally abandoned our imagination and sense of wonder for a hard world of utilitarian calculation?

Ken Goodman, among many other critics, observes that standardized education is a direct reflection of the mass-production mentality of the past century. "In the industrial view," he writes, "schools are factories taking children as raw materials, shaping them through controlled, uniform treatments, and delivering them as standard products." If we are truly interested in genuine teaching and learning, we will not mimic the processes of mass production; "We don't want interchangeable teachers, pupils, curriculum, and teacher education" (1994, 39). If education is so dominated by economic concerns that it cannot cultivate our individuality or the finer and deeper qualities of our humanity, then we — as a civilization and perhaps as a species — are in serious trouble.

The national goals agenda treats young human beings as objects rather than persons; students are defined as a national "resource" or, as Jeffrey Kane explains in his chapter, as "intellectual capital." The campaign for national standards rests upon a reductionistic, behaviorist image of the human being, and the advancement of this campaign can only fix this image ever more deeply in modern culture. Psychologist Blythe McVicker Clinchy has observed that

> what is striking about the Goals 2000 initiative is its virtual omission of the student. Of course, its proponents refer to students repeatedly. They speak of exposing students to important things and providing them with other things — all of this in the realm of "content standards." They talk about requiring students to do things that are good for them and evaluating them to see whether they did what they were supposed to do — this in the area of "performance standards." But in these pronouncements students are almost always treated as *objects*, rarely as *subjects*. Goals 2000 focuses almost exclusively on the external 'stuff' that is to be implanted in these apparently inert organisms. (1995, 383)

In an address he gave to the November 1994 conference on national goals, Douglas Sloan described how thoroughly this reductionistic mind-set has permeated education already:

> I asked a class of mine what was the image of education that they had experienced — what did they see to be the dominant image of the human being in the education they had experienced? Within a few minutes they came up with the phrase "units of production." They had experienced themselves as "units of production" — also the term that is used for factory farm animals. It says a lot about the kind of thinking that is dominating a lot of our educational theory today. (1994)

Once children are seen as a "national resource," we must ask a profoundly important question: To whom do children actually belong? To the state? To their families? To themselves? Just as Benjamin Rush (quoted earlier) considered individuals to be "public property," overzealous educators can proclaim that "children are the property of the state" (Wisconsin Teachers Association, 1865, quoted in Kaestle 1983, 158). This is not an appropriate basis upon which to build a democratic society — on the contrary, it is a primary foundation for a totalitarian society! It represents a complete disregard for the organic psychological and spiritual development of the growing child. In this volume, Jeffrey Kane eloquently points out the contrast between the state's and parents' views of children; parents, he says, do not send their children to school

> with the understanding that in so doing they, first and foremost, are developing intellectual capital as the central American resource in a global economic marketplace. More likely than not, parents see their children as children — as distinctive human beings with hopes and problems, strengths and difficulties to overcome — as growing persons attempting to learn about the world and themselves.

In their chapter, Seth Rockmuller and Katharine Houk make a similar point:

> It's parents who know their children best. In the final analysis, it's a question of trust. Will we as a society trust the family to look out for the best interests of its children?

We are facing a global environmental crisis that clearly demands more sustainable social and economic practices, yet the relentless push for productivity and competitiveness can only further drive our exploitation of the biosphere toward ecological catastrophe. The rhetoric of *A Nation at Risk*, Goals 2000, and the government and business leaders who persistently advocate for economic growth utterly fails to acknowledge the warnings that we have received over the past two decades from numerous observers, such as Wendell Berry, Donella Meadows, Lester Brown, Bill McKibben, Jeremy Rifkin, Jerry Mander, Theodore Roszak, Edward Goldsmith, and many others, who tell us that modern technology and excessive consumption are destroying the ability of the planet to support life as we know it. David W. Orr puts it this way:

> The truth is that many things on which our future health and prosperity depend are in dire jeopardy: climate stability, the resilience and productivity of natural systems, the beauty of the natural world, and biological diversity.... Something of earth-shattering importance went wrong in our lifetime, and we were prepared neither to see it nor to avoid complicity in it. (1994, 7, 156)

Orr (1992, 1994), along with Gregory A. Smith (1992), C. A. Bowers (1993, 1995), and a handful of other educational philosophers, strongly urges educators to recognize that the looming ecological crisis has tremendous implications for the aims and methods of education in a postindustrial age. If we are to prevent the devastation of the biosphere, they warn, we must challenge the deeply held cultural assumptions that undergird modern social and economic systems — assumptions that promote a mechanistic view of nature, a detached, competitive individualism, amoral technology, and uncontrolled growth and "progress." These are vitally important warnings, and for a nation to set long-term educational goals in complete ignorance (if not direct defiance) of them is woefully irresponsible.

Finally, we ought to consider Steiner's insistence that *cultural and intellectual life must be absolutely free of coercion because ultimately they arise from creative activity deep within the human spirit. Legislation, regulation, partisan politics, and majority rule reflect more superficial interests*. The modernist, reductionist worldview, as Jerry Mander (1991) and others have thoroughly explained, is proving to be highly destructive to the moral and physical health of individuals, to the social health of communities, and, as discussed above, to the ecological health of the natural world upon which our existence depends. Native American educator Gregory Cajete (1994) points out that in contrast to traditional, sustainable societies, modern culture completely lacks any "shared integrative metaphor of *Life*"; in other words, our institutions, careers, relationships, and values are not rooted in any deep, meaningful understanding of the mystery and miracle of life but merely in gross, superficial economic concerns and technical knowledge. To *impose* this shallow understanding on the intellect and spirit of developing human beings — as a program of national educational goals essentially does — is to perpetuate the spiritual emptiness of the modern age.

The essays that follow develop this multifaceted case for educational freedom, for a diverse democratic society, and for spiritual and ecological wisdom. The first chapter — a critique I wrote a few years ago — examines the ideological foundations of current educational policy. The next four authors — Moffett, Kane, Noddings, and Lamb — provide an overview of educational reform and standards. Then Ronald Milito gives a detailed description of the Goals 2000 legislation and analyzes its assumptions and implications. In the following chapters, Arons, Berlak, Purpel, Porter, and Shannon critique various aspects of Goals 2000 in considerable depth. Then, in the essays by Rockmuller and Houk, Farenga, and Dobson, we are asked to consider the consequences of national goals and standards beyond the schoolhouse in the lives of families. Finally, the chapters by Stoddard and myself explore a holistic philosophy of education that gives the notion of educational freedom a substantial and, I believe, deeply inspiring foundation. I believe that this is a powerful collection of writings with an immensely important message for educators, policymakers, and citizens at this critical historical moment. Arguably, we stand on the brink of tremendous social and ecological disaster, and the agenda of reductionism, efficiency, exploitation, and control that is represented by Goals 2000 and other efforts to impose national standards on education can only push us closer to the edge. Surely it is time to take a more careful look at where our culture is heading.

References

Arons, Stephen (1983). *Compelling Belief: The Culture of American Schooling*. New York: McGraw Hill.

Berman, Morris (1981). *The Re-Enchantment of the World*. Ithaca: Cornell University Press.

Bethel, Dayle M. (ed.) (1994). *Compulsory Schooling and Human Learning: The Moral Failure of Public Education in America and Japan*. San Francisco: Caddo Gap Press.

Bowers, C. A. (1993). *Education, Cultural Myths, and the Ecological Crisis: Toward Deep Changes*. Albany: State University of New York Press.

Bowers, C. A. (1995). *Educating for an Ecologically Sustainable Culture: Rethinking Moral Education, Creativity, Intelligence, and Other Modern Orthodoxies*. Albany: State University of New York Press.

Cajete, Gregory (1994). *Look to the Mountain: An Ecology of Indigenous Education*. Durango, CO: Kivaki Press.

Callahan, Raymond (1962). *Education and the Cult of Efficiency*. Chicago: University of Chicago Press.

Clinchy, Blythe McVicker (1995). Goals 2000: The Student as Object. *Phi Delta Kappan* 76: 5, pp. 383–384, 389–392.

Daniels, Harvey A. (1994). Let Them Eat Standards: Controversy over English Standards Teaches Some Lessons. *Rethinking Schools* 9: 2, pp. 22–23, 25. Originally published by the National Council of Teachers of English in the *English Journal*, November 1994.

Doll, William E. (1993). *A Post-Modern Perspective on Curriculum*. New York: Teachers College Press.

Fulk, Barbara Mushinski, Panayota Y. Mantzicopoulos, and Marilyn A. Hirth (1994). Arguments against National Performance Standards. *The Educational Forum* 58, 4, pp. 365–373.

Glenn, Charles Leslie, Jr. (1988). *The Myth of the Common School*. Amherst: University of Massachusetts Press.

Goodman, Kenneth S. (1994). Standards, NOT! The Movement is Being Used as Cover for an Attempt to Centralize Power. *Education Week*, September 7, 1994, pp. 39, 41.

Kaestle, Carl F. (1983). *Pillars of the Republic: Common Schools and American Society 1780–1860*. New York: Hill and Wang.

Mander, Jerry (1991). *In the Absence of the Sacred: The Failure of Technology & the Survival of the Indian Nations*. San Francisco: Sierra Club Books.

Miller, Ron (1992). *What Are Schools For? Holistic Education in American Culture* (2nd edition). Brandon, VT: Holistic Education Press.

Miller, Ron (ed.) (1993). *The Renewal of Meaning in Education: Responses to the Cultural and Ecological Crisis of Our Time*s. Brandon, VT: Holistic Education Press.

Nasaw, David (1979). *Schooled to Order: A Social History of Public Schooling in the United States*. New York: Oxford.

Nieto, Sonia (1992). *Affirming Diversity: The Sociopolitical Context of Multicultural Education*. White Plains, NY: Longman.

Noddings, Nel (1995). A Morally Defensible Mission for Schools in the 21st Century. *Phi Delta Kappan* 76: 5, pp. 365–8.

Orr, David W. (1992). *Ecological Literacy: Education and the Transition to a Postmodern World*. Albany: State University of New York Press.

Orr, David W. (1994). *Earth in Mind: On Education, Environment, and the Human Prospect*. Washington, D.C.: Island Press.

Palmer, Parker (1993). *To Know as We Are Known: Education as a Spiritual Journey*. San Francisco: Harper San Francisco.

Perkinson, Henry J. (1968). *The Imperfect Panacea: American Faith in Education, 1865–1965*. New York: Random House.

Perry, Theresa, and James W. Fraser (1993). *Freedom's Plow: Teaching in the Multicultural Classroom*. New York: Routledge.

Purpel, David E. (1989). *The Moral & Spiritual Crisis in Education: A Curriculum for Justice & Compassion in Education*. New York: Bergin & Garvey.

Reitman, Sanford W. (1992). *The Educational Messiah Complex: American Faith in the Culturally Redemptive Power of Schooling*. Sacramento: Caddo Gap Press.

Renyi, Judith (1993). *Going Public: Schooling for a Diverse Democracy*. New York: New Press.

Rifkin, Jeremy (1991). *Biosphere Politics: A Cultural Odyssey from the Middle Ages to the New Age*. New York: Crown.

Rudolph, Frederick (1965). *Essays on Education in the Early Republic*. Cambridge: Harvard University Press.

Sloan, Douglas (1983). *Insight-Imagination: The Emancipation of Thought and the Modern World*. Westport, CT: Greenwood Press.

Sloan, Douglas (November 11, 1994). Unpublished keynote address at a conference on "National Educational Goals and Standards: A Critical Review and Dissent." Harlemville, New York.

Smith, Gregory A. (1992). *Education and the Environment: Learning to Live with Limits.* Albany: State University of New York Press.

Spring, Joel (1972). *Education and the Rise of the Corporate State.* Boston: Beacon Press.

Steiner, Rudolf (1977). *Towards Social Renewal.* London: Rudolf Steiner Press.

Steiner, Rudolf (1985). *The Renewal of the Social Organism.* Spring Valley, NY: Anthroposophic Press.

Stoddard, Lynn (1990). The Three Dimensions of Human Greatness: A Framework for Redesigning Education. *Holistic Education Review* 3:1, pp. 4–10.

Stoddard, Lynn (1992). *Redesigning Education: A Guide for Developing Human Greatness.* Tucson: Zephyr Press.

Stoddard, Lynn (1995). *Growing Greatness: Six Amazing Attitudes of Extraordinary Teachers and Parents.* Tucson: Zephyr Press.

Welter, Rush (1962). *Popular Education and Democratic Thought in America.* New York: Columbia University Press.

Wood, George H. (1992). *Schools that Work: America's Most Innovative Public Education Programs.* New York: Dutton.

"Treating education as a political tool rather than as a pedagogical art is at the very core of most problems in modern education. Education cannot serve the needs of human development when it is used as an instrument for inculcating the established beliefs, values, and prejudices of a given community in a new generation, en masse."

— *Ron Miller*

Schooling in the Modern Age: Core Assumptions Underlying the Standards Agenda

Ron Miller

The effort to nationalize and standardize how young people will learn about their world is not a passing political fashion but represents deeply rooted assumptions about the meaning and purpose of education in modern society. These assumptions were vividly evident in papers delivered by 20 leading scholars and researchers at a 1987 conference on educational reform held at Trinity University in Texas and publish-

This article was originally published as a review of Sergiovanni and Moore's *Schooling for Tomorrow: Directing Reforms to Issues That Count* (1989) in the Summer 1991 issue of the *Holistic Education Review* (P.O. Box 328, Brandon, VT 05733-0328). It has been revised by the author for publication in this volume.

ed in the book *Schooling for Tomorrow: Directing Reforms to Issues That Count* (Sergiovanni and Moore, 1989). Most of the authors are well known liberal theorists (many of them directly influenced by John Dewey's ideas), and throughout the book they argue against top-down bureaucratic control of schools and for a more democratic, decentralized approach to educational reform. A few chapters, notably Donald A. Schön's paper on reflective practice and Roland S. Barth's discussion of school leadership, are impor- tant contributions to our thinking about education in a democratic society. Yet most of these liberal educators fail to recognize that their own assump- tions about education and schooling — often clearly implied and some- times explicitly stated — plant the roots of a national standards agenda that is highly *anti*democratic.

Because the authors do not consider their own foundational assump- tions, what they present as a profound and far-reaching critique of contem- porary educational policy is in fact a shallow attempt to shore up the status quo. Like previous generations of mainstream educational reformers, these well-connected scholars seek to ameliorate (i.e., tinker around with) some of the more egregious problems in public schooling, without addressing or even raising the most essential, foundational questions underlying modern education. Reading their essays, I was reminded of a story told by Abraham Maslow to illustrate the failure of reductionistic psychology, about a man who comes upon a drunk walking in circles under a street lamp. The man asks the drunk what he is doing. "I'm looking for my keys," the drunk replies. Seeing that he obviously isn't finding them, the man asks if he is sure that he lost them in that spot. "No, I didn't," replies the drunk, "but the light's better here."

The keys that these authors seek — the keys to a genuinely humane, democratic, and liberating education — have to do with the inner, creative, spontaneous energies of the human spirit, with the quality of relationships between human beings, and with the complete transformation of our materialist, hierarchical culture. They will not — cannot — be found under the street lamp of the established educational system, no matter how hard we look. But the editors announce right at the beginning that this book has a "pragmatic bent"; in other words, the authors are looking at what is practical, given the dominant culture and structure of education, not at what is truly necessary. None of these scholars wishes to rock the educational boat too vigorously. Arthur E. Wise, who calls his approach a "new paradigm," nevertheless states, "It is wrong to think that restructuring means a totally different school structure" (p. 308).

However, if we are genuinely to move toward a "new paradigm" that is democratic, person-centered, and concerned with meaning rather than efficiency, we will need to root out the basic assumptions that have, for the past 150 years or so, defined the old paradigm. Let us begin that task here.

Assumption #1: *Education is primarily a political matter.* Because it is a state institution, public education is expected to embody the dominant ideals and ideologies of society at large. "Within our political system," writes editor Thomas J. Sergiovanni, "the 'whats' [the content of the curriculum] are appropriately decided by the policy process in response to the wishes of the people, directly and through government" (p. 6). Wise concurs: "It is, of course, a legitimate expectation that schools and teachers be accountable to the public. After all, schools are a public enterprise, publicly financed and serving public purposes. The public has a right to demand accountability in schools..." (p. 303).

In today's political climate, it is heretical to maintain that schools should *not* be accountable to the public will. But (as Rudolf Steiner long ago recognized), treating education as a political tool rather than as a pedagogical art is at the very core of most problems in modern education. Education cannot serve the needs of human development when it is used as an instrument for inculcating the established beliefs, values, and prejudices of a given community in the new generation, en masse. This is a fundamentally constraining process rather than a liberating one. It necessarily makes education an agent of control rather than an aid to growth, and it riddles the delicate art of education with the crude demands of politics.

Who is "the public," anyway? What gets passed down in schooling is not what everyone wants for their children, but what the most influential or powerful segments of the community succeed in forcing into the curriculum. As legal scholar Stephen Arons has demonstrated (1983), public education by its very nature will always reflect conflicts within the community over whose values are to be established. This is recognized by some of the authors in *Schooling for Tomorrow* as well. Judith E. Lanier and Michael W. Sedlak observe that schools "serve many different purposes for many different people.... Schools have conflicting, competing goals..." (p. 141). Likewise, Larry Cuban recognizes that "the public" is actually composed of various factions who "compete for their versions of how tax dollars should be spent for the children of the community" (p. 253). Given this conflict, education cannot be designed fully according to pedagogical concerns, but requires political savvy: "The key to the changes that I recommend will be the creation and sustenance of an influential political constituency," admits Michael W. Kirst (p. 87). The 20 authors in the book, assuming that education is essentially a matter of public policy, fail to consider whether it ever can be possible to design a truly humane, nurturing education so long as schooling remains an instrument of the state. This failure is most unfortunate.

Assumption #2: *Education should serve the economic interests of the nation*. Reflecting the dominant motivation of the school reform movement of recent years, editor John H. Moore states, "Perhaps never before in the history of the republic has the success of this nation and people been linked so inextricably to the quality of education available to young people in the nation's elementary and secondary schools" (p. 394). But of what does "national success" consist? Does it mean a society in which all people are leading meaningful, satisfying lives in healthy communities, a society that seriously endeavors to meet people's basic needs and to provide opportunities for their personal and spiritual development? Or does "national success" mean military power projected around the globe, economic domination over less developed nations, and the opportunity to consume a grotesquely disproportionate share of the Earth's resources? It is obvious which vision of "national success" has inspired leading educational reformers and the national standards movement. Although there are thousands of parents and citizens who dissent from this vision, who seek a more just, ecologically balanced culture instead, none of the authors in the book addresses this question. The implicit assumption is that the nation has economic goals and interests under which we all should be united, and that it is a primary task of schooling to get us marching in step.

Assumption #3: *Education should serve the employment needs of American corporations*. Former Secretary of Education Lamar Alexander is quoted as a major spokesman for the education reform movement: "To meet stiff competition from workers in the rest of the world, we must educate ourselves and our children as we never have before" (p. 23). As Kirst puts it, politicians such as Alexander "are concerned about economic competition, and state legislatures have therefore felt compelled to step in and preempt local discretion. State actions have been directed at the heart of the instructional process in order to upgrade the qualifications of the basic U.S. labor force" (p. 65). This is a chilling statement, which captures the gross reductionism of recent reform movements. Our children are not to be educated as human beings, with feelings, ideals, dreams, and unknown spiritual resources; they are to be reduced to a "labor force" that will work intelligently and diligently enough to keep their corporate employers competitive.

It is no secret that corporate elites have played a major role in the education reform movement. (Indeed, the conference at which the book's chapters were presented was underwritten by Southwestern Bell and called the "Bell Conference.") If education is in fact a political process, then we do not need to look far to see who exerts the most pressure and power in determining its course. The educational restructuring movement is obsessed with economic issues, with competitiveness, with the preparation of a productive work force. The authors in *Schooling for Tomorrow* never ask what kind of society, what kind of economic system, what kinds of cultural values would best bring out the talents and productiveness of people; they assume that the hierarchical corporate economy is here to stay and so the only question is how to prepare dependable workers for that economy.

Assumption #4: *State schooling is an appropriate means of promoting democratic values and traditions*. The authors all seem deeply committed to democratic values. But the discussion of democracy in the book is consistently abstract, academic, and far removed from the realities of American life. In none of the 400 pages is there serious recognition of the very real and severe limitations to democracy that have been perpetrated according to race, class, gender, ethnic heritage, and other human differences. There is no discussion of the myriad ways in which educational policies have, for a century and a half, served the interests of economic and political elites at the expense of local communities, people of color, the working class, and ethnic subcultures.

For example, in an essentially technocratic analysis, Douglas E. Mitchell attempts to describe the "legitimate interests" that vie for political influence over schooling. (Yes, we're back to assumption #1; we have never left it.) He lists these "stakeholders" as students, families, teachers, school administrators, local-school-district citizens, state governments, "the national civic community," and "corporations, universities and the military" (pp. 55–56). Most of these are abstract sociological categories that completely overlook the very diverse interests among students (such as different learning styles or different life goals), families (religious or ethnic values), and many others. Who is to determine which of these are "legitimate" interests? Mitchell argues that so long as all stakeholders "have a reasonable chance" to influence educational policy, then the system is democratic. But having a "reasonable chance" does not mean that different individuals and communities will get what they need out of their education, or what they desire! It means that whoever can control the policy process gets to impose their vision of schooling on everyone. And with policymaking becoming more concentrated at higher governmental levels, it is increasingly difficult for families or local communities to influence that process, and increasingly easy for more powerful entities such as "corporations, universities and the military."

In another revealing passage, Lee S. Shulman argues that teachers should not be "empowered" without carefully defining their roles. "Societies," he declares, "should not grant power to those who do not have the intellectual commitments and moral capacities to wield it justly" (p. 169). He does not apply this stricture to corrupt politicians or corporate raiders and speculators who put thousands of people out of work; apparently it is important to keep employees in line, but not important to hold the nation's elite to the same standard. Perhaps this is not what Shulman means, but his incomplete analysis is characteristic of the book. Public education embodies America's antidemocratic shadow side as much as it expresses democratic ideals, and to tinker around with the system as it stands is to leave the shadow side dangerously intact. We must stop pretending that this shadow is not present.

Assumption #5: *Teachers are professionals; students are their clients.* A large portion of the book is devoted to the topic of professionalism. In these sections, the authors are sincerely interested in freeing teachers from excessive control by bureaucratic superiors; they see educators as important moral leaders in society, not merely as technicians. But as the concept of "professionalism" is developed in these essays, a hierarchical, role-bound relationship between teacher and learner is firmly established. None of the chapters adequately addresses questions of pedagogical approach, the design of the learning environment, or the human relationship between adult and child; instead, several authors assert that teachers-as-professionals will simply know what is best for their students, and therefore should have the autonomy and authority to implement their knowledge.

But "professionals" are not immune from the political and cultural pressures on schooling, nor from the common tendency in modern culture to maximize their own professional power. Karl E. Weick and Reuben R. McDaniel, Jr., explicitly recognize that professional values — as opposed to personal values — "are 'owned' by and supportive of the larger society" (p. 334). According to Weick and McDaniel, professionals ought to "participate in the dominant coalition" that makes the political decisions about schooling. They explicitly refer to decision-making bodies as "these elites." In the "nonroutine" daily life of the classroom, teachers may be tempted to "apply personal rather than professional values" but must not do so because "outsiders" will view such decisions as "arbitrary" and "capricious" (p. 338). Here again is assumption #1: Education cannot be rooted in authentic human encounter, but must be controlled by politically determined standards.

In short, the professionalism advocated here is highly elitist. Weick and McDaniel define professionals as "those who through special training and socialization have gained a unique set of understandings that set them apart from nonprofessionals.... The power of the professionals is, in part, a function of their special knowledge and skills. If these are eroded and the mystery surrounding the professionals' work disappears, then the power of the professional is reduced" (p. 333). Arthur E. Wise similarly asserts,

"Knowledgeable professionals must make decisions on behalf of less knowledgeable clients" (p. 304). But should the human relationship between
teacher and learner be shrouded in the "mystery" of the teacher's presumably special knowledge? Should the teacher hold special "power" in the
educational encounter? Are these appropriate models for a humane, democratic education? These are crucial questions, which none of the authors in
the volume even bothers to ask.

On the contrary, Lanier and Sedlak put forth a concept of "teacher
efficacy," which they define as "the power one has to bring about a desired
effect" — in this case, "the desired student learning" (p. 131). The professional teacher needs to "manage both the social relations of the classroom
and the cognitive development of students" (p. 137). Nearly every author
in *Schooling for Tomorrow* takes these definitions for granted, as the very
essence of good teaching. They fail to realize that they are advocating a
pedagogy of control, a "banking" conception of education, as Paulo Freire
calls it, in which the adult is seen as the supreme authority, the source of
knowledge, and the final judge of success — while the students are seen as
empty vessels needing to be filled with the adults' superior wisdom.

The alternative to this assumption of teacher control is not, as we are
led to believe, pedagogical chaos. The alternative is a recognition that every
human being has a personal identity that unfolds according to organized,
meaningful patterns. Obviously, children do not know as much about the
world as do most adults, but neither are they empty vessels! Learning is a
meaningful engagement between the unfolding person and the vastly
complex world, a personal encounter, which a teacher may facilitate but not
"manage." The only author in the book who even remotely recognizes that
there are inherent patterns in child development that ought to be followed
is Harvard psychologist Howard Gardner (of "multiple intelligence" fame).
His chapter offers some welcome relief from the adult-controlled pedagogy
advocated elsewhere in the book. Yet even he ultimately supports such a
conception of education; in a revealing statement he says, "Education has
always been a struggle against human finitudes," such as limited mental
capacities or lack of motivation (p. 163). But only a society trying to inculcate
its preferred beliefs into presumably empty vessels — thus going against
the grain of human development — would see education as a struggle

against our own humanness! From a holistic perspective, our human identity — with all of its needs and potentials — is the irreducible starting point, and education then becomes a struggle on behalf of our human identity against cultural prejudice and repression.

A number of insightful psychologists, philosophers, and educators have made this criticism of mainstream education over the past two centuries. From Rousseau, Pestalozzi, Froebel, and Emerson, through Montessori, Steiner, Jung, Rogers, and Maslow, to recent radical educators Paul Goodman, John Holt, George Dennison, Ivan Illich, Paulo Freire, and many others, the holistic tradition has strongly emphasized the root meaning of education — to nurture and draw forth the intellectual, moral, social, and aesthetic qualities that reside in the human spirit. Yet none of these people — *none of them* — is considered by today's leading educational reformers to have anything relevant to say about "directing reforms to issues that count." The underlying reason for this is found in their last, and most fundamental, assumption.

Assumption #6: *The only valid knowledge is empirical, analytical, intellectual, and utilitarian.* Almost every author draws upon research studies in the social sciences to support his or her claims. Good education, as conceived in *Schooling for Tomorrow* and by the leaders of the standards movement, is not defined by its moral value, its vision of human potentials and a desirable society, but by the measurable results it produces in scientifically controlled tests. One contributor, Kenneth A. Sirotnik, does launch a good critique against reductionistic science and offers a credible phenomenological approach instead. But, as if to reassure his professional, scholarly audience that phenomenological research is legitimate, he contrasts empirical knowledge with "divine inspiration and mystical intervention" and insists that he relies only on empirical knowledge (p. 91).

It is easy to ridicule "mystical intervention" while safely ensconced in the materialist worldview of the modern age. It is easy to dismiss the "romantics" who talk about the child's spiritual essence, to consider them simply irrelevant. It is easy, but it is wrong. The modern worldview has suppressed a vital part of our human identity by relegating spirituality, intuition, imagination, and creativity to the out-of-bounds realm of "romanticism" and "mysticism." The authors in *Schooling for Tomorrow* do absolutely nothing to reclaim this vital part of the human spirit. Not only do they limit their own approaches to empirical models, but their conception of education is decidedly rational and intellectual. There is virtually nothing in these pages about the arts, music, theatre, dance, or playfulness — nothing about imagery or meditation, about the complementary functions of the left and right hemispheres of the human brain. Schooling is to be concerned with "constructive mental action" (Lanier and Sedlak), with instrumental and utilitarian uses of reason, with problem solving and higher-order thinking skills. That the human being is a complex, integrated whole, involving physical, emotional, transpersonal, and social as well as intellectual aspects of experience, is simply not considered.

In conclusion, I would claim that it is not the "romantics" who are irrelevant to the true reconstruction of education — it is the reductionist worldview shared by the scholars who participated in the 1987 Bell Conference and in all the conferences, commissions, and committees that have paved the way to Goals 2000. Standards and accountability do not address the severe economic, ecological, and cultural challenges humanity faces over the next few decades. We shall soon be forced to recognize that the reign of materialism, nationalism, and corporate control over resources is turning our culture as well as our planet into a wasteland. We may soon realize that the schools of tomorrow need to be grounded in a deep appreciation for the interconnectedness of all life on Earth. They need to be based on a profound understanding of human potentials — including the spiritual essence that transcends our cultural and nationalist prejudices. The schools of tomorrow need to hold a clear vision of an ecologically healthy and economically just world, a world in which conflict and competition are replaced by cooperation in pursuit of our common survival. The reformers who met in 1987 did not offer a vision of "schooling for tomorrow," but rehashed a version of schooling from the past, stubbornly imposed on the future. Their book does not direct reforms "to issues that count" but away from the issues that count most: justice, peace, ecological sensibility, genuine community, and true human fulfillment.

References

Arons, Stephen (1983). *Compelling Belief: The Culture of American Schooling*. New York: McGraw-Hill.

Segiovanni, Thomas J., and John H. Moore (eds.) (1989). *Schooling for Tomorrow: Directing Reforms to Issues That Count*. Needham Heights, MA: Allyn & Bacon.

"For at least a hundred years, education has been thought of as akin to mass production and mass marketing, as if the job of schools is to turn out as efficiently as possible the reliable, quality-controlled products that the consumers — the parents and employers — are looking for. Much of the awful stuff that goes on in schools can be traced to this inappropriate analogy between learning processes and the procedures by which inert physical materials are manufactured and sold."

— *James Moffett*

Reforming School Reform

James Moffett

I have spent about 30 years working to change schools — a full-time career effort that began during the reform of the 1960s and has lasted into the reform of the 1990s. The main thing that has been borne in on me is that most schooling problems are not learning problems. They are institutional and political problems, many of which are the same that plague the larger culture. That is, most of what schools struggle with are not difficulties inherent in learning to read and write or do science and math. Their difficulties stem from the society at large and are merely reflected in schools.

Institutionalitis. First of all, school systems are bureaucracies, and second, they are *public* bureaucracies. Schools share some problems with many other large institutions, which tend notoriously to standardize, mechanize, and compartmentalize whatever materials or procedures they are dealing with. Institutionalism makes its own rules and tends to appro-

Adapted from *The Universal Schoolhouse: Spiritual Awakening Through Education*, chapters 5 and 6. © 1994 by Jossey-Bass Publishers, San Francisco. This excerpt is reprinted by permission of the publisher.

priate more and more resources for its own functioning. It's a parasite that feeds itself first.

Schools play out a tragicomedy. Learning language and literacy, for example, are extremely personal, and yet schools are supposed to pull this off in absurdly public circumstances. Since the 1960s I have, along with other curriculum developers, advocated that the language arts curriculum move toward more individualization, interaction, and integration. This would make learning more personal, interpersonal, and holistic. Learning to speak is more difficult than learning to read and write, but it occurs successfully at home (unless the child is defective or totally ignored) without any failures or dropouts because those three conditions characterize the spontaneous verbal life of the family. Schools could find no better model for teaching literacy, but individualization, interaction, and integration run exactly counter to the standardization, mechanization, and compartmentalization that are the hallmark of large institutions.

Commercialization. Ours is a society that seldom values something that has not been run through the market. Anything free and natural is suspect. If it were any good, it would cost something and be advertised. We're a nation trained to solve problems by purchasing something, whether the problem is how to get relief from hemorrhoids or how to get along with your spouse or teenager, to the point that managers of institutions think just like other good consumers.

The most direct determinant of curriculum is some form of commercial materials. The great majority of schools *buy* their curriculum; they don't create it. To this fact alone a major portion of their ills may be attributed. The curriculum-adoption conditions set by school districts and state departments of education constrain drastically what textbooks and other commercial school materials may contain or do. And the corporations who produce those materials for them should not be entrusted with anything so important as learning.

The worst aspect of materials created to pass adoption is that they are expected to accommodate the standardization, mechanization, and compartmentalization that characterize institutionalitis. Thus they militate against the individualization, interaction, and integration that learning requires. This fits the assembly-line mentality of both the public bureaucracies that are the consumers and the corporate manufacturers that are the producers. Adopted materials are also expected to mesh with various standardized tests, which always shrink the curriculum to fit their extremely narrow measures. Testing itself is one of those scourges of schooling that adoption keeps firmly locked into place.

Most textbooks come in series and packages because they constitute entire courses and even whole programs spread over many years. These series and packages are in fact *managerial systems*, usually replete with teacher and student directions and with tests. They do not just contain information about the subject, they install certain methods and procedures in the classroom that preempt the curriculum and remove choice from both teachers and students. For example, they render group process and individual inquiry virtually impossible, though they may make pretenses of including these, and they displace some of the content itself with excessive procedure designed to make the materials "teacher-proof" and to establish tight control over student activities. These commercially packaged curricula manipulate both students and teachers outrageously. It is *this* that makes them hopelessly boring even when the actual subject matter is not bad. It is well known that the more experienced, creative, and successful public school teachers become, the more they ignore commercial materials and devise their own curricula.

There is another way in which public education has to be decommercialized. A major reason that schools look to commercial companies for the curriculum they should be forging themselves is that the very concept of public schooling in this country derives from industrial engineering and business.

For at least a hundred years, education has been thought of as akin to mass production and mass marketing, as if the job of schools is to turn out as efficiently as possible the reliable, quality-controlled products that the "consumers" — the parents and employers — are looking for. Much of the awful stuff that goes on in schools can be traced to this inappropriate analogy between learning processes and the procedures by which inert physical materials are manufactured and sold.

What this dehumanized schooling prepares students for is to be manipulated like objects by governments and corporations as adults. Schools did not invent this materialism — the society thrust it on them — but it is impossible to understand why schools are the way they are and which direction change must take unless one grasps the full import of asking schools to function like commercial companies. This unseemly metaphor equating education with business has adversely affected the curriculum, the administration, and the relationship of schools to the outside world. It is assumed that schools are in the business of certifying people for employment (or for higher education toward the same end), but employers should determine at their own expense who is qualified to work for them. The effort to certify students for the job market spoils education, which is swamped by all the rites and tests that this entails. People have to develop as human beings before they can learn objective skills and be of any great use to employers.

The Public Will. When I began my career, I naively thought that bright ideas, good sense, and clear research indications would suffice to change curriculum. It was a turning point when I realized that the biggest obstacles to improving schools were political and mostly beyond the reach of educators alone.

The public has just the awful schools it "wants." Through the political chain of state legislatures and state and local boards of education, it controls schools much more than it admits and is therefore much more responsible for the negative results than appears. My own field of English education, for example, has been especially hard to reform because popular public prejudices about reading and writing often determine which methods and materials teachers may use. A book by some zealot can inflame the public about why kids can't read and cause a craze for one reading method at the expense of a balanced approach. And of course community censorship has increased dramatically in recent years, intimidating teachers more and more, even though the complainers almost never represent the majority.

The public has schools in a double bind. On the one hand, it stays apart from them, complains about them, and expects them to do an important job for their children as if schools should bear the whole responsibility for education. On the other hand, the public runs schools themselves in important ways by electing state and local officials who set policy according to popular notions about education and to political expediency. School administrators have to practice a lot of public relations. Teachers often complain to me that their principals try so hard to please every faction of the community that they make a mishmash of schooling. I know that many, if not most, teachers are doing many things they do not believe in and omitting much that they do believe in because they are not free to make many of the decisions about methods and materials.

Top-Down Posing as Bottom-Up

Official School Reform. The governmental school reform initiative of the early 1990s based itself on precisely two of the assumptions most responsible for the problems that reform aims to solve. One is that assessment is the instrument of change, because schools teach to tests. The second is that business knows best, because public education is really just another business.

American educators began to speak of "restructuring" about the same time Soviet leaders began to speak of *perestroika*. Both had come to realize that when officials too far from the scene of an action make key decisions about that action, disaster results. So both embarked on a campaign of decentralization, the Kremlin by deregulating the market and granting autonomy to provincial governments, American school districts by instituting site management and parental choice.

When George Bush decided to become an "education president" and set goals with the governors, however, this decentralization of the local school district was surmounted by a new federal centralization grafted onto an old state centralization. The supporters of his initiative, "America 2000," claimed that a national assessment and a national curriculum would be voluntary, but this was not honest, for state and district school constituencies always clamor for their officials to get on board the Washington train, so strong is the fear of being left out and so great is federal prestige even when not backed up by federal money.

Moreover, *state* governments were locked into the implementation of America 2000 via the governors' National Education Goals Panel and other activities of the National Governors' Association (a member of which was president-to-be Bill Clinton, who helped develop the initiative). Bush bypassed the Democrat-dominated Congress, which he didn't want to ask for money and with which he didn't want to share credit. He allied himself with the governors, because states have increasingly come to control schools. In my experience, the biggest single stumbling block to educational improvement are the state legislatures, because they wield far too much power in education for the little they understand about it. Since the United States Constitution does not empower the federal government to administer education, Washington cannot legally enforce national assessment or a national curriculum. So any proposal like America 2000 must depend on the states to carry it out.

Federal and state officials share a common investment in standardized testing: Along with funding, it constitutes the main way they can control or just get a handle on schools, since local school districts traditionally determine public education in this country. External exams mean external leverage, which elected or appointed officials can always justify on grounds that it is they whom the public is holding accountable for education. But the public usually blames school personnel, and state officials promise to reform schools as if their own decision making were not implicated in school failures. Not conversant with the actual processes of education, not involved in the means, politicians grab hold of the one thing that they can think about and speak to and that concerns their job — the bottom-line results, preferably in the quickly perusable form of test scores.

For little money and less thought, you can become an education president just by claiming to set higher standards. The broad goals that Bush and the governors fantasied for America 2000 constituted a wish list that everybody had been dreaming of for years — schools free of drugs and violence, drastic reduction in dropouts, all adults literate and able to compete in a global economy, all children starting school ready to learn, and all students of grades four, eight, and twelve scoring well on national tests. A press secretary can draft such a list in a half hour. How to accomplish these in the face of massive problems is quite something else. Such a proclamation implied, moreover, that schools had never thought about accomplishing these things and were simply waiting for the president and the governors to tell them what to do.

Unfortunately, this thoughtless initiative is not merely an insincere way of garnering votes but the principal way by which policy makers of good faith also propose to reform education. In 1993, the Clinton administration renamed America 2000 as "Goals 2000: Educate America Act" and asked Congress to enact it by passing into law Bush's national goals, federally chartering the National Educational Goals Panel, and creating a federal body to certify "voluntary" national curriculum standards and assessment. The last was immediately objected to by Janet Emig, chair of the English Standards Board, formed by the National Council of Teachers of English and the International Reading Association to write standards within their professions: "No federal body can legislate our success or failure (Emig 1993)."

The Bush/Clinton initiative implied that schools had failed in large measure because their standards were too low. Good teachers have always had high standards but have been thwarted in implementing them by external testing. The initiative sacrificed *teacher* standards to standardizing itself, which requires referencing to some old "norms" or to some threshold criteria ensuring that most students will pass. If school standards need to be raised, it is because external testing has set them too low. It was managers, not educators, who saddled schools with "minimal standards," whose original purpose was to protect schools from malpractice suits and other charges of graduating illiterate and ignorant students. "Demonstrating competence" benefits the institution, not the individual, and constitutes more the problem than the solution. *Citizens have no obligation to demonstrate their competence to the institution or the state.*

By stipulating only certain "core" subjects — math, science, English, history, and geography — Goals 2000 narrowed the concept of curriculum and therefore also limited choice. Arts and foreign languages, for example, were not included in the assessment planned at grades four, eight, and twelve. Nor would proposals to "reinvent schooling" that didn't echo such emphasis and priority be likely to receive development funding. National exams force schools to emphasize these "core" subjects first, the result of which, as all educators know, is that in order to cover themselves securely, schools will neglect other subjects like the arts and foreign languages. Actually, giving the *arts* high priority would be the best means to reverse the depersonalization of schooling that constitutes its largest single problem. Whether considering emotional issues such as alienation and low self-esteem or the intellectual and motivational difficulties of math and science, the arts provide the best growing medium. But state and federal government is not interested in the arts because it is dominated by business, which thinks math and science will serve its interests best, along, of course, with literacy, and a bit of history for patriotism and "our heritage."

Furthermore, stipulating tests of *separate* subjects (a built-in assumption) showed how little authors of Goals 2000 had thought about the crucial issue of *integrating* learning across the curriculum. Such national exams discourage learning that cuts across traditional subject divisions, whereas the current thinking in professional organizations for teaching the various school subjects emphasizes interdisciplinary education. It's hypocritical to push a strategy based precisely on teaching to tests and still claim that educators remain free to integrate learning so long as students do well on the tests of separate subjects.

Prioritizing and separating subjects also militates against individualization, which requires organizing curriculum around learners rather than subjects. (In fact, integrating learning naturally goes with individualizing it.) By reinforcing the old subject-centered approach, Goals 2000 thwarts the student-centered approach that real choice and school reform require. Exploiting the appeal of choice aimed to realize the old conservative goal of funding private schools with public funds. This is why it defined choice merely as family selection among some competing schools, not as learner selection of daily activities from alternatives arrayed across many possible sites and situations.

Theoretically, however, according to the 1991 request for proposals of the New American Schools Development Corporation, experimental schools applying for funding might integrate or individualize the curriculum or even dissociate education from school sites and deploy it across a whole community, as I advocate. But, interestingly, the authors of this manual were inspired to say yes to such possibilities only after their consultants specifically queried about them (NASDC 1991: 50–52). Naturally the authors could not exlude such possibilities and still call for proposals to "reinvent schooling." But they either didn't see or wouldn't acknowledge the contradictions between this call and their ultimate goal of a national assessment and national curriculum. It was surely these contradictions that prompted their consultants to question how far they would actually go.

The fact is that reinventing schooling is not consistent with a national curriculum, which already dictates what the subjects shall be, nor with national assessment, which in limiting itself to these subjects and to standardizable forms of testing takes any serious meaning out of "reinventing." You can't have it both ways — choice *and* standardization. Enforcing *conformity* as a way to *innovate* characterizes this centralized approach masquerading as grass roots experimentation: "You are free to use any means to reach our goals as measured by our tests."

Testing, Testing, Testing. America 2000 did not arise in education quarters, conspicuously bypassed educators, and was heavily criticized for being pushed through with very little debate even among policy makers themselves. "Go Slow on National Curriculum, Tests, ASCD Warned" read the headline of the May 1991 issue of *ASCD Update,* which featured a report on the annual conference of its parent organization, the Association for Supervision and Curriculum Development, the chief national organization for school principals and superintendents, other district or state administrators, curriculum specialists, and researchers. "With remarkably little deliberation or involvement of practicing educators, the United States appears to be rushing headlong toward a new national assessment system and its implied national curriculum, speakers warned participants." Chris Pipho, an analyst with the Education Commission of the States, which represents governors no less, declared, "I feel very strongly that at this point it is unbridled, running loose, rampant, and so far undebated... If you're opposed to a national test, now's the time to get in gear and head them off at the pass (ASCD 1991: 1, 6–7)." Other speakers "presented a number of potential problems with a system of common exams: that exams won't be made part of a comprehensive plan to improve curriculum, teaching, and textbooks; that the 'authentic' performance-based exams called for as part of a national assessment are unproven on a wide scale and will be costly;

that exam results will not be used to improve instruction for students who do poorly; and that U.S. schools already devote too much time to assessment (ASCD 1991)."

Students and teachers don't need tests. Assessment for *learning* purposes is no problem, because the data can be as rich as the learning activities themselves. Teachers can easily monitor performance when they examine student products and witness their processes. Because they work with students over a long period of time, teachers can make *composite judgments* based on continuous observation on numerous occasions supplemented by periodic conferences. Portfolios and projects are best assessed on site, and no one has any idea of how to standardize the assessment of them for purposes of comparing results around the country or the globe. Good education simply does not require comparing students or schools with each other, which is the only point of standardized evaluation. The real problem is to get going the kind of *productive* classrooms where authentic performances, portfolios, and projects do in fact thrive. The right curriculum solves the problem of assessment. The reverse is not true, that the right assessment solves the problem of curriculum.

Everything in assessment depends on *how much time and space* it encompasses, on how big the arena of action is. For extremes, compare a problem specific enough for a student to solve in 15 or 20 minutes on one rare occasion in exam-room conditions with, on the other hand, continuous observation of a student's problem-solving abilities across numerous different circumstances. Advocates of behavioral objectives insisted on assessing acts specific enough to manifest entirely on one short occasion and soon enough after a lesson to establish cause and effect. But the higher and more intricate the mental activity, the more difficult it is to capture on one short occasion. Consider the many long-range projects out of school that best represent complex thinking and creative problem-solving. Moreover, the accuracy of assessment increases with the number of samples, which is also a factor of spreading performance over time and space. Taking quick samples every four years as in national assessment, or even once or twice a year, makes for skimpy, shoddy assessment even for its senseless purpose of comparing scores around the nation or the world.

Tests are for outsiders, for *their* purposes, some of which are legitimate. In writing and consulting, I suggest that parents and administrators
should assess how good their schools are by taking slice-of-life samples of
what's going on there, that is, by examining performance for themselves as
this manifests in portfolios and other products or as they can hear and see
student activities in audiotapes and videotapes. In the long run, however,
the laity judges schools mainly by practical outcomes — by how well
graduates can handle their lives, their children's lives, their jobs, and their
civic responsibilities. It is not by test scores but by real-life behavior that the
public, including employers, is assessing education. Fair enough. Testing,
on the other hand, really just provides fodder for a system of institutional
self-monitoring that indicates cheaply and simply where teachers and
students should be placed and when they should be moved on. This is a
system of routing and promoting, qualifying and disqualifying, including
and excluding that should itself be reformed.

Since the whole system of testing comes down ultimately to certifying
graduates of all educational institutions for jobs, it is a colossal example of
how the private sector foists onto the public sector, at public expense,
something that it should be doing, at its own expense. Employers — and
colleges too for that matter — should screen applicants themselves by their
own means. If they did, schooling could in fact send them better-educated
applicants. If that is not ironic enough, consider that school certification
now indicates so poorly who to admit or hire that it serves badly anyway
even the purpose for which this intolerably high price is paid. The real
problem for colleges and businesses is that the education of virtually all
applicants has been crippled by the very testing system that is supposed to
do their screening for them.

In addition to being obliged to accommodate the College Board and
various governmental directives at all levels, school districts *buy* their
curricula and most of their tests from national manufacturers, whose first
principle is to sell what has sold. These and other uniformizing forces long
ago combined to create a *de facto* national curriculum and national assessment. America *already* has what government is urging today as innovation.

It is the *users* who should assess schooling, not the state. This is the
only pertinent and honest accountability. Since to assess is to control, user

assessment would restore power to the citizenry. People using public libraries and museums don't take tests. They assess such institutions by saying what they want or what they want changed, by praising and complaining, by supporting them or not. Schools are public facilities that should satisfy their users. Admittedly, the problem is circular in that good public education depends on educating the public. Ignorant people may want some ignorant things. But the way to solve this problem is to educate for choice by helping learners make their own decisions, not to use their ignorance as an excuse to patronize them and decide for them.

Public accountability does not depend on centralized assessment. In fact, accountability loses meaning exactly in the measure that the public allows district, state, and federal governments to structure education from the outside and yet blame schools for poor results. When users set and assess their own curricula, moreover, whatever need there may have been for state and federal intervention to offset local bureaucracy is obviated, along with the need for *any* government to safeguard individual rights.

Why should education be mobilized anyway around the question of national assessment? Why should we even assume that assessment of any sort is a major way to reform schools? Why not mobilize for things that experience *does* indicate, like personalizing learning, integrating the curriculum, renovating teacher training, or organizing community networks? Why not, in other words, focus on the learning environment and learning processes themselves? Why on *assessment*? When you think of all the factors that enter into the success or failure of schooling — many intrinsic to mass public education, many inflicted on schools by an ailing society — to single out assessment seems so arbitrary as to be downright bizarre even without its long history of implication in school failure. Nothing in experience, research, or logic warrants this assumption. It exemplifies quintessentially how the main problem of schooling is still being used as the main solution.

"Business Knows Best." The government's conviction that business can show schools how to set their house in order derives not only from a concern about the employability of the populace but from the old false analogy that running schools is like manufacturing and marketing commodities. When Lee Iacocca addressed the Association for Supervision and Curriculum Development at its annual convention in May 1991, he said,

"Your product needs a lot of work, and in the end, it's your job." His tough attitude on the problem of the increasing numbers of children in poverty was that "your customers don't want to hear about your raw materials problem — they care about results." So children are raw materials. After complaining that Chrysler spends $60 million for school taxes and still has to teach basic skills to many workers, he likened graduating a student who can't read to selling a car without an engine: "It's a massive consumer fraud." (How good it must have felt to be able to level against another "industry" the charge that has so often been leveled at his.) He pursued the theme of consumerism: "Right now, American education has a lot of dissatisfied customers (Iacocca, 1991)."

Comparing children to metal, rubber, and plastic is hard to forgive. Comparing human growth to factory production implies the putting together of inert parts into subassemblies that eventually go into that final assemblage, the product. This applies an inorganic, particle approach to an organic, holistic process. But what irrational thinking anyway to compare students to products when these "products" are also the "consumers," both as students and later as parents and taxpayers. Furthermore, these consumers are tax-paying voters who also *run* schools — much more, as I've tried to show, than we admit. Chrysler's customers don't run the company. What possible sense can this analogy between school and business make when the raw materials, the products, and the consumers are all one and the same — the citizens?

Unfortunately, it is part of current executive thinking to lump all large enterprises together from a purely managerial viewpoint and thus to ignore the actual nature of each enterprise. Managing is managing, it is thought, regardless of whether the organization is a foundation, a government agency, a for-profit company, or a public institution. Manufacturing executives think they can tell an education system what it ought to do because they look on schooling as just another outfit to run. But what the outfit *does* is critical.

The idea that business knows best and that education should imitate the secret of its "success" — competition — underlies the movement toward national assessment. This approach to reform is faulty from one end to the other — from the initial assumptions to the consequent strategies. If rationalization were not standing in for rationality, and were it not backed by government and business, this line of thinking would not even have to be refuted.

It is simply not true that educational change awaits new ideas or higher goals or more information. What we know to do far exceeds what we are free to do. Neither more research nor assessment data nor bright ideas will improve public education if we can't act on what we already know. The blockages are the key. Thus I have dwelt on *why* known good things do not occur. Unless you analyze and remove the obstacles to the good ideas we have, educational reform is impossible. From years of working with educators in the classroom, I know very well what constitute obstacles within the profession, but the more deeply I've been forced to consider the roots of professional inadequacy, the more I'm led back out into the society. From a shallow critique of schooling we could easily blame poorly qualified teachers. But until schooling begins to metamorphose into a humane, creative garden of learning, public education will continue to attract too few of the best people into the profession and thus force itself to accept many who are poorly qualified. Many heroines and heroes do go into schools, and some of the more saintly among them even stay, but too many of them burn out and leave or sell out and resign themselves to doing a lot they do not believe in and to not doing what they know to do.

Merely blaming school people will change nothing. They need help from a society that will take responsibility for what they cannot control. Current cries for reform appear to them as "teacher-bashing," as not only ascribing educational failure entirely to them but also as demanding that they penitently shoulder the burden of reform *in addition to* an already impossible set of responsibilities. When leading teacher workshops on innovation, I am very careful to make clear that school reform has to be part of a bigger social reform that goes beyond teachers' jurisdiction and that innovation must solve the problems teachers already face, not merely add a new level of difficulty and frustration. Successful reform will work in the measure that it changes educational conditions so as to attract more of the people who will *make* it work.

The mandate to reinvent schooling does not mean we have to scrap everything and start from scratch. Most of the desired reform could be achieved simply by throwing out unjustified practices now filling the curriculum and pulling together into a unified learning field the many excellent practices that generations of educators have advocated, a few of which certain schools have already managed to implement in bits and pieces, often under special circumstances. Imagine the exasperation of those educators who *have* begun successful changes only to have government announce with a flourish of trumpets that it is going to reassert even more strongly the standardized testing and other centralization that such experimental enclaves have fought to waive in order to succeed.

The best ways of learning are not recondite exotica. They are taking place all around us all the time, if not often in public schools, then in some private schools. But if not in any schools at all, then everywhere else — at home, in the workplace, on the playground. People are learners, and they are learning all the time. We already know what works. More practical evidence exists for effective learning than special research could ever tell us. The prospect for reform is much more positive than it looks: find out how to act on what we know about learning, and don't let politics and economics obscure this obvious practical knowledge staring us in the face from the whole environment.

References

ASCD (Association for Supervision and Curriculum Development) (1991). Go Slow on National Curriculum, Tests, ASCD Warned. *ASCD Update.* May 1991: 1, 6–7).

Emig, Janet (1993). Quoted in "Curricular Standards: Federal or National?" *Reading Today* (June/July 1993): 40.

Iacocca, Lee (1991). Quoted in "Sound Bites." *ASCD Update.* May 1991: 5.

NASDC (New American Schools Development Corporation) (1991). *Designs for a New Generation of American Schools.* Arlington, VA: Author.

"The assumptions embedded in the language of reform over the past dozen years offer a distorted view of the child and the nature of education. The child, indeed, has become 'a mere creature of the state' by the systematic elimination of any aspect of an individual's humanity beyond the intellectual capital he or she may provide for the nation and the nation's economy."

— *Jeffrey Kane*

Educational Reform and the Dangers of Triumphant Rhetoric

Jeffrey Kane

One of the great ironies of federal educational reform since the publication of *A Nation at Risk* is that it has virtually nothing to do with children. Predictably, federal reform efforts, lacking recognition of the most essential element of the educational process, the child, have been impractical and ineffective. Compounding the irony, the increasingly strident efforts to assure "our very future as a Nation and a people" (National Commission on Excellence in Education [NCEE] 1983, 5) are undermining the ideal of democracy where government is instituted to secure certain "unalienable rights" rather than a supply of labor.

These ironies are embedded in the presuppositional structure on the discourse of federal educational policy during the last three presidential administrations. They are bound up in primary and unexamined assumptions about (1) the economic risks to our nation, (2) the need for trained intelligence to serve national economic interests, (3) the role of high standards of academic achievements in the development of such intelligence, and (4) children as a national economic resource open to governmental development much like coal and oil reserves. The purpose here is to clearly illustrate and challenge these assumptions.

Education in the Absence of Children

A Nation at Risk established the conceptual foundations for federally sponsored educational reform initiatives since 1983. The report described the need for educational reform in terms of perceived economic risks stemming from international competition and low productivity on the part of the American work force. Low labor productivity was interpreted as a consequence of inadequate educational preparation — a particularly vexing problem at the dawn of an "information age."

Absent from *A Nation at Risk*, and the subsequent federal discourse on reform, is any definition or insight into how children grow; what they need; how they learn; how schooling affects their perceptions, values, interests, aspirations, and beliefs; or how education affects their contributions to the American economy and the nation. Absent is any recognition that intelligence is an essential, defining element of a growing human being. Absent is any understanding of the emergence of an individual human being with a unique and evolving sense of identity, with a desire to understand what the world is and how it works, with unique aesthetic, moral and personal sensibilities, with needs to create, communicate, and belong, and with a complex range of emotions from anger to wonder.

The whole of federal educational reform since the early eighties identifies "childhood" as an impersonal state of intellectual potential and "education" as a means of actualizing economically valuable intellectual skills. The error here is in assuming that children *have* intelligence rather than that they *are* intelligence — that intelligence is an essential attribute of their being rather than a possession of something distinct from themselves. If reform is to be successful, it will require us to develop a refined and comprehensive image of children, individually and collectively. If we are successful in applying current assumptions underlying reform, we may well create a generation of distorted individuals with narrowly conceived and overly developed capacities for thought and action.

While one may argue that the concept of the child described in the paragraph above is romantic, the fact remains that children are profoundly complex and that effective teaching requires an understanding of the fundamental dynamics and subtleties of growing children. To insist otherwise is to deny the reality that teachers face daily as they work with children. No, the concerns here are not romantic; rather, the economic model of the child as potential skilled intelligence is political chimera. For all the hard-headed language of business and weighty concerns about the future of our nation, the federal educational reform initiatives over the past dozen years have failed. And, as a body of evidence for such failure mounts, the federal response has been to redouble its efforts rather than to question its assumptions and objectives. Where Reagan exhorted the nation to reform education, Bush developed strategic plans. Where Bush developed strategic plans, Clinton implemented legislative measures backed by federal funds. Reason demands we reexamine the beliefs and aims of this most recent era of federal educational reform initiatives.

The Transition from Assumptions to Action

The assumptions underlying the current era of federal policy initiatives are evident in the opening declaration of *A Nation at Risk*, "Our nation is at risk. Our once unchallenged preeminence in commerce, industry, science and technological innovation is being overtaken by competitors throughout the world" (NCEE 1983, 5). The report went on to explain that the international challenges to the American economy were not confined to specific industries such as Japanese auto-making, South Korean steel production, or German machine tools. These instances of international competition illustrated only the intensity of the industrial marketplace. Far more problematic competition was expected as we moved further into the "information age" (NCEE 1983, 7). Whereas our previously industrial economy was grounded in "an abundance of natural resources and inexhaustible human enthusiasm," the information age would require a new economic foundation, one in which, "Knowledge, learning, information and skilled intelligence [were] the new raw materials of international commerce.... " (NCEE 1983, 7).

This conceptualization of national economic peril placed education at the center of our national struggle for prosperity. Economic culpability and the possibility of economic renewal were placed in the school. Regarding culpability, the report stated, "[T]he educational foundations of our society are presently being eroded by a rising tide of mediocrity that threatens our very future as a Nation and a people ... others are matching and surpassing our educational attainments" (NCEE 1983, 5). Regarding the possibility for renewal, the report argued that American schools had always assumed a significant role in building the American economy from the land grant colleges that "provided the research and training that developed our national natural resources and the rich agricultural bounty of the American farm" in the nineteenth century and the educated work force necessary for American industry from the "late 1800s through mid-twentieth century" (NCEE 1983, 33). With the dawn of the information age, the schools would need to supply the economy with individuals with the capacity to process information. Where the nation's economic capital was once primarily measured in terms of natural, agricultural, industrial, and monetary resources, the capital of the new economic age would be the collective and individual minds of all citizens, particularly children.

The report stated that the problems of American education resulted from "a rising tide of mediocrity" and insisted that we had "allowed this to happen to ourselves" (NCEE 1983, 5). We had allowed ourselves to "*squander* the gains in student achievements made in the wake of the Sputnik challenge" (NCEE 1983, 5; emphasis added). It added, "History is not kind to *idlers*" (NCEE 1983, 6; emphasis added). Clearly American schools were perceived as the victims and purveyors of self-indulgence.

The suggested remedy to the perceived problem of self-indulgence was "excellence." The report defined excellence for individual learners in terms of "performing on the boundary of individual ability in ways that test and push back personal limits, in the school and in the work place" (NCEE 1983, 12). Institutionally, the term was defined relative to high expectations and commitment to help students achieve them. At the societal level, it was described as the adoption of these policies so that "through the education and skill of its people [our nation could] respond to the challenges of a rapidly changing world" (NCEE 1983, 12). The recommendations offered for national action were based on the premise that, "We must demand the best effort and performance from all students, whether they are gifted or less able, affluent or disadvantaged, whether destined for college, the farm, or industry" (NCEE 1983, 24). The nation could no longer suffer the self-indulgent, "diluted," and "diffused" "cafeteria style" curricula "in which the appetizers and desserts can easily be mistaken for the main courses" (NCEE 1983, 10). Rigorous academic standards, intellectually-based curricula and high student achievement were said to be required.

The educational problems of our nation were not described in terms of poverty, a lack of educational resources, poor systems of educational accountability, bureaucratic organizational structures, or curricular and instructional models unresponsive to the needs, interests, or developmental characteristics of children. The national educational imperative was not to develop greater insight into the growth of children, exercise greater creativity and efficacy in working with them, design more specific and effective means of accountability for the education of individual children, or restructure schools to give them the flexibility they needed to guide the education of the children of the community they serve. Rather, the imperative was to set high arbitrary standards with the demand that they be achieved.

Crystallizing its conception of the federal government's interest, the report concluded that, "It is ... essential — especially in a period of long-term decline in educational achievement — for government at all levels to affirm its responsibility for nurturing the nation's intellectual capital" (NCEE 1983, 17).

The notion of children as "intellectual capital" did not begin with the publication of A Nation at Risk. It derived from the concept of "human capital" which made its way into federal policy as early as the 1960s when it was reasoned that healthy, well-fed and well-educated people are likely to be economically productive. Alan J. DeYoung indicates that "such arguments were instrumental in the creation of a variety of compensatory programs mounted in the schools and communities as part of President Johnson's War on Poverty programs in the 1960s" (DeYoung 1989, 91).

When defining children as human capital, we assume that they are a public resource and open to development for economic, political, or social objectives. They acquire the attributes of other inanimate objects like raw materials for production, machine tools, or electrical energy. In a manufacturing plant, the conception of the individual as capital, as a particular set of economically valuable skills, is reasonable, albeit short-sighted. Once an individual has agreed to take a job in, let us say, an industrial plant, he is not there as an autonomous agent, as a person with rights to determine his own role, set his own objectives, or chart a unique course with destiny. However, if the American ideal of democracy is to have meaning, the individual, beyond the laborer, *is* an autonomous agent with all the rights and privileges guaranteed by the American Constitution. The concept of human capital is, at best, appropriate only within the confines of a contract of employment (loosely defined) and cannot be used to substitute for a definition of a human being socially, politically, or culturally.

A Nation at Risk refined the notion of human capital for a post-industrial economy; it introduced the concept of "intellectual capital" and placed it at the very heart of our hopes for national economic recovery. In an "information age" human capital was not measured in physical but intellectual terms. The danger here is that *A Nation at Risk* assumed not only that the concept of human capital is appropriate in education but that the human mind itself — the quintessential element of humanity reserved from the powers of government — the source of freedom protected by the American Constitution — is a public resource. The report asserted "the right" of government "at all levels" to shape the development of children's minds in order to meet prescribed economic goals.

Three years subsequent to the publication of *A Nation at Risk*, the Carnegie sponsored Task Force on Teaching as a Profession issued the most influential non-governmental report of the decade, *A Nation Prepared: Teachers for the 21st Century*. Building upon the concepts of a nation endangered by international economic competition and the pivotal role of education in providing a productive work force in an "information age," the report argued that

> [t]he 1980s will be remembered for two developments: the beginning of a sweeping reassessment of the basis of our nation's economic strength and an outpouring of concern for the quality of American education. The connection between these two streams of thought is strong and growing. (Task Force on Teaching as a Profession [TFTP] 1986, 11)

Like *A Nation at Risk*, the report identified low productivity as the sources of America's weakness in the international marketplace. The Task Force concluded, "America's ability to compete in world markets is eroding. The productivity growth of our competitors outdistances our own" (TFTP 1986, 2). Low productivity was believed to have been the consequence of an educational system ineffective in providing labor with the knowledge and skills necessary for the post-industrial workplace. Arguing that "Advancing technology and the changing times of international trade are remolding the basic structure of international economic competition" (TFTP 1986, 13), the Task Force emphasized the national need for highly skilled workers. Such workers in a "Knowledge-Based Economy" would be identified by, "a cultivated creativity that leads them to new problems, new products and new services before their competitors get to them" (TFTP 1986, 20). Given this perception of the circumstances, the report concluded that the American people "rightly demand an improved supply of young people with the knowledge, the spirit, the stamina and the skills to make the nation once again fully competitive" (TFTP 1986, 2).

The notion of "an improved supply of young people" implied that schools should ensure that their graduates were equipped with the intellectual skills desired by American corporations. The function of schools was not to guide students in their development as human beings, as autonomous thinkers with unique values, aspirations, and life goals; the function of schools was not to help students discover a sense of meaning in their work, a sense of purpose in their lives, or a sense of moral responsibility to humanity. With children defined as "intellectual capital" and a generation perceived as a "supply," the concept of improvement related to the limited range of intellectual skills thought to be necessary to the productivity of American labor. Continuing the transition from human capital to intellectual capital first begun with *A Nation at Risk*, the Task Force concluded, "The American mass education system, designed in the early part of the century for a mass-production economy, will not succeed unless it not only raises but redefines the essential standards of excellence" (TFTP 1986, 3). The heightening and redefinition of standards had nothing to do with the academic needs of students or the effectiveness of schools in leading children toward the development of their full potentials as human beings;

such actions related to the perceived needs for trained intelligence to increase corporate productivity, competitiveness, and profitability.

In September of 1989, President Bush called the nation's governors to an education "summit." Accepting, as given, the economic models of education undergirding the educational reforms of the 1980s, the group's "Joint Statement" argued that the United States needs "an educated work force, second to none, in order to succeed in an increasingly competitive world economy" (U.S. Dept. of Education 1989, 1). The President and Governors declared, "We believe that the time has come, for the first time in U.S. history, to establish clear, national performance goals, goals that will make us internationally competitive" (U.S. Dept. of Education 1989, 1).

Where previously the federal role in education, constrained by the Tenth Amendment, had been to "identify" the national interest in education, and where such interest when articulated in the private sector lacked legislative clout, the Summit was intended to set a national strategy for action. In describing this "federal/state partnership," the statement explained, "The President and the Governors are committed to achieving the maximum return possible from our investments in the nation's educational system" (U.S. Dept. of Education 1989, 3). Employing the language of business, the federal and state governments were seen as investing in intellectual capital — children's minds — and as having the authority to demand a return on the outlay of their resources.

The president and governors assumed that children were intellectual capital and intellectual capital alone. There was no pretense about the dignity, freedom, and sanctity of the human being beyond the intellectual resources individuals could provide to American corporations. Unrestrained by such considerations, the participants of the summit asserted that government at the federal and state levels, investing in the development of a purely public resource (the minds of children), had the right to insist upon a maximum return on investment. Their commitment was not to young American citizens; their responsibility was not to ensure an education responsive to childrens' needs, interests, and capacities; their sole objective was to produce refined intellectual capital with maximum economic efficiency.

In April of 1991, the U.S. Department of Education issued *America 2000: An Educational Strategy* built upon the federal and state commitments made in 1989. The document was defined as "A National Strategy, not a federal program" to achieve key national educational objectives by the year 2000 (U.S. Dept. of Education 1991, 1). Confirming the importance of local control in education and states' rights, the role of the federal government was limited but included its responsibility to set standards (U.S. Dept. of Education 1991, 2).

The need for such standards was summarily expressed in terms consistent with what had by this time become the common language of the prevailing internationally oriented intellectual capital approach to educational policy. The need was identified as "America's skills and knowledge gap" (U.S. Dept. of Education1991, 5). *America 2000* explained that in the eight years since the publication of *A Nation at Risk* "we haven't turned things around in education. Almost all our education trend lines are flat. Our country is idling its engines" (1991, p. 5).

The statement suggested that the rest of the world was not "sitting idly by" while American "employers [could not] hire enough qualified workers" (1991, 5). In keeping with the assumptions of educational reform of the 1980s, *America 2000* proposed a strategic plan to secure the supply of intellectual capital believed to be necessary to power America's economic engines. The six goals set educational objectives for various populations in accordance with their possible contributions to the perceived American need for intellectually skilled labor. Goal 5 explicitly called for every American adult to be literate with the "knowledge and skills necessary to compete in a global economy and exercise the rights and responsibilities of citizenship" (1994, 9). Goal 1 proposed that "All children in America will start school ready to learn" (1994, 9).

Goal 1, at first blush, seems to represent a national concern for the health, safety, and well-being of young children. However, *America 2000* depicts children in need as "innocent victims of adult misbehavior" (1994, 7), rather than as members of families beleaguered by poverty, racism, personal tragedy, or the isolation and hopelessness that accompany unemployment and underemployment. Given this perception of the problem, what the strategic plan offered amounted to nothing but an exhortation for communities "to discover the timeless values that are necessary for achievement" (U.S. Dept. of Education 1994, 21). The "specific strategy" was to mobilize the "'little platoons' that have long characterized well-functioning American communities" (U.S. Dept. of Education 1994, 21) to (1) adopt the six national goals, (2) establish plans for achieving them, (3) measure their progress, and (4) support the development of a new American school. No national plan was presented to encourage the growth of communities, to enhance the quality of child care, to enrich the educational value of the home, or to promote nutritional programs. The notion that children should "start school ready to learn" referred to the values preschoolers should be taught so as to increase their disciplined efforts to achieve academically. It did not refer to their health, security, or sense of well-being.

Far more specific, far reaching, and instrumentally defined was Goal Three. It stated:

> American students will leave grades four, eight, and twelve having demonstrated competency in challenging subject matter including English, mathematics, science, history, and geography; and every school in America will ensure that all students learn to use their minds as well, so they may be prepared for responsible citizenship, further learning, and productive employment in our modern economy. (1994, 9)

Here, we do not find a delineation of national risks but a declaration of national requirements. The education of children was to be guided and held accountable by "New World Standards" intended to keep America competitive in a new, technologically-based economic world. These standards were to "incorporate both knowledge and skills, to ensure that, when they leave school, young Americans [would be] prepared for further study and the work force" (U.S. Dept. of Education 1991, 11).

America 2000 also proposed the creation of the National Education Goals Panel to establish a "new (voluntary) nationwide examination system ... based on the five course subjects, tied to the New World Standards" (U.S. Dept. of Education 1991, 11). The tests were to serve as the cornerstone of a national system of accountability to allow parents as well as governments at all levels to read the "report cards" of children, schools, local communities, and the nation. It was also hoped that the tests would be given additional clout by colleges using them in admissions and employers using them in their hiring practices.

The Bush administration maintained that the American Achievement Tests would not establish a national curriculum. They were concerned only with educational "results." "They [The New World Standards and the associated American Achievement Tests] have nothing to say about how those results were produced, what teachers do in the classroom from one day to the next, what instructional materials are chosen, what lesson plans are followed" (U.S. Dept of Education 1991, 32). The argument was, at best, educationally naive; it lacked recognition of assessment as a fundamental force in shaping instructional methods and it confused freedom to select pedagogical technique with curricular authority. It is unreasonable to claim that one has the authority to determine what students "need to know and be able to do" without establishing a curriculum.

The American Achievement Tests proved politically problematic, stalling *America 2000* before it made its way into legislation. Presidential politics took their course and Bill Clinton took office.

The national shift from right to left occasioned changes in federal educational strategy rather than intention. Clinton, as governor, had strongly supported the goals movement, with its fundamental intellectual capital orientation. His agenda was clearly stated in *Goals 2000: Educate America Act* — to promote "coherent nationwide, systematic education reform" (1994, p. 4). More specifically, the Act was (and is) intended to assist "in the development and certification of high-quality assessment measures that reflect the internationally competitive content of student performance standards" (U.S. Dept. of Education 1994, 4) and to support new initiatives to provide "equal education for all students *to meet high academic and occupational skill standards and to succeed in the world of employment and civic participation*" (U.S. Dept. of Education 1994, 5; emphasis added).

Admittedly, *Goals 2000* puts a distinctly Democratic spin on the national goals. For example, reminiscent of the Johnson administration's War on Poverty, the school readiness objectives include provisions for preschool programs, parent education, and initiatives for nutritional and health programs. However, the fundamental context for educational reform remains economic — in this case, the central focus is less on the needs of employers than the interests of individuals seeking productive employment as a means to securing their own happiness and well-being. As Governor of

Arkansas Bill Clinton explained, "…if we expect to compete in important areas with those who pay their people [a fraction] of what we pay to assure a decent living standard in our state and our nation, it is absolutely imperative that we do what we can to develop the only major resource we have left, the mind of the people of the U.S. and of Arkansas" (TFTP 1986, 10).

Goals 2000 operates on the assumption that an enhanced development of individual minds relative to the labor requirements of a postindustrial economy will benefit individuals and the prosperity of our nation as a whole. Its economic focus relies on the same faulty interpretation of the international economic environment as *A Nation at Risk, A Nation Prepared*, and *America 2000*: to wit, its uncritical belief that education should be driven by economic considerations, and that we, as a nation, have a cohesive and unitary set of economic interests in a competitive global economic environment.

On the Disjunction of Economic and Political Interests

"Nation" is foremost a political concept and secondarily an economic one. As technology has progressed and as trade barriers have faded, the borders separating nations do not serve as they had in the past to draw sharp economic distinctions. While a nation is composed of a people in a territory bound by a single government (including, possibly, a single economic system), economic interests in a postindustrial economy are not bound to a region, a system of government, or a single economic system. Economic entities, such as multinational corporations, identify their interests relative to their own profit both in their home nation and abroad. McDonald's will sell hamburgers wherever they find it profitable, will seek labor wherever it is most efficient and cost-effective, and will purchase resources wherever the supply is most consistently abundant and inexpensive. Such corporations are not concerned with national interests as much as they are obliged to serve their shareholders. They are not concerned with citizens as much as they are with shareholders, consumers, and labor.

Historically, in agrarian and industrial times, the concept of nation incorporated the notion of a common economic base; "the people" were rooted in the soil or bound up in the industrial development of natural resources. The difference in the perception of our nation as a political and as an economic community, if not subtle, was virtually irrelevant to defining American interests.

However, the oil embargo of the late 1970s and the skyrocketing prices for crude oil (in part precipitated by an American initiative to ensure the financial resources of the Shah of Iran to purchase American military goods) demonstrated in terms that every American could understand at the gas pump and supermarket counter that our nation's economy was subject to international events. The reindustrialization of Japan and Germany as well as the emergence of other industrialized nations highlighted our vulnerability with a wide range of highly marketable goods.

Our national economic well-being could not be isolated from international politics and economics. At the same time, new information technologies were beginning to revolutionize the storage, management, and communication of previously unimaginable bodies of data. New products and services found their way to the market on a daily basis. In addition, new technologies provided American corporations with the data management capacities to allow them to greatly extend their management beyond our domestic borders. American companies began to see the opportunities in foreign nations and to greatly expand their internationalized investments. This invigorated international emphasis enabled American corporations to greatly expand their markets and decrease their labor costs with little benefit to the vast majority of Americans. Joel Spring indicates that such factors, in combination with others such as changes in the tax law, "contributed to a decline in after-tax income for the lowest 60% of wage earners and an increase for the top 20%" (Spring 1993, 66).

American-based corporations now invest in projects overseas that import goods and services into the United States. In the same way, but to a lesser extent, corporations based in foreign nations invest in American projects resulting in exported goods and services. Japanese auto manufacturers have opened manufacturing plants in the United States for domestic sales and American corporations have opened plants throughout the world for distribution in foreign nations. Restrictions on free trade are diminishing and the borders between nations. Nations, as peoples bound by a common

territory and common government, are becoming economically anachro-
nistic.

Spring explains, "Workers, corporate leaders, and companies increasingly move from country to country in search of higher wages or, in the case
of companies, in search of a cheap labor supply" (Spring 1993, 66). He also
argues, following Robert Reich, that the upper strata of the new international work force "are losing allegiance to any particular nation and are
withdrawing support from national infrastructures" (Spring 1993, 66).
Simultaneously, corporations identified themselves less with national political interests than with their unique international economic interests.
While American economic and political interests are deeply entwined, the
needs and interests of "Corporate America" are not the same as those of our
nation and people.

In this context, recall the national risks identified by the National
Commission on Excellence in Education. American productivity was perceived as low due to inadequate knowledge of skills of the American work
force. No mention was made of ill-advised trade policies, corporate investment strategies, monetary policies, or banking legislation. No risks were
noted with regard to the problems posed by poverty, racism, child abuse
and neglect, or social injustice. The risks identified referred primarily to
corporate rather than our national interests. While references abound in the
rhetoric of reform about "our nation and our people" and the democratic
requirement for an informed citizenry, such concerns were economically
derived. Furthermore, national economic prosperity was and is misper-
ceived as a function of the competitiveness of American-based corporations
in a global economy.

Given the narrow and misguided conceptions of the risks faced by our
nation, it is not surprising to find inconsistencies with respect to the role of
education in increasing national economic productivity. In the 1970s and
1980s, American economic productivity was in decline at the same time
American students were increasing their educational attainments in terms
of their years of schooling. While it may be argued that such an apparent
contradiction was the result of decreased academic standards, there is no
evidence to indicate that low standards lead to low productivity or that high
ones have the opposite result. Alan DeYoung notes that the "classic studies

linking increased economic productivity with years of formal education …
[have not yielded] sophisticated econometric data on return to G.N.P. from
different types of formal education" (DeYoung 1989, 129). Economist Jesse
Burkhead notes,

> If we accept, as seems indisputable, the proposition that investment in
> education is "productive" for society as a whole, then it should be
> possible to apply microanalytic techniques to discover those combina-
> tions of resources, decision structures, or educational practices that are
> more productive or less productive of specific outcomes. Unhappily, to
> date, it hasn't worked…. The efforts to analyze schooling as a system have
> not, as yet, been useful for policy purposes. (in DeYoung 1989, 130)

The relationship between educational standards and economic productivity is particularly difficult to discern when we look at the relationship
between the two in the late 1980s and the early 1990s. In 1991, President
Bush stated that, "Almost all our educational trend-lines are flat." The data
provided in *The National Educational Goals Report: Building a Nation of
Learners* lead to a similarly dismaying conclusion. However, American
economic productivity has increased dramatically. In February of 1995, *The
New York Times* reported that productivity grew for the fifth year in a row.
"American business productivity improved in 1994 for the fifth consecutive
year, pushed up by the largest growth and output since 1984, the Labor
Department reported today. At the same time, business held labor costs to
the smallest gain in thirty years" (*New York Times*, 1995, D2). *Fortune* magazine in June of 1994 indicated that national productivity increased by "a
whopping 5.1% annual rate during the second half of 1993. Manufacturing
productivity, rising at an average of 2.4% a year in the 1980s, surged 3.8%
annually from 1991 through 1993" (Magnet 1994, 79). The conclusion
reached was that "whatever the absolute growth rate of U.S. productivity
in both manufacturing and services, it has been sufficient to keep America
number one on this front, well ahead of Japan and Europe" (Magnet 1994,
80).

A reasonable question here is why American productivity has shown
such dramatic growth — so as to keep us first in competition among nations
— while American education — as measured by standardized examinations — has accumulated such a dismal track record. If the answer lies in
the restructuring of American businesses to make them more "lean and
mean" or in the repositioning of American products and services to make

them more marketable or in the restructuring of tax laws to encourage long-term investment and risk-taking or in any number of similar factors, then we must ask if the "low productivity" of labor was and is the essential risk to our economic and national well-being. The connection between the development of intellectual capital and American economic productivity is, at best, obscure.

Children as Persons

In the midst of this maze of competing nations, interests, and theoretical perspectives, children walk into American classrooms. Their parents likely do not send them there with the understanding that in so doing they, first and foremost, are developing intellectual capital as the central American resource in a global economic marketplace. More likely than not, parents see their children as children — as distinctive human beings with hopes and problems, strengths and difficulties to overcome — as growing persons attempting to learn about the world and themselves. In this context, education begins with an appreciation of the distinctiveness and importance of the individual child. While many parents may send their children to school in the hopes they will acquire the knowledge and skills they need to be gainfully employed, many focus their concerns on their children as persons not as labor, not as consumers, not as citizens. The point here is to remind us, as once did the Supreme Court in *Pierce vs. Society of Sisters* (1925), that "The child is not a mere creature of the state."

The assumptions embedded in the language of reform over the past dozen years offer a distorted view of the child and the nature of education. The child, indeed, has become "a mere creature of the state" by the systematic elimination of any aspect of an individual's humanity beyond the intellectual capital he or she may provide for the nation and the nation's economy (however problematically interpreted). Given this context, the prime impetus for reform with its narrow conception of achievement has been to ensure — quoting President Bush and the governors once again — "the maximum return possible from our investments in the nation's educational system" (U.S. Dept. of Education 1989, 3). Through the schools and the investment they represent, government has asserted a proprietary interest in the development of public intellectual capital otherwise known as children, individually and collectively.

The rhetoric of reform has assumed that schools serve political and economic functions but has failed to recognize that schools are cultural institutions to the extent that they serve children as whole human beings learning to understand themselves, the world, and their place therein. While schools are often defined in terms of curriculum, instructional methods, organizational structures, and educational objectives, the concepts we employ embody substantial and often unrecognized assumptions. The definitions we use in creating curriculum, designing instructional methods, organizing schools or selecting objectives are predicated upon the belief systems we have developed in response to fundamental questions.

> What is knowledge? What is intelligence and how may it best be developed? What is learning and how can it be measured? What is the nature of the world? How shall it be studied and interpreted? Is truth to be found through revelation or scientific process, or is it knowable at all? What is it to be human? Is the very foundation of human identity to be found in the divine or are we social animals? What values or "valuing" processes would we teach? Are there responsibilities incumbent upon virtue of our humanity or are our relations with ourselves, one another, and the larger world circumscribed by questions of "the common good?" (Kane 1992, 47).

The language of reform has virtually eliminated discussion of the educational needs of children *qua* children, and questions such as these have been answered in terms purely political and economic. But answered they have been. Federal educational reform initiatives have charged the schools with a cultural function — to inculcate the language, modes of thought, standards of measure, and values of business. Whether a particular initiative focuses upon the needs of corporate America, the potential labor market for individuals, or simply consumerism, the cultural message is the same and the notion of the individual maintains a constant, narrow definition.

When we recognize the growing child as more than intellectual capital and understand that schools are primarily cultural institutions, we can see that the language of reform has extended the authority of government over the minds of individuals while simultaneously reducing the concept of human beings with "unalienable rights."

As John Stuart Mill (1963) states in "On Liberty," "There is a limit to the legitimate interference of collective opinion with individual independence" (p. 131). Mill elaborates the boundary between public authority and the liberty of individual minds as follows:

> It comprises, first, the inward domain of consciousness; demanding liberty of conscience, in the most comprehensive sense; liberty of thought and feeling; absolute freedom of opinion and sentiment on all subjects, practical or speculative, scientific, moral, or theological. (p. 137)

Recognizing the role of education in developing the intellectual tenets that underlie an individual's perspectives, modes of thought, judgments about values and conceptualization of the problems and purposes of life, Israel Scheffler (1976) concludes, "To choose the democratic ideal for society is wholly to reject the conception of education as an *instrument* of rule: it is to surrender the idea of shaping or molding the mind of the pupil" (p. 311). Stephen Arons argues that it is a fundamental contradiction of commitments for government at any level in a democracy to use schooling for purposes of shaping the minds of children. He states, "If the First Amendment protected only the communication and not the formation of ideas, totalitarianism and freedom of expression could be characteristic of the same society" (Arons 1983, 206).

This is not to suggest that government has no proper interest in education — for there are complex questions relating to the financing of education, the enforcement of civil rights, and the safety and well-being of children. Rather it is to argue that a commitment to democracy is a commitment to the sanctity of the individual mind and to withhold from the powers of the body politic the authority to develop that mind according to political, economic, or social objectives. Government may introduce itself into this reserved sphere of human consciousness when and only when it demonstrates "a compelling interest" for doing so — such as in the matter of the abuse or neglect of children (see Arons, 1976).

During this most recent period of reform, federal educational policy has been guided by a concern for the development of intellectual capital capable of increasing economic prosperity and assuming the responsibilities of democratic citizenship. At the same time, the rights, needs, and developmental characteristics of children as individuals — not laborers, consumers, or citizens — have become virtually inarticulable given a language of reform. The assumptions and language of reform greatly endanger the survival of the concept of the democratically sanctified human mind. As Mill concludes,

> Apart from the peculiar tenets of individual thinkers, there is also in the world at large an increasing inclination to stretch unduly the powers of society over the individual, both by the force of opinion and even by that of legislation, and as the tendency of all the changes taking place in the world is to strengthen society, and diminish the power of the individual, this encroachment is not one of the evils which tend spontaneously to disappear, but, on the contrary, to grow more and more formidable (Mill 1963, 139).

So it has and does.

References

Arons, S. (1976). The Separation of School and State: Pierce Reconsidered. *Harvard Educational Review*, 46: 76–104.

Arons, S. (1983). *Compelling Belief: The Culture of American Schools*. New York: McGraw-Hill.

DeYoung, A. J. (1988). *Economics in American Education*. New York: Longman.

Kane, J. (1992). Choice: The Fundamentals Revisited. In P. W. Cookson, Jr. (Ed.), *The choice controversy* pp. 46–64. Newbury Park, CA: Corwin Press.

Magnet, M. (June 27, 1994). The Productivity Payoff Arrives. *Fortune* 129: 79–84.

Mill, J. S. (1963). *The Sixth Grade Humanistic Essays of John Stuart Mill*. New York: Washington Square Press.

National Commission on Excellence in Education. (1983). *A Nation at Risk: The Imperative for Educational Reform*. Washington, D.C.: U.S. Government Printing Office.

New York Times. (1995). U.S. Productivity Grows for Fifth Year in a Row. 28 January. p. D2.

Pierce vs. Society of Sisters, 268 U.S. 510 (1925).

Scheffler, I. (1976). *The Moral Content of American Public Education in Educational Research: Prospects and Priorities*. Washington, D.C.: U.S. Government Printing Office.

Spring, J. H. (1993). *Conflicts of Interest: The Politics of American Education* (2nd ed.). New York: Longman.

Task Force on Teaching as a Profession. (May 1986). *A Nation Prepared: Teachers for the 21st Century: The Report of the Task Force on Teaching as a Profession, Carnegie Forum on Education and the Economy*. Washington, D.C.: The Forum.

U.S. Department of Education. (September 27–28, 1989). *The President's Education Summit with Governors*. A joint statement issued by the Education Summit.

U.S. Department of Education. (1991). *America 2000: An Educational Strategy*. Washington, D.C.: U.S. Government Printing Office.

U.S. Department of Education. (1994). *Goals 2000: Educate America Act*. Washington, D.C.: U.S. Government Printing Office.

"In a real and ultimate sense, teachers do not have control over what students do — unless they are willing to use the methods of a drill sergeant or one who 'washes brains' through physical and emotional coercion."

— *Nel Noddings*

Goal Setting in
Education

Nel Noddings

Opponents of national goals and a national curriculum give many reasons for their opposition: distrust of federal control, fear that the movement will result in mediocrity and uniformity, objections to giving priority to the knowledge of privileged groups, concern over the likely futility of goal-setting at a long distance, and worry that such goals will hurt those already at-risk.[1] However, even those of us who oppose the movement most strongly have to admit that there is something wrong in our public schools. We too shudder when we hear of high school graduates who can't read, who cannot place the Civil War in the correct century (never mind give its exact dates), who do not know that the United States used atomic bombs in the war with Japan. But we do not believe that establishing national goals will cure the problem or even remove its superficial symptoms. Indeed, we argue, the items just listed are already in the school curriculum virtually everywhere. Every school in the nation already states as a goal that its students will be able to read. The vast majority of schools

---

[1]For a discussion of these views and others, see the special issue on national curriculum standards of *The Educational Forum* 58:4 (1994).

also have stated objectives describing the historical knowledge students should acquire. How will national goals accomplish what local goals have failed to do?

There is an inherent problem in setting goals or objectives for other people. The people for whom the goals are set must *want* to achieve those goals. John Dewey wrote,

> Plato once defined a slave as the person who executes the purposes of another.... There is, I think, no point in the philosophy of progressive education which is sounder than its emphasis on the participation of the learner in the formation of the purposes which direct his activities in the learning process, just as there is no defect in traditional education greater than its failure to secure the active cooperation of the pupil in construction of the purposes involved in his studying (Dewey 1963, 67).

In perhaps the vast majority of adult occupations, workers must meet externally established goals, and so advocates of national goals for schools and learning objectives for classrooms can argue that such strategies are "real world" — clear and efficient. However, in the occupational world, workers have immediate reasons for accepting the objectives laid on them: they need the pay and benefits. Less immediate but still almost tangible for many workers is the possibility of greater pay, promotion, or recognition. For many students, no such immediate or tangible rewards exist.

Fields in which success is defined in terms of what happens to other people or what other people do are especially difficult. For example, a physician may have as an objective to cure Mr. A of disease, but she may not succeed at this if Mr. A does not share the objective. Overwhelmingly, in the health field, patients *want* to get well; they embrace the objective before even consulting a doctor. Teaching, as Aristotle noted long ago, is (like medicine) a set of activities in which success appears in those taught, not in the teachers themselves. But, unlike patients in medicine, students do not always come to teachers with the objective of learning. When they do come with such objectives — as most students do in professional schools, optional sports, chosen arts, etc. — teaching is still challenging and success is not guaranteed, but students and teachers share at least some goals.

At the pre-college level, students are too seldom involved in the construction of the purposes for their own learning. They are compelled to attend school and required to take courses they have not freely chosen. The

only pay-off discussed today — better jobs and more money — is too uncertain and too far in the future to influence many youngsters. If a student
sees that her parents are flourishing and that they attribute their success to
education, she may accept the educational objectives set for her. Or if
parents who are not doing well believe they would have done better with
more education, they may convince their children to stick with schooling.
But for the youngsters we want most to reach, our coercive methods of
establishing and assessing objectives fail; our objectives bear no resem-
blance to the objectives of our student captives.

Advocates of national goals and curriculum might respond to my line
of argument by agreeing that the pay-off is often too uncertain and too far
off. But surely, they argue, we need not change the goals. Rather, we must
bring the pay-offs closer, make them more real. Consider the programs that
promise middle school children a free college education if they study
academic subjects and graduate from high school. These programs have
found a way to induce kids to buy into their schools' learning objectives,
and that's what national goals are meant to do — inspire or prod states and
local districts to devise ways to secure the cooperation of their students.

Let's consider these success stories more closely. First, they are heroic
in the sense that few localities and few individuals can offer them. As a
result, they reach a mere handful of students. Second, even with heroic
measures, they often lose a surprising number of their target groups. But
most important is that a careful examination of these programs reveals that
objectives other than academic ones are being met. The kids are buying our
objectives because we are acknowledging theirs. There is often pay-off here
and now in the form of enjoyment, satisfaction, adult trust and companion-
ship, increased self-understanding, understanding of others, group support, and extracurricular involvement. Sometimes there is even help in
finding a safer, more supportive home environment.

Such possibilities suggest that the goals themselves have shifted. In
interaction with the kids, new and more significant goals have been constructed. These goals tend to be varied, flexible, adapted to situations as
they develop. Further, it is not at all clear that students in successful
alternative or incentive programs master the kind of material that would
appear in a national curriculum. For example, some obviously do not

master standard English, and my guess is that many cannot answer the kind of factual questions that some social studies educators insist they should be able to answer. On these criteria, they are neither better nor worse than other high school students. But they have learned some things: On the positive side, they have learned something about their own competence, that they can do well enough (and sometimes superbly well) to "make it" in the system. On the negative side, many have learned to depend on external prodding — rewards, punishments, and admonitions — to stick it out, to do enough of what is required to get by. The positive results are almost certainly products of variable goals co-constructed by caring adults and students who have learned to trust them. The negative ones are the fruits of coercion.

If this account is at all accurate, establishing national performance goals and a national curriculum is a very unwise thing to do. Goals and objectives for students must be set in concrete situations *with* concrete students. Even teachers, close as they are to the student setting, must be wary about establishing goals *for* students. The best they can do is to say, "If you want to achieve X, then you will probably have to show your competence in X_1, X_2, . . ., X_n." For example, if a student wants to be an engineer, she will have to show some competence in elementary mathematics, and that means a mastery of basic algebraic operations, knowledge of geometric relations, and the ability to use trigonometric functions. The more abstract or global X is, the more tentative are the connections to X_1, X_2, and X_n. It is not clear, for example, that a student who wants to be an elementary school teacher really needs the same mathematical preparation as her friend who plans to be an engineer. Understanding teachers may sympathize with such a student, admitting that they do not see the connections between the little Xs and the big X either. The connections are more political (gatekeeping) than intellectual or practical.

Thus a student who wants to major in mathematics or a closely related field will almost certainly have to master the rudiments of algebra. However, a student who simply wants to go to college (a more distant and global X) may not need to follow one particular sequence of steps. He or she may not need algebra at all. Still, such students may be forced to follow the sequence simply because academic rules require it. Although there certainly should be, there may not be a multitude of paths to choose among. Thus teachers and students should work together to lay out a mutually satisfactory path within the established constraints.

In a real and ultimate sense, teachers do not have control over what students do — unless they are willing to use the methods of a drill sergeant or one who "washes brains" through physical and emotional coercion. Teachers have control over what they themselves do. Old-fashioned lesson plans were couched in such self-referring language: I will demonstrate the mean value theorem and assign practice exercises, p. 101, 1–12; I will read aloud parts of *Heart of Darkness*; I will construct, display, and demonstrate a device for the production and collection of chlorine gas. Of course, teachers hoped that students would be able to do things as a result of their teachers' doings, but few were so foolish as to suppose that their doings could command specific performances (under specific conditions, to specific criteria). Followers of Dewey frankly offered their doings as invitations to be accepted, revised, replaced, or rejected as students worked to construct their own objectives. They did not always ask whether their students learned a specific set of facts or skills as a result of the teacher's acts (sometimes, of course, they did). Rather, they asked a more open question: What *did* the student learn? This question acknowledges the initiative, the full participation, of the student. Other, more traditional, teachers simply tested their students over the full range of possibilities. ("What will be on the test?" "Everything!") This approach produced an enormous range of achievement and was often exercised cruelly, without regard to individual difference in either capacity or interest. But at least it recognized the student's role as a semiautonomous agent. It recognized that what the student *will* do depends in great part on what the student *wants* to do.

Wise teachers, then, try to establish conditions in which students with multifarious interests, capacities, and needs can achieve things that are educationally worthwhile. These "things" are skills, attitudes, dispositions, understandings, habits, and constellations of facts that will contribute to further learning and education.[2] Teachers can make use of biographical anecdotes to broaden their subjects and connect to possible student inter-

---

[2] See the discussion of "habits of mind" in Sonia Nieto, "What Are Our Children Capable of Knowing?" *The Educational Forum*, 58:4 (1994).

ests. For example, mathematics teachers might discuss the theological interests of Descartes, Pascal, Newton, and Leibniz; the musical interests of James Sylvester; the aesthetic interests of David Birkhoff; the psychological interests of Poincaré; the humanitarian interests of Bertrand Russell. Only a very few of these interests can be pinned down and universalized for all students, but any one of them might connect with a student who would otherwise be unmoved by mathematics.

In many ways, good teachers are more heteronymous than their students; that is, they are often responsive and reactive. They pick up on and build on their students' interests. They accept what some postmodern philosophers call local or situational obligation. They are *claimed* by the needs of their students. Alternating between inviting and responding, they present, suggest, answer, lead, or assist.[3] They may be led to material they hadn't thought to present — to recollect material half-forgotten or to learn brand new material.

If my account of the relationship between teacher and student goal-setting seems right, then surely the argument holds at every level of educational policy making, for at every level, we are faced with the temptation to set goals for others. If we succumb to the temptation, we fall into deeper and deeper levels of coercion, demanding accountability because we neither expect nor encourage *responsibility*.

What should the federal government do? What role should it play? If it is to play a role, it should begin by establishing goals for itself, not for others. What will it pledge itself to do in order to establish conditions under which education may flourish? It might provide funds for decent school facilities in poor urban neighborhoods. It might facilitate the coordination of activities between social agencies and schools. It might provide resources for groups such as NCTM and NCTE to continue their work in developing a wide range of materials for possible (not mandatory) use. It might also provide resources to competing curriculum groups to ensure choice and the free play of ideas. In short, it should ask the question: What can *we* do? If it cannot answer that question, then it should remain decently silent.

---

[3] For an account of heteronomy as "being claimed," see John D. Caputo. *Against Ethics* (Bloomington: Indiana University Press, 1993); for a discussion of response and relation in teaching, see Nel Noddings, *Caring* (Berkeley: University of California Press, 1984) and Noddings, *The Challenge to Care in Schools* (New York: Teachers College Press, 1992).

Early in this century, Dewey made a remark about moral theory that can be translated aptly into one about national goals. He wrote:

> Moral principles that exalt themselves by degrading human nature are in effect committing suicide. Or else they involve human nature in unending civil war, and treat it as a hopeless mess of contradictory forces. (Dewey 1930, 2)

Adapting his language, we might say:

> National goals that exalt themselves by degrading the competence of local institutions, teachers, and students to establish their own goals are in effect committing suicide. Or else they involve educators in unending civil war, and treat education as a hopeless mess of contradictory forces.

National goals for local enactment do suggest a form of educational suicide. They will induce mere compliance, not vigorous innovation. Further, they ignore the reality of contradictory forces. These forces cannot all be reconciled, and educators must be free to meet them in locally effective ways if education is not actually to deteriorate into a "hopeless mess." For example, will a national curriculum include provisions for moral education, critical thinking, and various forms of affective education? Or, because these are controversial areas, will they be omitted from national discussion? If so, will that omission provide justification for deleting such topics from local schools?

Some groups today are making demands that most responsible educators want to resist. Among these are demands that moral education be taught in exactly one way, that critical thinking not be fostered in public schools, that certain books be removed from school libraries, that self-esteem and its equivalent at the ethnic or racial level not be promoted in schools. Against such demands, educators who believe that freedom of thought is the very essence of education must be encouraged to press their case. National goals can only distract attention from matters of great local importance.

Finally, precisely because there are contradictory forces and a great variety of problems to be addressed, we need to foster creativity and responsible experimentation. We should support responsible and creative forms of vocational education, alternative routes to college entrance, curricula centered on special talents, interdisciplinary programs, service learning and other forms of community involvement, education for parenting, and education for peace — to name only a few promising possibilities. Let there be many goals, and let all those directly involved in the local enterprise establish their own goals.

References

Dewey, John. 1930. *Human Nature and Conduct* New York: Modern Home Library.

Dewey, John. 1963. *Experience and Education*. New York: Macmillan/Collier.

" 'In exchange for freedom, the charter school is held to strict accountability on student outcomes. The overall focus is on outcomes, not inputs.' This is indeed a very narrow and warped concept of freedom, where teachers and families give up all hope of self-determination in regard to the meaning and goals of education. This is called procedural freedom. As long as you agree to the government's predetermined goals and standards, you will have a certain measure of freedom from rules and regulations determining how you will achieve those goals."

— *Gary Lamb*

Charter Schools and Procedural Freedom

Gary Lamb

T he *Nation at Risk* report that was issued by the National Commission on Excellence in Education in 1983 created a conceptual basis for the nationwide dissatisfaction with our public education system. Hundreds of studies and reports followed that tried to analyze the problem in graphic, empirical terms. Most states issued some type of reform measure. Tens of thousands of business and education partnerships were created over the next four years. But student test scores, attendance figures, and desired outcomes showed little or no progress. In 1989 George Bush called for an educational summit, which all 50 state governors attended. The result of the summit was a unanimous endorsement of six national educational goals that the states would use to develop unified, coherent reform programs. These national educational goals have necessitated in turn the development of national curriculum standards and assessments to provide

Adapted from an article in *The Threefold Review* (PO Box 6, Philmont, NY 12565), no. 12 (Summer/Fall, 1995). Reprinted with permission.

the pathway to reach the goals, and a method to determine how schools and students in all the states are progressively marching toward them.

At the same time, a call arose out of academic circles and the business community for a shift to an educational method that has become widely known as Outcome-Based Education (OBE).[1] For the most part our present public educational system depends on teachers and students complying with procedural standards such as teacher licensing requirements, student attendance requirements, and syllabus guidelines. Conformity to dictated rules and regulations is an indication of compliance and a fulfillment of one's accountability, but often, in the end, with little control over what the children actually learn. The OBE approach takes the intended student performance outcomes as a starting point and works backward to form standards and assessments to ensure that the goals are met. What a student should know and be able to do is clearly and specifically defined.

Since the *Nation at Risk* report, political and economic forces are in the process of becoming welded into a unified national force seeking to determine what the predominant educational outcomes should be.

> Perhaps the single most important effort to turn the focus toward outcomes was that of the National Governors' Association (NGA). They gave the outcome approach far-reaching policy attention beginning in the mid-1980s.... They focused on education for one direct and simple reason: "Better Schools mean better jobs. To meet stiff competition from workers in the rest of the world, we must educate ourselves and our children as we never have before...." In short, the governors cast their lot with those arguing that the time had come to place primary emphasis on what people learn, the outcomes they achieve. The approach endorsed by the governors gathered further momentum in 1989, when President Bush invited them to meet at an Education Summit in Charlottesville, Virginia. The President and the governors agreed to set six ambitious national educational goals — outcomes — from early childhood through lifelong learning that they would work to achieve by the year 2000. (Hudson Institute, 1994, 2)

The National Business Roundtable, consisting of the chief executive officers of the 200 leading businesses in the United States and who are also active in shaping educational policy in the U.S., has stated: "Too often, our school staffs are asked, 'Did you do what you were told?' The right question is, 'Did it work?' Trying hard is not enough. What students actually know and can do is what counts. Thus, we must define, in measurable terms, the

---

[1] The term itself has become tainted and is being removed from some reform measures because of opposition to certain outcomes. The method itself is, however, still the basis of virtually all reform measures.

outcomes required for achieving a high-productivity economy and maintaining our democratic institutions" (The Business Roundtable, n.d., 4).

The Goals 2000: Educate America Act, signed into federal law on March 31, 1994, by President Clinton, has embraced and codified the original six national educational goals and added two more.

The Act provides for the creation of federal agencies and councils to certify national content standards and national student performance standards and national opportunity-to-learn standards and embraces the OBE approach. One of the appeals of the OBE approach is that it provides a mechanism to hold specified individuals accountable for a child's education in a way that was not possible under the old input system. Previously, as long as teachers and administrators adhered to the bureaucratic rules and regulations — get certified, teach this subject, administer that test, use these books, take attendance — they fulfilled the requirements of their profession. But many children were simply not learning, even when everyone was complying with the required procedures.

With the OBE approach incorporating specified outcomes defined in measurable terms, a whole new approach to accountability is possible. Teachers and schools will no longer fulfill their responsibilities through mere adherence to procedures, rules, and regulations but individuals and schools will be held accountable for specific, measurable results.

In the present system, as the Business Roundtable (1990) expresses it,
[w]ith so many people responsible, no one is responsible. And without clear goals and outcomes, the tendency is to rely on procedural standards to impose order and protect pockets of authority. It is precisely this maze of administration that has led many reformers to stress accountability for performance outcomes rather than endless wrangling over procedure. By focusing on results and providing the incentive to achieve results, a performance-driven system theoretically can escape the need for elaborate bureaucracies to establish and enforce complex procedural requirements. (p. 21)

Once the clear, definite, measurable outcomes are established, then procedural regulations can be relaxed as long as educators have a commitment to achieve the outcomes and a method of assessing student performance.

It was in this context of national educational goals, standards, and assessment, undergirded by the OBE approach, that experimental outcome-based schools, later to be called charter schools, were first begun.

The charter school phenomenon first appeared at the state level in 1991 in Minnesota. This was two years after the establishment of the original six national educational goals; the drive for performance-based educational reform at the academic level and within the business community was in full swing nationwide. In fact, the wording of the Minnesota law does not use the term "charter school," which came later in legislation in California, but used the term "outcome-based school." Charter schools are prototype experiments in developing the outcome-based educational approach that is seen to be necessary to nationalize education in the United States.

Charter schools are in essence public schools in which a group of individuals or an organization contracts with the state to create a school in which students must achieve specific educational outcomes. In this arrangement the accountability issue is clear. Whoever signs the contract is held accountable. Legally speaking there can be no placing of the blame elsewhere. The consequence of noncompliance is also clear — termination of contract and school operations.

The Morrison Institute for Public Policy defines charter schools as follows:

> In its purest form, a charter school is an autonomous educational entity operating under a charter, or contract, that has been negotiated between the organizers who manage the school, and a sponsor who oversees the provisions of the charter. The organizers may be teachers, parents, or others from the public or private sector, while the sponsors may be local school boards, state education boards, or some other public authority.
>
> Charter provisions address issues such as the school's instructional plan, specific educational outcomes and how they will be measured, and the management and financial plan for the school.
>
> Once granted approval, a charter school becomes an independent legal entity with the ability to hire and fire, sue and be sued, award contracts for outside services, and control its own finances. Funding is based on student enrollment just as it would be for a school district. With a focus on educational outcomes, charter schools are freed from any (or all) district and state regulations often perceived as inhibiting innovation (e.g., excessive teacher certification requirements, collective bargaining agreements, Carnegie Units, and other curriculum requirements).
>
> When the term of a charter school's contract expires, it may be renewed — providing the school has met its student outcomes, has not violated

any laws or grossly mismanaged its affairs or budget, and continues to attract students, parents, and teachers. Failure in any of these areas puts the school out of business. (Bierlein and Mulholland, 1994)

Charter schools appear to address certain public issues concerning education. According to the Morrison Institute the appeal of charter schools includes enhanced educational choice options, true decentralization, autonomy in exchange for accountability, the maintenance of common school ideals, new professional opportunities for teachers, and a more market-driven educational system.

Here, I would like to focus on the issue of autonomy and accountability as depicted in the Morrison Institute report: "In exchange for freedom, the charter school is held to strict accountability on student outcomes. The overall focus is on outcomes, not inputs." This is indeed a very narrow and warped concept of freedom, where teachers and families give up all hope of self-determination in regard to the meaning and goals of education. It is called procedural freedom. As long as you agree to the government's predetermined goals and standards, you have a certain measure of freedom from rules and regulations determining how you will achieve those goals.

For many teachers and schools hemmed in by the present bureaucratic system and for parents who find the local public school is failing to meet the needs of their children, the charter schools may appear to be a liberation from all the present system's failings. In addition, due to the extreme financial pressure that many private schools are experiencing, the charter school concept is now cautiously being reviewed by them as a way to obtain state money. But we are only experiencing the beginning of the plans for a nationalized, technology-based educational system in the United States. The environment in which charter schools will find themselves and, consequently, their character will evolve as plans unfold. It is not only important to consider the outer manifestations of charter schools as they are now but also what are they becoming.

As of this writing, nine states have passed charter school legislation: Minnesota (1991), California (1992), Colorado (1993), Georgia (1993), Massachusetts (1993), Michigan (1993),[2] New Mexico (1993), Wisconsin (1993), and Arizona (1994). All of the laws embrace the OBE approach and hold schools accountable for state-determined student outcomes. It was not until

1994 [Arizona and Jersey City (proposed)] that there was direct reference to national standards and assessments. The states themselves are only beginning to formulate and have their standards reviewed by the federal government as provided for under Goals 2000. These standards will be a key factor in determining the required outcomes students in public schools will have to achieve. As public schools, charter schools will be required to meet any new standards that are imposed by the state.

Illustrative Passages from Some of the Charter School Laws

- Minnesota, 1991, Chapter No. 224 H.F. No. 350: "A school board may sponsor one or more outcome-based schools." "The purpose of this section is to ... require the measurement of learning outcomes and create different and innovative forms of measuring outcomes."

- California, 1992, Chapter 781, Part 26.8: "[The law] holds the schools established under this part accountable for meeting measurable pupil outcomes, and provide the schools with a method to change from a rule-based to performance-based accountability systems.... Charter schools shall meet the statewide performance standards and conduct the pupil assessments pursuant to Section 60602.5."

- Massachusetts, 1993, M.G.L. Chapter 71, Section 89: "The board of trustees of a charter school... shall be deemed to be public agents authorized by the Commonwealth.... The purposes for establishing charter schools [include] ... to encourage performance-based educational programs [and] to hold teachers and school administrators accountable for students' educational outcomes.... Students in charter schools are required to meet the same performance standards, testing and portfolio requirements set by the board of education for students in other public schools."

- Colorado, 1993, Senate Bill 93-183: The law will "improve pupil learning by creating schools with high, rigorous standards for pupil performances.... Charter schools [will be held] accountable for

---

[2] The Michigan charter school law has been declared unconstitutional. Efforts are underway to redraft the legislation to comply with the state constitution.

meeting state board and school district content standards" and be designed to "enable each student to meet such standards."

- Arizona, 1994, Chapter 2, House Bill 2002: [Charter schools must design] "a method to measure pupil progress toward the pupil outcomes adopted by the state board of education...including participation in the essential skills tests and the nationally standardized non-referenced achievement test as designated by the state board...."

- Jersey City, New Jersey, 1994 (Proposed, not enacted): The Jersey City proposal provides for both charter schools and a voucher program, and the following references apply to both. The law makes provisions for establishing academic standards and assessments "to evaluate each student's progress in each school year..." "The academic standards adopted ... must reflect defined levels of competency that a student should be capable of demonstrating in each subject [English, mathematics, science, history, geography, and government] at each grade level from grades K through 12. These academic standards must be at least as high in rigor and quality as national standards in this country."

Charter schools reflect the latest thinking regarding the performance-based educational approach. They dovetail very neatly into the drive to nationalize education. But the charter school movement is not uniform throughout the nation. Only nine states have enacted charter school legislation. Each law is worded differently and was enacted in the period from 1991 to 1994 when the national standards movement was itself rapidly evolving and eventually evolved into the Goals 2000: Educate America Act. On the one hand, the provisions for curriculum standards and testing are called voluntary, but, on the other, for the states to chart an independent course is inconceivable at this point. Either the states continue with the existing arrangements or push forward with goverment dictated OBE and national educational goals.

The teachers' union perspective is ambivalent in relation to charter schools. They are certainly preferred over voucher programs, and they offer some enticing features, such as local deregulation. But the major concern as expressed by Albert Shanker, President of the American Federation of

Teachers, is the necessity for the rigorous uniform standards being promoted through the Goals 2000 legislation to be clearly in place before
charter school legislation is passed:

> We are in the process of defining our education "product" through Goals
> 2000, and when we do so and want to pull the education system together
> to achieve it, what effect will charter schools have on this effort? Suppose
> the Coca-Cola Company put a number of independent units in business
> without telling them what kind of drink they should be making. And
> then, after some had started making beer and others wine, it came along
> and said, "You're supposed to be making Coke!" Will the schools we have
> liberated be willing to accept the goals of public education? Will we see
> a coalition of schools that have gotten their independence and are no
> longer willing to pull with the rest?
>
> Many of our schools now suffer because of bureaucratic, top-down
> management, but giving them the freedom to do whatever they choose
> will not solve the problems of our education system. Indeed, encouraging
> them to do their own thing before we have decided what we want our
> students to know and be able to do could be very destructive. The real
> question is not whether schools should be independent but when and
> under what circumstances. (Shanker, 1994)

Charter schools only make sense to Shanker and everyone else pushing for national standards if every school is required to produce a defined
uniform product. He wants to be sure that before the teachers' local bureaucratic chains are broken, national standards are securely in place. Only then
should teachers be turned loose. When the teachers are required to churn
out the right student product, they are free to be creative in how to go about
it — they will have procedural freedom.

When assessing charter schools it is essential to understand the mentality of those promoting them and the political, economic, and cultural
context in which they are inextricably enmeshed — Outcome-Based Education, uniform national education goals and standards, and many desperate people trying to save our crumbling, outmoded public educational
system.

References

Bierlein, Louann, and Lori Mulholland (1994). *Charter School Update: Expansion of
    Viable Reform Initiative.* Tempe: Morrison Institute for Public Policy, Arizona State
    University.

Manno, Bruno V. (1994). *Outcome-Based Education: Miracle Cure or Plague?* Indian-
    apolis: Hudson Institute.

Shanker, Albert (1994). Charter Schools: More Mediocrity? *American Teacher* 79(2), 5.

The Business Roundtable (n.d.). *Essential Components of a Successful Educational System: The Business Roundtable Education Public Policy Agenda.* New York: Author.

The Business Roundtable (1990). *The Business Role in State Education Reform.* New York: Anchor.

"Those creative in the cultural sphere, such as scientists, teachers, doctors, artists, and those engaged in religious work, all require freedom to create, while the others must be left to accept or reject their services. Whenever government provides these services, it takes away freedom. If it supports any one variety of these services over another, it is unfair to the remainder. If it tries to support multiple varieties of each of these services, it makes them dependent on government standards."

— *Ronald Milito*

"Goals 2000": What Have We Done With Our Freedom?

Ronald Milito

The "Goals 2000: Educate America Act" was passed into law on March 21, 1994.[1] Merely stating the eight national education goals fails to convey the full complexity and pervasiveness of the 156-page law with its emphasis on increased federal responsibility for education. In the debate over what ails education and what the remedies should be, the role of freedom is typically ignored or underrated. While the United States has played a major role in the historical development of liberty, it has typically misunderstood freedom's role in education. It is all too easy to lose sight of this central issue by getting caught up in more narrowly focused debates. For example, we may argue about the validity of a particular goal and overlook the issue of who should set goals for education in a free society. In discussing what kind of educational system we should

This chapter originally appeared in *The Threefold Review*, No. 12 (Summer/Fall 1995), pp. 31–35, and is reprinted with permission in its original style.

have, we forget to ask if we should have a system at all. Why can't different kinds of schools be permitted to exist? In discussing how to educate poverty-stricken children, we may fail to ask why poverty exists in the first place. These are questions that "Goals 2000" skirts by diverting our attention elsewhere. In effect, the framers of the "Act" cling to the outmoded concept of government control of education. Thus, when the educational system fails they can only call for more regulation and external controls to improve the system. In this way they resist the winds of change, refusing to see that regulation itself is becoming the problem. A careful reading of the legislation and statements of the National Education Goals Panel reveals many contradictions and unsavory implications. Oddly enough, the legislators themselves periodically recognize the need for freedom in education, but their primary response is to create more regulations.

Let us turn to the statements of the National Education Goals Panel: "In September 1989, an historic turnaround began. The President and the nation's Governors met in Charlottesville, Virginia, for an unprecedented, bipartisan 'Educational Summit.' At that summit, they laid the groundwork for the National Educational Goals, a vision of the education results toward which we should strive.* Equally important, they developed a timetable for attaining the Goals."[2] Here we have a prime example of the implication-laden statements characteristic of "Goals 2000." In one fell swoop it is implied that politicians, not educators, should determine the goals of education. The same politicians in dictatorial fashion assume the power of determining what teachers, parents, and students should strive for. And we are told that setting a timetable is equal in importance to choosing our goals, the implication being that a goal not achievable in one lifetime is not worth striving towards.

The Goals Panel reveals its capacity for contradiction when it states: " 'We' means all of us. Educators, learners, parents, policymakers, employers, and other community leaders allowed what was once an exemplary education system to stagnate and decay. For many years, employers and college officials criticized the low skills and knowledge of high school graduates. But when international academic assessments showed that Am-

---

*At this meeting six national goals were agreed upon. With the passage of the "Act," two more were added: the current goals numbered four and eight.

erican students were not measuring up to students in other industrialized countries, it rocked the foundations of business and the education system."[3]

Why did government ignore the warnings of the employers and the college officials and only respond after such assessments were made? The Panel is a bit unfair when it glibly asserts that all of us were responsible for the decay of a once exemplary system. If the system was once truly exemplary, why doesn't the Panel tell us when it was so; then we could determine what has changed. This would be more practical than re-inventing the wheel by activating the massive engine of "Goals 2000." Simply asserting that all of us are responsible for the decay of the system overlooks the role that TV-watching, poor nutrition, increasing poverty, drug abuse, broken families, and other factors may have in crippling human beings in ways that are impossible to overcome under any system of education.

The Panel's assertion that all of us are responsible is also misleading in light of the fact that state governments acting through departments of education have the legal control of education. Voters have no direct influence on appointed officials of government agencies, a serious problem when such agencies regulate more and more of life and elected officials often fail to carry out campaign promises.

Furthermore, over the last three decades the states have been injecting behaviorism into schools and teacher education programs and continue to do so despite valid objections.[4] The behavioristic assumptions that man is an unfree animal determined by conditioning and that all learning must be broken into steps, objectives, goals, and assessments are also the basis for "Goals 2000."[5] Yet what has been failing at the state level will now be encouraged at the federal level. Behaviorism appeals to those who wish to control others, but it is precisely such control that is inimical to a healthy education. Government control of education is based in part on the belief that educators are impractical and need the conditions of their work set for them. Such a belief overlooks the fact that depriving educators of control of their work leads to their lack of practicality and further weakens education. The Goals Panel's belief in the impracticality of educators is indicated in the above phrase, "business and the education system." The term *business* stands alone connoting independence, free initiative, and the necessity for practicality in order to survive. Instead of the term *education*, they use the

THE NATIONAL EDUCATION GOALS

By the year 2000:

1. "all children* in America will start school** ready to learn."

2. "the high school graduation rate will increase to at least 90 percent."

3. "all students* will leave grades 4, 8, and 12 having demonstrated competency over challenging subject matter including English, mathematics, science, foreign languages, civics and government, economics, arts, history, and geography, and every school in America will ensure that all students learn to use their minds well, so they may be prepared for responsible citizenship, further learning, and productive employment in our Nation's modern economy."

4. "the Nation's teaching force will have access to programs for the continued improvement of their professional skills and the opportunity to acquire the knowledge and skills needed to instruct and prepare all American students for the next century."

5. "United States students will be first in the world in mathematics and science achievement."

6. "every adult American will be literate and will possess the knowledge and skills necessary to compete in a global economy and exercise the rights and responsibilities of citizenship."

7. "every school in the United States will be free of drugs, violence, and the unauthorized presence of firearms and alcohol and will offer a disciplined environment conducive to learning."

8. "every school will promote partnerships that will increase parental involvement and participation*** in promoting the social, emotional, and academic growth of children."

(Sec. 102; pp.7-10; STAT. 130-133)

* "the terms 'all students' and 'all children' mean students or children from a broad range of backgrounds and circumstances, including disadvantaged students and children, students or children with diverse racial, ethnic, and cultural backgrounds, American Indians, Alaska Natives, Native Hawaiians, students or children with disabilities, students or children with limited-English proficiency, school-aged students or children who have dropped out of school, migratory students or children, and academically talented students and children" (SEC. 3. Definitions, (a), (1); p. 5; STAT. 129). *Please note that page numbers from the Conference Report and STAT. numbers from Public Law 103-227 are provided for ease of reference since both of these documents contain the "Goals 2000: Educate America Act."* Free copies are available by request from the House of Representatives' Document Room (202-225-3456).

** "the term 'school' means a public school that is under the authority of the State educational agency or a local educational agency or, for the purpose of carrying out section 315 (b), a school that is operated or funded by the Bureau" (SEC. 3, Definitions, (a), (12), p. 6; STAT. 130).

*** If "school" really means a public as opposed to a private school, then "parents," in the sense of this "Act," can refer only to parents of children attending a public school ("all children," as already noted above, means every kind of child, not every child). Yet according to SEC. 401 (a), (2); p. 66; STAT. 187, the federal government seeks "to strengthen partnerships between parents and professionals in meeting the educational needs of children aged birth through 5 and the working relationship between home and school." How is the government to know at birth that a particular child shall attend a public and not a private school? Or will the lack of such knowledge be used as justification for including every parent and child in this activity?

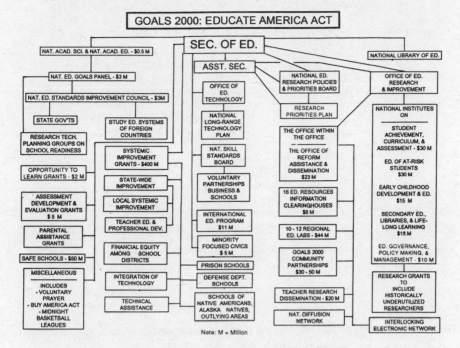

Note: M = Million

phrase "education system," reinforcing the idea that education must be set up, organized, and directed by a central agency. A full exposition of the danger of persisting in such arrangements was first presented by Rudolf Steiner in 1919:

> *This book* [Towards Social Renewal] *must assume the unpopular task of showing that the chaotic condition of our public life derives from the dependence of spiritual life on the political state and economic interests. It must also show that the liberation of spiritual life and culture from this dependence constitutes an important element of the burning social question.*
>
> *This involves attacking certain widespread errors. For example, the political state's assumption of responsibility for education has long been considered to be beneficial for human progress. For people with socialistic ideas it is inconceivable that society should do anything but shape the individual according to its standards and for its service.*
>
> *It is not easy to accept a very important fact of historical development, namely, that what was proper during an earlier period can be erroneous for a later period. For a new era in human relations to emerge, it was necessary that the circles that controlled education and culture be relieved of this function and that it be transferred to the political state. However, to persist in this arrangement is a grave social error.*
>
> *...The administration of education, from which all culture develops, must be turned over to the educators. Economic and political considerations should be entirely excluded from this administration.... No one should make decisions who is not directly engaged in the educational process. No parliament or congress,*

nor any individual who was perhaps once an educator, is to have anything to say. What is experienced in the teaching process would then flow naturally into the administration. By its very nature such a system would engender competence and objectivity.

Of course one could object that such a self-governing spiritual life would also not attain to perfection. But we cannot expect perfection; we can only strive toward the best possible situation.... To what extent a child should be taught one thing or another can only be correctly determined within a free cultural community.... The state and the economy would be able to absorb vigor from such a community, which is not attainable when the organization of cultural institutions is based on political and economic standards.[6]

The Goals Panel assures us that "National Goals are neither a political ploy nor a hollow promise" and in the very next sentence informs us that National Goals "represent the educational centerpieces of both the Bush and the Clinton administrations, and serve us as a nationwide compact by which we can marshal our best efforts and measure our shortcomings and accomplishments."[7] But massive federal rescue efforts in response to national emergencies, with their concomitant increase of federal spending and bureaucracy, are not without precedent or political overtones.[8] The Depression evoked the New Deal, Sputnik evoked the space race, and educational decay has evoked "Goals 2000." When Russia launched the first space satellite in 1957, we wanted education to enhance technology. Now, technology is to enhance education, and an Office of Educational Technology has been created to further this purpose (SEC. 231; p. 29; STAT. 151; see middle col. of chart on p. 101).

Turning to the "Act" itself, we see in the chart (upper left) the six-million-dollar organization near the top of the power pyramid: the National Education Goals Panel whose writings we have already sampled, and the National Education Standards and Improvement Council. The nineteen appointed members of the Council will certify and periodically review voluntary national standards submitted by the states. They will also study other countries' education systems to get insights for establishing voluntary standards. In addition they will identify areas that need the development of voluntary standards, although it is hard to imagine that they will find an area that doesn't need them. All such voluntary standards must be submitted to the Goals Panel. The eighteen appointed members of the Panel will review these voluntary standards to see if they support the eight national goals and then approve or veto their adoption. In characteristic behavioristic style, the voluntary standards are divided into voluntary national content standards, voluntary student performance standards, and voluntary national opportunity-to-learn standards—in other words, what teachers will be compelled to teach, how teachers will be compelled to evaluate students, and how the grading process will be justified, since opportunity to learn will be well documented. Furthermore, it should be made very clear that these voluntary standards are only voluntary for the state governments. Once a state adopts the standards, they are no longer voluntary for those controlled by that state. In the following discussion we shall generally omit repetition of the adjective *voluntary* because it is redundant, misleading, and inconsistent with the behavioristic underpinnings of "Goals 2000." And what can the term *voluntary* mean to those who believe that human freedom is scientifically meaningless?

Examining the composition of the Goals Panel, we find that sixteen of its eighteen members must be high-ranking politicians (see Sec. 202; p.11; STAT. 134). The Panel has veto power over the Standards Council composed of representatives from education, business, industry, and labor (SEC. 212; p. 16; STAT. 139). What is implied when even at this level educators do not have the final say? The Panel will set up and oversee Resource and Technical Planning Groups On School Readiness (chart, col. 1), which in support of Goal 1 will study and monitor efforts to assess school readiness and collect data for establishing policy (SEC. 207; p. 15; STAT. 138). If the Groups decide that all children should read as early as possible or should sit in front of computer terminals as early as possible, what recourse will exist for those who maintain that such practices are harmful? Some may assert that these standards are voluntary, but that misses the point if families can't afford to send their children to a private school when their public school must accept what they object to. And if some can afford private schools, how long will these schools be able to resist the pressure to conform, especially if such practices receive the imprimatur of official science? Furthermore, notwithstanding the fact that in "Goals 2000" the word *school* means public school, each state could require all its private schools to submit to its voluntary plans.

"Goals 2000" also empowers the Secretary of Education (hereafter called the Secretary) to grant a half-million dollars to the National Academy of Sciences or the National Academy of Education to conduct evaluations of the Goals Panel and the Standards Council, which, if positive, will lend them further scientific credibility (SEC. 221; p. 28; STAT. 151). The Secretary is charged to collaborate with other agencies such as the National Science Foundation and NASA to establish a National Long-Range Technology Plan (chart, col. 3) to "encourage the effective use of technology to provide all students the opportunity to achieve State content ... and student performance standards ... [and] promote the use of technology in education, and training and lifelong learning ... [and] the educational uses of a national information infrastructure ... [and] professional development of teachers in the use of new technologies" (SEC. 232, (b), (3); p. 30; STAT. 153).

The Secretary is also to establish an Office of Educational Technology within the Department of Education (chart, col. 3) to develop, research, and promote the use of technology in education in coordination with the Technology Plan (SEC. 233; p. 31; STAT. 154). The use of computers, for example, in education is generally taken as an unquestionable good to which all should submit. The paralyzing action of cathode-ray tubes in the form of television or computer monitor screens can easily be verified through direct experience and has been discussed by a number of authors.[9,10,11] When young children are placed in front of such mesmerizing screens they are trained to become illiterate consumers of programs that do not deserve the name of culture. The newest computers come equipped with CD-ROM, which allows the computer monitor to deliver television entertainment in the guise of multimedia programming. If children are really supposed to start school ready to learn (Goal 1), why greet them with the very influence that should be discouraged in the first place? How is promotion of computers with its concomitant TV watching going to help every American to become literate (Goal 6)? Is a literate person one who develops himself by reading great works or one who is able to read instructions, but who prefers television and movies to books? The *Sesame Street* television approach to learning creates more desire for television than for books. Remember, once the states accept the standards, they cease to be voluntary. School attendance is compulsory and private schools and home educators must also meet state standards. Those who find the standards objectionable will have little recourse.

The Secretary has two million dollars for competitive Opportunity-to-Learn grants to broadly based consortia of individuals and organizations at the state level (chart, col. 1). These consortia, which should include, among others, state and local officials, parents, teachers, secondary school students, businessmen, advocacy groups, and accrediting associations, shall develop opportunity-to-learn standards and make lists of model programs (SEC. 219; p. 26; STAT. 149). The Secretary has another five million dollars for Assessment Development and Evaluation grants to state and local agencies to examine the validity of assessments made by the state to insure they are consistent with national standards (chart, col. 1). In other words, the state will evaluate how it evaluates, but such assessments "may not be used for decisions about individual students relating to program placement, promotion, or retention, graduation, or employment for a period of 5 years from the date of enactment of this Act" (SEC. 220, (c),(2); p. 28; STAT. 151).

Why will millions be given to the states for making standards when the Standards Council is already doing it at the federal level and has veto power over the states? Won't the states in essence just copy the Council's standards? Yet this is the kind of illusory consensus that "Goals 2000" hopes to achieve. The illusion of consensus is also furthered by having broadly based consortia, but a broad sampling of the population on these committees is not the same thing as equal representation by law. In either case an appeal is made to the mistaken notion that education should be decided by democratic principles, which is the antithesis of free self-determination by educators with parents determining who shall educate their children. The framers of "Goals 2000" cannot grasp the idea of freedom. Thus, throughout the "Act," the assurances to different groups that their interests will be represented in the new system. Appeals are made to minority groups, the poor, the disenfranchised, those seeking democratic representation, and, last but not least, to those who want progress through science. But what is scientifically true is not a matter for democratic decision. Forcing a teacher to follow programs statistically proven to produce better group averages on standardized tests is an abuse of the scientific method and a clever diversion from addressing the teacher's need for freedom to work from immediate insight into the children before them. Hence, education should be liberated from democratic rule as well as from bureaucratic tyranny.

In the chart (col. 2) we see that the Secretary has 400 million dollars to grant to state educational agencies for creating statewide systemic improvement plans, but the agencies must give assurances of forming broadly based panels, eliciting public input, and creating student performance standards no less rigorous than before the passage of this "Act" (SEC. 306; p. 38; STAT. 160). The state agencies are authorized in turn to make subgrants available on a competitive basis to local education agencies that shall in turn make a local plan via broadly based panels (SEC. 309, (a); p. 47; STAT. 169). Subgrants can also be made to local agencies in cooperation with institutions of higher learning and nonprofit organizations to train teachers and administrators to better carry out the local plans (SEC. 309, (b); p. 50; STAT. 172). Thus college and university faculty who need to bring in money for research and publications in order to get tenure can be pressed into the service of local plans, but, of course, voluntarily.

The Secretary has also been endowed with waiver power "Except as provided in subsection (c) ... [to] waive any statutory or regulatory requirements applicable to any program or Act described in subsection (b) for a State educational agency, local educational agency, or school if [certain conditions are met] ... for a period not to exceed 4 years" (SEC. 311, (a); p. 52; STAT. 174). A program carried out under this subsection is designated "an education flexibility demonstration program" (SEC. 311, (e), p. 55; STAT. 176). We witness here a frank admission by the legislators that regulation of education can be counter-productive, but only when regulations obstruct the Secretary's purposes, namely, the achievement of the national goals. Specifically, he can temporarily bend the federal laws listed in section 311, (b); p.54; STAT. 175, but only for national goals and standards, and only for four years with very careful monitoring. You never can tell when a slight cessation of bondage might unleash repressed yearnings for freedom. If after four years the new program is not a success, the laws that were stretched will snap back into place. Either way, rigidity reigns.

A real flexibility demonstration would constitute a permanent dissolution of government control or influence over education by a constitutional amendment: Congress (or any other level of government) shall make no law respecting an establishment of education or any cultural activity, or prohibiting the free exercise thereof. Instead, Congress confuses the issue when it "finds that leadership must come from teachers, related services personnel, principals, and parents in individual schools, and from policy makers at the local, state, tribal, and national levels, in order for lasting improvements in student performance to occur" (SEC. 301, (3); p. 34; STAT. 157). But if all are leading, who is following? What Congress really wants is followers from every level. Congress finds that "simultaneous top-down and bottom-up education reform is necessary to spur creative and innovative approaches by individual schools to help all students achieve internationally competitive standards" (SEC. 301, (4); p. 35; STAT. 157), but creativity and innovation do not flourish under slavery. If a student's creativity is sparked by some aspect of knowledge, and the teacher tries to nurture it, then what do they care about internationally competitive standards? How many geniuses had to overcome the standards of their day and were abused for their creativity?[12] Why should creativity and innovation require simultaneous top-down and bottom-up reform? Simultaneous top-down and bottom-up reform is a euphemism for a blitzkrieg attack on the cultural life. Money falling left and right for those who would reform and promises to each faction and advocacy group that they can influence the outcomes if they get involved will make it hard to resist on principle and difficult in practice.

Those who receive systemic improvement grants from the Secretary under Title III to develop, "standards or State assessments described in a State improvement plan submitted in accordance with section 306 shall not be required to be certified by the [Standards] Council" (SEC. 316; p. 62; STAT. 184). Is this a case of double standards? Or does it mean that since the Secretary won't approve anything that the Council wouldn't, it's pointless to involve it? Besides, the Council will be busy certifying all of the states who did not receive grants under Title III who can submit standards directly to it (SEC. 211; p. 16; STAT. 139). Referring to the chart (col. 2) we see that the Secretary may support systemic improvement by giving grants for technical assistance in achieving, "a greater degree of equity in the distribution of financial resources for education among local educational agencies in the State" (SEC. 313; p. 58; STAT. 179); National Leadership grants for technical assistance in the integration of standards, the implementation of plans, the dissemination of research on systemic education, and the support of demonstration projects" (SEC. 314; p. 58; STAT. 180); and grants "to assist each State to plan effectively for improved student learning in all schools through the use of technology as an integral part of the State improvement plan" (SEC. 317; p. 62; STAT. 184). Under "Goals 2000" the Secretary is not to deprive the American Indians, the Alaska Natives, and the peoples of the outlying areas (Guam, American Samoa, the Virgin Islands, the Common-wealth of Northern Mariana Islands, Palau, the Republic of the Marshall Islands, and the Federated States of Micronesia) of the system's benefits (chart, col. 3). Four million dollars is reserved for making "an agreement between the Secretary and the Secretary of the Interior containing such assurances and terms as the Secretary determines shall best achieve the provisions of this section and this Act" (SEC. 315, (a), (1); p. 59; STAT. 181). Under section 315, (b), (2); p. 60; STAT. 181 entitled VOLUNTARY SUBMIS-SION, the Indians are to be brought under the auspices of the Standards Council.

No government school or educational program will escape the sys-tem. For example, "The Secretary shall consult with the Secretary of Defense to ensure that, to the extent practicable, the purposes of this title are applied to the Department of Defense schools" (SEC. 315, (d); p. 62; STAT. 183). The phrase "to the extent practicable" reveals more hypocrisy. If this new system is going to be at world-class standards and internationally competitive, then surely our military must not be deprived of such an opportunity to learn. Or does the term *practicable* imply that if the system interferes with the military schools' effectiveness, exceptions can be made for national security reasons? But if such is the case, why doesn't the nonmilitary educational system adopt the more effective approach of the military schools? How can national security be the reason for national education reform and the reason why the military can be exempted from the same reform? The limping logic of "Goals 2000" casts doubt on the competence and integrity of purpose of the reformers. And in SEC. 931, (h); p. 121; STAT. 240, we read that "The more than 1,000,000 men and women incarcerated in the prisons and jails in the United States are among the most severely educationally disadvan-taged." That these should not be left out of the new system, the Secretary is supposed to work with the Office of Correctional Education and the Bureau of Prisons of the Department of Justice.

"Goals 2000" takes a new tack by allowing the Secretary to award parental assistance grants (chart, col.1) "to nonprofit organizations, and nonprofit organizations in consortia with local educational agencies, to establish parental information and resource centers that provide training, information, and support to parents [especially] of children aged birth through 5 years" (SEC. 401; p. 66; STAT. 187). Will these parents be advised to introduce their children to early reading, educational TV, and computers?

Perhaps you are thinking that one can escape the long tentacles of the Goals Panel and the Standards Council after leaving school. Think again, for the Secretaries of Education, Commerce, and Labor, as well as the chairman of the Standards Council, will become part of the twenty-eight members of the National Skill Standards Board (chart, col. 3) "to serve as a catalyst in stimulating the development and adoption of a voluntary national system of skill standards and of assessment and certification of attainment of skills standards" (SEC. 502; p. 70; STAT. 191). Fifteen million dollars can be spent to "identify broad clusters of major occupations that involve 1 or more than 1 industry in the United States and that share characteristics that are appropriate for the development of common skill standards" (SEC. 504, (a), (1); p. 74; STAT. 195). What does not fit into this category? Will they really find an area that doesn't need standards? The Skill Board shall establish Voluntary Partnerships with broad representation including business, industry, labor, educational institutions, and civil rights groups, for the purpose of creating standards (SEC. 504, (b); p. 74; STAT. 195). The Skill Board is for the economic realm what the Standards Board is for the educational system, and both boards are to work with each other. The hoped for result is "increased productivity, economic growth, and [increased] American economic competitiveness" (SEC. 502, (2); p. 70; STAT. 191). The real result will be that if a school doesn't submit to the system, its graduates may have less chance of getting a job, since most job standards will be linked to school standards. Consequently, parents will experience even more pressure to send their children to schools that have adopted the standards. Of course, the standards will be voluntary.

In the two right-hand columns of the chart we see an overview of Title IX of "Goals 2000," which is also known as the "Education, Research, Development, Dissemination, and Improvement Act of 1994." Just as the man-on-the-moon project needed NASA, so the launching of "Goals 2000" needs its organ of research and development. The new Office of Education Research and Improvement within the Department of Education is based on the premise that "quality education requires the continual pursuit of knowledge about education through research, development, improvement activities, data collection, synthesis, technical assistance, and information dissemination" (SEC. 912, (a), (1); p. 93; STAT. 213). But this presupposes and fosters the notion that research done by such agencies is intrinsically better than the insights that a teacher who is free can develop through his own work with students and on himself. The approach of these national institutes is to view the teacher as merely the delivery vehicle; what is taught, when it is taught, and how it is taught is best determined by others engaged in scientific research. The Assistant Secretary of Education will work with the National Education Research Policy and Priorities Board composed "of 15 members appointed by the Secretary" including research-ers, educators, and knowledgeable individuals (which may be parents) (SEC. 921, (g); p. 106; STAT. 226). The Board and the Assistant Secretary will set up a Research Priorities Plan (chart, col. 4). The Board will review and approve both the Research Priorities Plan and standards for the conduct and evaluation of all research, development, and dissemination (SEC. 921, (b); p. 104; STAT. 224) and create standing subcommittees for each of the National Institutes to be created within the Office of Educational Research (chart, col. 5): the National Institute on Student Achievement, Curriculum, and Assessment; the National Institute on Education of At-Risk Students; the National Institute on Educational Governance, Finance, Policy-Making, and Management; the National Institute on Early Childhood Development and Education; and the National Institute on Postsecondary Education, Libraries, and Lifelong Education (SEC. 931, (a); p. 108; STAT. 227).

In total, these institutes will receive 68 million dollars in 1995 and one billion dollars per year from 1996 through 1999 (SEC. 911, (m); p. 101; STAT. 221). They can award research grants, but the Assistant Secretary shall "increase the participation ... of researchers and institutions that have been historically underutilized in Federal education research activities, including researchers who are women, African-American, Hispanic, American Indian and Alaska Native, or other ethnic minorities" (SEC. 931, (c), (5); p. 111; STAT. 231). But shouldn't the ability of the researcher be the primary consideration? Does the law of gravity depend on the race, gender, or ethnic background of the scientist? Furthermore, it is rather ironic that within the current Congress there is a movement to terminate affirmative action.

Thirty million dollars will go to the Institute on Student Achievement, Curriculum, and Assessment because Congress has found that "During the last 20 years, relatively little changed in how students were taught. Despite much research suggesting better alternatives, classrooms continue to be dominated by textbooks, teacher lectures, short-answer activity sheets, and unequal patterns of student attention" (SEC. 931, (d), (1), (B); p. 112; STAT. 232). We question how our once exemplary system alluded to earlier by the Goals Panel managed to succeed with teacher lectures and textbooks? Furthermore, with the exception of Waldorf schools and some alternative schools, almost all private and public schools insist upon textbooks. Textbook companies, knowing that teachers are overloaded and expected to test and grade regularly, create multiple-choice machine-gradeable worksheets to accompany their texts. The pressure to do well on these standardized tests (Goal 3) will discourage the teaching of valid topics not covered by them, let alone not in the text. And perhaps lectures are usually boring these days because the lecturers are no longer inspired after being force-fed the grim fare of behaviorism.

Classroom instruction is dominated by external control, and more is on the way via "Goals 2000." When the National Institute on Student Achievement, Curriculum, and Assessment sets out to improve "the working conditions of teachers ..., which may include ... the reduction of stress in the teaching profession" (SEC. 931, (d), (2), (A), (x); p. 113; STAT. 233), it should consider the effects of teachers being dictated to in their work. What inspiration can a teacher draw from this Institute's research on "test security, accountability, validity, reliability, and objectivity" and "relevant teacher training and instruction in giving a test, scoring a test, and in the use of test results to improve student achievement" (SEC. 931, (d), (2), (D), (i),

(X-XI); p. 115; STAT. 234)? It does not require thirty million dollars to gain the insight that testing is inimical to education.[13]

While in section 931, (g); p. 119; STAT. 238, Congress recognizes that, "many ... schools ... are structured according to models that are ineffective and rely on notions of management and governance that may be outdated or insufficient for the challenges of the next century," it cannot grasp Steiner's insight that only active teachers should have any say in education. Congress recognizes a problem, but can only conclude three sentences later that "Not enough is known about the effects of various systems of school governance and management on student achievement to provide sound guidance to policymakers as such policymakers pursue school restructuring and reform." How long will it take the policymakers to realize that they are part of the problem? Yet ten million dollars will be granted to reinforce the idea that there should be policymakers (chart, col. 5). When Congress asserts that not enough is known, it projects its own blind spot and consistently misses the sources that do know enough and are accessible to any good-willed thinker.[14, 15]

The National Institute on Early Childhood Development and Education is going to spend fifteen million dollars (chart, col. 5) on items such as, "effective learning methods and curriculum for early childhood learning, including access to current materials in libraries ... [and] the impact that outside influences have on learning, including television, and drug and alcohol abuse" (SEC. 931, (f), (2), (G) & (L); p. 119; STAT. 238). The potential here is great for involving ever-increasing numbers of children in early learning, which is actually harmful to the development of the human being.[16] Why do we need more research to realize that television, drugs, and alcohol are not appropriate for children? If television is questionable, why is the newly created Office of Technology going to fund "the development and evaluation of software and other products, including multimedia television programming" (SEC. 234, (a), (6); p. 33; STAT. 155). Furthermore, we should be working to free students from their addiction to the cathode-ray tube, not to foster a stronger dependency in the guise of education. Television and computers relegate teachers to the role of monitors and encourage their passivity. Once a media program is certified as meeting standards, the pressures to use it will be greatly enhanced.

In addition to the billion dollars a year for research, an almost equal amount will be spent on dissemination (SEC. 912, (m) (2); p. 101; STAT. 221). The Secretary is to create, within the Office of Educational Research, an Office of Reform Assistance and Dissemination that may also be referred to as the Office within the Office, or the Dissemination Office (chart, col. 4), whose director is to be chosen by the Assistant Secretary (SEC. 941, (b), (1); p. 125; STAT. 244). The Dissemination Office's duties include the following: to "disseminate relevant and useful research ... operate a depository for all Department of Education publications and products ... coordinate the dissemination efforts [of the Department of Education] ... carry out a program of research on models for successful knowledge dissemination, and utilization, and strategies for reaching education policymakers, practitioners, and others interested in education" (SEC. 941, (b), (2); p.125; STAT 244). The Assistant Secretary shall set up a system of sixteen Educational Resources Information Center Clearinghouses (chart, col. 4) which shall synthesize and provide information to their respective locales (SEC. 941, (f); p. 128; STAT. 247), establish an electronic network connecting relevant libraries, institutes, centers, entities engaged in research, and so on (SEC. 941, (g); p. 129; STAT. 248), and establish a networked system of ten to twelve Regional Educational Laboratories for Research, Development, Dissemination, and Technical Assistance (chart, col. 4) (SEC. 941, (h); p. 131; STAT. 250). These Regional Laboratories shall promote systemic improvement, collaborate with the five new institutes, set up a broadly based governing board to guide these activities, and consult with the Assistant Secretary. In addition, the Secretary is charged to create a national library of education within the Office of Educational Research and Improvement (chart, col. 5) (SEC. 951; p. 142; STAT. 260).

"The Assistant Secretary is authorized [for "Goals 2000" Community Partnerships] to make grants to eligible entities to support the establishment of Learning Grant Institutions and District Education Agents and the activities authorized under this subsection within eligible communities" (chart, col. 4)(SEC. 941, (i); p. 136; STAT. 255). An eligible entity may include, for example, any institution of higher education, regional educational laboratory, national research and development center, or public or private nonprofit corporation. An eligible community must have a population between 200,000 and 300,000, with at least half of the school-age children from poverty-stricken families. Each partnership shall create plans and appoint a District Education Agent to direct the plan's implementation. This approach bears a similarity to the land-grant college and the district agricultural agent, which have had a powerful but not necessarily beneficial effect on agriculture. The Assistant Secretary is to provide much technical assistance to these partnerships and "plan for the expansion of the "Goals 2000" Community Partnerships program throughout the remainder of the United States, beginning in fiscal year 1999" (SEC. 941, (i), (11), (D); p. 140; STAT. 259). Eventually the whole country could be divided into separate organizational cells with District Agents overseeing the local plans. This is reminiscent of the Sovietizing of Russian agriculture with its farm collectives, five-year plans, and commissars.

The broadly sweeping system of "Goals 2000" also includes a wide variety of other programs and resolutions to ensure that no potential influence on education has been missed. For example, under Title VII, the "Safe Schools Act of 1994" (chart, col. 1), the Secretary is authorized to spend 50 million dollars in grants to local agencies to help schools become free of drugs and violence. In addition, "The Secretary shall designate the District of Columbia as a national model city" and shall sufficiently fund a local agency "to carry out a comprehensive program to address school and youth violence" (SEC. 706, (b); p. 88; STAT. 208). Here we have a case of a double standard. Washington is automatically honored as a model city, but a panel has to be established to decide if a promising educational program should officially be designated as exemplary (SEC. 941, (d); p. 127; STAT. 246). Under Title VIII, Gun-Free Schools, we find that in order to get assistance a local educational agency must have "a policy requiring the expulsion from school for a period of not less than one year of any student who is determined to have brought a weapon to a school under the jurisdiction of the agency" (SEC. 8001, (a), (1); p. 152; STAT. 270). It seems as if Congress is getting tough on schools who are soft on gun offenders, but let us not forget who has allowed guns to become so readily available.

Besides exercising its power of pervasion throughout the United States and its outlying areas, the Secretary, along with the Secretary of State and the Director of the United States Information Agency, under Title VI of the "Act," is to establish an International Education Program (chart, col. 3). The Secretary shall "award grants for the study, evaluation, and analysis of education systems in other nations, particularly Great Britain, France, Germany, and Japan," our economic competitors (SEC. 601, (b); p. 79; STAT. 200). The Secretary may spend ten million dollars to establish an International Education Exchange Program, but only with an "eligible country," that is, "a Central European country, an Eastern European country, Lithuania, Latvia, Estonia, Georgia, the Commonwealth of Independent States, and any country that formerly was a republic of the Soviet Union whose political independence is recognized in the United States" (SEC. 601, (c), (6); p. 83; STAT. 204). Under the exchange program, the Secretary is to "make available to educators from eligible countries exemplary curriculum and teacher training programs in civics and government education and economic education developed in the United States" (SEC. 601, (c), (1), (A), (i); p. 80; STAT. 201), and shall "provide support for research and evaluation to determine the effects of educational programs on students' development of the knowledge, skills, and traits of character essential for the preservation and improvement of constitutional democracy; and effective participation in and the preservation and improvement of an efficient market economy" (SEC. 601, (c), (1), (A), (v); p. 80; STAT. 201).

Clearly the framers of the "Act" want to influence these countries to adopt our forms of government and economy, but wouldn't it serve them better to imitate Germany, Japan, and Great Britain? Wasn't the premise of "Goals 2000" the supposed falling behind of the U.S. in the world economy? The U.S. will offer the eligible countries exemplary programs in civics and government while it intends to become first in the world in mathematics and science (Goal 5). This hardly constitutes a fair exchange. Furthermore, an exchange program of truly international character would not limit itself to Europe and the former Soviet Union. Yet the Goals Panel previously asserted: "The National Goals are neither a political ploy nor a hollow promise."[17] To assist the exchange there shall be a "translation of basic documents of United States constitutional government for use in eligible countries, such as *The Federalist Papers*, selected writings of Presidents Adams and Jefferson and the Anti-Federalists, and more recent works on political theory, constitutional law and economics" (SEC. 601, (c), (3), (v); p.

82; STAT. 203). Herein lies a great potential embarrassment for the Secretary and the framers of the "Act," since, as Richard Webb has meticulously demonstrated, the above documents show that many of our federal laws and programs are in frank contradiction to the U.S. Constitution.[18]

The same problem occurs when Congress justifies its authority to carry out "Goals 2000." In section 319 Congress correctly states that "in our Federal system the responsibility for education is reserved respectively to the States and the local school systems and other instrumentalities of the States" ((a), (3); p. 65; STAT 186); whatever is not among the enumerated powers is reserved to the states. Thus when Congress also states it "is interested in promoting State and local government reform efforts in education" (SEC. 319, (a), (1); p. 65; STAT. 186), it clearly enters the realm of impropriety. How can a legal entity express a desire to promote what it has just stated is outside its constitutional jurisdiction? This is a public statement of the desire to violate the Constitution. And it is disingenuous for Congress to declare that "the purpose of the Department of Education was to supplement and complement the efforts of the States, the private sector, public and private educational institutions, public and private nonprofit educational research institutions, community based organizations, parents and schools to improve the quality of education" (SEC. 319, (a), (4); p. 65; STAT. 186) because Congress has no jurisdiction to do so, no matter how noble its intentions may be or how much a state might desire it.

What can it possibly mean when Congress states that "with the establishment of the Department of Education, it intended to protect the rights of State and local governments and public and private educational institutions in the areas of educational policies and administration of programs and to strengthen and improve the control of such governments and institutions over their own educational programs and policies" (SEC. 319, (a), (5); p. 65; STAT. 186)? What agencies were taking away or limiting the rights of the states over education, which necessitated the formation of the Department of Education to protect the states? From whom do state's rights, not to mention the rights of private educational institutions, need protection? How did it come about that state governments could not control their own educational programs and policies? Furthermore, how could the Department of Education help restore this control if it has no power? When

Congress argues that establishing the Department of Education will protect the rights of the states to control education, we question why the first Congress didn't establish a department of religion to strengthen the rights of states to control state religions or why establishing a federal department of religion today wouldn't strengthen the rights of individuals to control their own religious life? In any event, it is apparent that the Department of Education did not fulfill its mission, since Congress found it necessary to pass "Goals 2000" in 1994, decades after the formation of the Department. As Webb has demonstrated, lack of resistance to each extension of federal power under misconstruction of the Constitution signals the public's readiness for the next step, and "Goals 2000" may well be the last great step necessary to totally control the cultural life of this country.[19]

Despite grant monies for those who cooperate with the Department of Education, we find that "The Congress agrees and reaffirms ... that no action shall be taken under the provisions of this Act by the Federal Government which would, directly or indirectly, impose standards or requirements of any kind through the promulgation of rules, regulations, provisions of financial assistance and otherwise, which would reduce, modify, or undercut State and local responsibility for control of education" (SEC. 319, (b); p. 65; STAT. 187). How can billions for bribery not be considered at least an indirect form of coercion? Thus Congress agrees and reaffirms that it shouldn't do what it will do through "Goals 2000."

Regarding its jurisdiction over education, we also find Congress asserting that "While the direction of American education remains primarily the responsibility of State and local governments, the Federal Government has a clear responsibility to provide leadership in the conduct and support of scientific inquiry into the educational process" (SEC. 912, (a), (1); p. 93; STAT. 213). Whereas earlier (SEC. 319, (a), (3); p. 65; STAT. 186) Congress stated that responsibility for education is reserved to the states, it has now added the qualifier *primarily*, which implies that there is some aspect of education not reserved to the states, a portion reserved to the federal government. Congress would find it impossible to cite the Constitutional basis for this reapportionment in the enumerated powers of Article 1, Section 8, or in any amendment to the Constitution. And even though Congress stated earlier (SEC. 319, (a), (3); p. 65; STAT. 186) that responsibility for education is reserved to the states, we find that the term *education* has been cleverly replaced by the phrase "the direction of education."

Step by step, the federal government extends its powers if unchecked. It may be clear to Congress that "the Federal Government has ... responsibility to provide leadership in the conduct and support of scientific inquiry into the educational process" (SEC. 912, (a), (1); p. 93; STAT. 213), but once again there is no basis for it in the enumerated powers of Article 1, Section 8, of the U.S. Constitution. The only item in the enumerated powers that relates to scientific research is the power "To promote the progress of science and useful arts, by securing for limited times to authors and inventors the exclusive right to their respective writings and discoveries."[20] Please note that only copyrights and patents may be granted, not funds! Congress has neither the responsibility nor the power to fund any scientific research, including the education research of "Goals 2000." Those who argue that Congress is merely doing what it has done many times before would replace constitutional democracy with rule by decree based on expediency. In light of the confused and contradictory statements concerning its Constitutional authority to enact "Goals 2000," Congress appears to be both ignorant and condescending when under Title VIII of "Goals 2000," the "Minority-Focused Civics Education Act of 1994," it proposes "improved instruction to improve minority and Native American student knowledge and understanding of the American system of government" (SEC. 802, (2); p. 89; STAT. 209).

Let us turn to section 912 (a), (1); p. 93; STAT. 213 where Congress erroneously justifies taking responsibility for providing leadership in educational research. At the section's beginning , "Congress declares it to be the policy of the United States to provide to every individual an equal opportunity to receive an education of high quality regardless of race, color, religion, sex, age, disability, national origin, or social class. Although the American system has pursued this objective, it has not been attained. Inequalities of opportunity to receive high-quality education remain pronounced."

The means proposed by Congress to achieve its goal are puzzling: "To achieve the goal of quality education requires the continued pursuit of knowledge about education through research ..." (SEC. 912, (a), (1); p. 93;

STAT. 213). Whether this is true or not misses the point. Congress errs by confusing equality of opportunity with quality of education and reasons like a man who, upon hearing that poor folks did not have an equal opportunity to obtain high-quality food, initiated a research program to improve the quality of food. And even if educational research is the solution, it is not, as we have seen, a constitutional prerogative.

Congress claims that "The failure of the Federal Government to adequately invest in educational research and development has denied the United States a sound foundation of knowledge on which to design school improvements" (SEC. 902, (3); p. 92; STAT. 212). Not content with an apparent confession, Congress repents with "Goals 2000." We are faced with the curious situation of Congress having sinned by failing to exercise a power it didn't have, and making amends by exercising the same. However, mere confession to a crime is as insufficient to establish guilt as mere denial is to establish innocence. Either case needs supporting evidence. The true sin of omission by Congress has been its failure to adequately protect human rights which in turn caused the current inequality of opportunity. Parents should be free to choose an education for their children as conscience dictates, but this is generally not possible because they lack a sufficient income.

Those creative in the cultural sphere, such as scientists, teachers, doctors, artists, and those engaged in religious work, all require freedom to create, while the others must be left to accept or reject their services. Whenever government provides these services, it takes away freedom. If it supports any one variety of these services over another, it is unfair to the remainder. If it tries to support multiple varieties of each of these services, it makes them dependent on government standards, which negates freedom. In either case the essence of a free society is denied. The injustice is exacerbated when those taxed must support cultural activities to which they object. The fallacy is made clear in Article 121 of the 1936 Soviet Constitution: "The citizens of the U.S.S.R. shall have the right to education. This right shall be ensured by universal compulsory eight-year education."[21] Denying freedom does not protect rights!

When Congress states that "demographers project that by the year 2005 almost all urban public school students will be minority children or other children in poverty" (SEC. 901, (3); p. 92; STAT. 212), the appropriate response is to seek the elimination of poverty, not to establish a thirty million dollar National Institute of At-Risk Students. Welfare recipients will always resent the indignity of their position and the social negativity is enhanced by the resentment of those who are forced to give through taxation. Many of these unwilling donors look down upon the welfare recipients, but fail to realize that they too are welfare recipients when it comes to the education of their children, insofar as they must send them to public schools. But many of these welfare recipients do not consciously sense the indignity of their situation. Now that international studies have shown that our public schools, more accurately called welfare schools, are not what they should be, Congress has passed one of the most comprehensive welfare programs ever devised, "Goals: 2000." Ironically, the current Congress diverts our attention from this by proposing to get tough on welfare recipients.

When "Goals 2000" promises to support "the implementation of high-performance management and organization strategies [for schools], such as site-based management, [and] shared decision making" (SEC. 308, (b), (2), (B); p. 46; STAT. 168), it should be asked what could be more site-based than Steiner's concept that only active teachers in a school should have any say in its running. When "Goals 2000" calls for "performance-based accountability and incentive systems for schools" (SEC. 308, (b), (2), (F); p. 47; STAT. 169), it should be asked what could make schools more accountable than parents financially able to support the school of their choice. When "Goals 2000" suggests "promoting public magnet schools, public 'charter schools,' and other mechanisms for increasing choice among public schools" (SEC. 308, (b), (1), (I); p. 47; STAT. 169), it should be asked: Why not the choice of any school? Isn't the choice of any school the maximization of the equal opportunity principle espoused by Congress (SEC. 912; p. 93; STAT. 213)? And won't the choices be greatest when educators are freest? (These statements should not be misconstrued as an argument for government vouchers. The latter will always have strings attached because the government will have to decide which schools are valid recipients. Recipients would have to demonstrate accountability.

Thus, government control of education would have to continue in full force.)

If Congress is to stand wholeheartedly behind its declaration of a U.S. equal opportunity policy, then let it prove itself by withdrawing from the realm of education as it has withdrawn from religion and recognize that public education is as outdated as state religion. In our times numerous cynics abound who reject freedom because the masses may make poor choices. Whenever these cynics speak in private about the masses, they always exclude the present company, but they expect the present company to understand why they too must give up their freedom. At best these cynics may be viewed as self-styled aristocrats, but their noblesse oblige is as outdated and repugnant as the concept of the white man's burden. Today we are in danger of becoming the bureaucrat's burden, and we should ask ourselves along with Thoreau whether the freedom we inherited from the Founding Fathers was "a freedom to be slaves, or a freedom to be free"?[22]

Notes

1. Public Law 103-227; Mar. 31, 1994; H.R.1804.

2. *Summary Guide to The National Education Goals Report: Building the Best* (NEGP Communications, 1850 M Street NW, Suite 270, Washington, D.C. 20036; 1993), p. 3.

3. *Summary Guide to The National Education Goals Report*, p. 2.

4. Ronald Milito, "Homework Is a Sacred Cow," *The ThreeFold Review* (Issue No. 8), p. 35.

5. B. F. Skinner, *Beyond Freedom and Dignity* (Bantam/Vintage, NY, 1972), p. 191.

6. Rudolf Steiner, *Towards Social Renewal: Basic Issues of the Social Question* (Rudolf Steiner Press, London, 1977), pp. 11-13.

7. *Summary Guide*, p. 3.

8. Richard Webb, "Who Should Decide Whether Nuclear Reactors Are Safe?", *The Threefold Review* (Issue No. 6), pp. 37-47.

9. Ronald Milito, "TV Paralysis - Part I" (*The Kimberton Farms School News*, vol. 6, #12, Nov. 1983), pp. 19-22.

10. Marie Winn, *The Plug-In Drug* (Bantam, NY, 1977).

11. Jerry Mander, *Four Arguments for the Elimination of Television* (Morrow Quill Paperbacks, NY, 1978).

12. Ronald Milito, "Testing, Tracking, and Grading: The Woeful Trinity," *The Threefold Review* (Issue No. 10), pp. 26-31.

13. Ronald Milito, "Testing, Tracking, and Grading."

14. Rudolf Steiner.

15. Rudolf Steiner, *The Renewal of the Social Organism* (Anthroposophic Press, Hudson, NY, 1985).

16. Rudolf Steiner, *A Modern Art of Education* (Rudolf Steiner Press, London, 1972), pp.135-139.

17. *Summary Guide to The National Education Goals Report*, p. 3.

18. Richard Webb.

19. Richard Webb.

20. *Five Constitutions*, edited by S. E. Finer (Penguin Books, NY, 1979), p. 95.

21. *Five Constitutions*, p. 138.

22. Henry David Thoreau, "Life Without Principle," *Civil Disobediance and Other Essays* (Dover Publications, Inc., NY, 1993), p. 87.

"Goals 2000 is a reallocation of power over the content of schooling, away from individuals and communities. This reallocation is massive, systemic, and inconsistent with the basic principles of constitutional democracy.... In order for a system of majority rule to actually work effectively, and for the 'just consent of the governed' to be something other than a hollow phrase, it is necessary to prevent government from manipulating the content of schooling in particular and of intellect and belief in general."

— *Stephen Arons*

Goals 2000 Versus the Rights of Conscience and the Building of Community

Stephen Arons

Public education, I think in almost everybody's view, has fallen upon extremely hard times. The schools are beleaguered, over-reformed, deprived of public confidence. They are sterile, boring, often ineffective, and sometimes destructive. They've become a kind of giant sorting machine for an unequal society. And they are beset by conflict. The increasing intensity of this conflict over the last 10 to 15 years — something that I've been paying a lot of attention to — is particularly disturbing, especially the conflict over content.

This chapter is adapted from a talk given at a November 1994 conference on national goals in Harlemville, New York. More detailed references and a more thorough discussion of these issues will be found in the author's forthcoming book (University of Massachusetts Press).

Goals 2000 is, in effect, a symptom and a cause of these conflicts over schooling content. It is a symptom and a cause of the attack on conscience and on community in the United States. It's a symptom of our failure to understand the importance of applying basic principles of constitutional democracy and of the First Amendment to the structure of schools. Hardly aware that we have blinded ourselves to these constitutional freedoms under local control, we have now expanded our misfortune by raising our ignorance to the national level. These constitutional principles, I think, we ignore at our peril.

Nowhere is this made more clear than in the case of *Barnette vs. West Virginia*. This is the case from 1943 in which the United States Supreme Court overturned a 1939 decision and declared that the compulsory flag salute in public schools was unacceptable constitutionally because the state lacks the power to require "confessions of belief"; that's what the Court called the pledge of allegiance. To modernize this, bringing it 50 years into the present, we might say that the performance tests required under Goals 2000 are a kind of confession of belief. In two passages the *Barnette* majority talks about the basic constitutional principle, which I think is balked by Goals 2000. First, this:

> The very purpose of a Bill of Rights was to withdraw certain subjects from the vicissitudes of political controversy, to place them beyond the reach of majorities and officials, and to establish them as legal principles to be applied by the courts. One's right to life, liberty and property, to free speech, a free press, freedom of worship and assembly and other fundamental rights may not be submitted to [a] vote. They depend on the outcome of no elections.

In another passage, the Justices say:

> We set up government by consent of the governed, and the Bill of Rights denies those in power any legal opportunity to coerce that consent.

> Authority here is to be controlled by public opinion, not public opinion by authority.

I submit that we have lost track entirely of the Court's warnings in *Barnette*, and that Goals 2000 is a symptom of this willful ignorance.

Goals 2000 is also a cause of the infringement of individual conscience rights and of the undermining of community. It reconstitutes the power over schooling, moving it away from individuals and toward state government and the federal government. This change in power is systemically enforced in Goals 2000 by a system of performance examinations and assessments, by the expectation that all texts will eventually reflect the standards and goals established through political mechanisms, by teacher certification that is required to reflect the same standards and goals, and eventually by the requirement that state and federal funding also be made consistent with these standards and goals.

Now I want to speak not so much about the marginalization of conscience as about community — about community-building and community-sustaining. This is a problem of constitutional dimensions, but it also has important components related to our own personal consciousness as well as the structure of our politics. I want to begin with a quotation from Alexis de Toqueville, who is probably regarded by most people as among the most perceptive observers of the American character and American institutions; he was certainly a great admirer of the American experiment in democracy. He wrote this not long after his visit here in 1830:

> Despotism, which by its nature is suspicious, sees in the separation among men the surest guarantee of its continuance, and it usually makes every effort to keep them separate. No vice of the human heart is so acceptable to it as selfishness. A despot easily forgives his subjects for not loving him, provided they do not love one another. He does not ask them to assist him in governing the state; it is enough that they do not aspire to govern it themselves. He stigmatizes as turbulent and unruly spirits those who would combine their exertions to promote the prosperity of the community. And perverting the natural meaning of words, he applauds as good citizens those who have no sympathy for any but themselves.

That starts us off thinking about the importance of community, about cohesion among individuals, about shared values and worldviews. It also prompts us to think about the dangers of excessive individualism and the way in which excessive individualism can lead, not only to alienation, but to tyranny.

I'd like to read something from *Barnette* that I think comes at the same subject — community — but from another perspective:

> As government pressure toward unity becomes greater so strife becomes more bitter as to whose unity it shall be. Probably no deeper division of our people could proceed from any provocation than from finding it necessary to choose what doctrine and whose program public education officials shall compel youth to unite in embracing. Compulsory unification of opinion achieves only the unanimity of the graveyard.

These two quotations frame the issue of community and schooling in Goals 2000.

The rest of what I have to say I owe in part to a very interesting book that needs to be given credit here — *Responsive Schools and Renewed Communities* by Clifford Cobb. It seems pretty clear that a balance between individual conscience and the sustaining of community has to be struck if either is to survive. The balance, in part, is already struck by the United States Constitution, which protects individual conscience from government manipulation — not only for its own sake, but to protect the process of community decision making from being crippled by unresolvable conflict.

In this context, schooling becomes extraordinarily important. It is one of the few institutions that we have remaining to us in which, by participation, engagement, and contact with one another, we can compromise, we can find common ground, we can engage in finding and sustaining communities — communities that are necessary not only to education and the health of the culture but to resisting alienation and preserving diversity.

Somehow, as the numerous conflicts over school content indicate, we have arrived at a situation in which our primary institution for arriving at these compromises and shared community values has turned into a source of division and hostility. I want to suggest seven tentative ideas that might be considered conditions for our ability to sustain communities in the United States. I understand that by speaking about community I seem to be slighting the individual rights of conscience. I assure you that I understand that these are two sides of the same coin, that they are entirely inseparable. I have to say in my defense only what I remember being told shortly after I graduated from law school — that if two things are inextricably connected, and you can speak about one without speaking about the other, then you have the legal mind. Although my main point is that the balance between conscience and community has to be preserved if either is to survive, I do have the legal mind and so I'm just going to speak about community.

So, I offer seven conditions for the preservation of community:

First, *we need to abandon our exclusive reliance upon geography as the only definition of community*. I don't say that we need to deny geography as a definition of community, but that we need to abandon a structure for schooling that says that this is the *only* possible way to define community. That means we have to stop thinking about local control as a defense against national education goals. That means we have to broaden our thinking about the possibilities of community to include communities of belief, communities of heritage, communities of interest. And it means we have to resist the imposition of beliefs and the politicization of knowledge by government at *all* levels.

Second, I think we have to understand that *coercion of community, of cohesion, of unanimity, is a contradiction in terms*. It achieves, as the *Barnette* court said, only the unanimity of the graveyard. Coercion not only crushes individualism and individual freedoms, it also delegitimizes authority and, in a kind of anti-authoritarian rights-centered reaction by spirited individuals to this authoritarianism, we are at risk of becoming isolated and weakening the very idea and attraction of community.

Third, *we have to preserve and enhance individual freedom of intellect and belief*, lest community become repressive — the tyranny of the majority as de Toqueville named it — something to be feared, rather than something to be sought after. Again, we have to limit government power over school content.

Fourth, *we have to extend these freedoms of conscience, of intellect and belief, of worldview, to cultures as well as to individuals* if we are to preserve diversity and the integrity of communities.

Fifth, and this is something we might learn from the process of mediation, *it is primarily when concerted action and community membership are voluntary — especially in schooling — that there is a chance of finding common ground, a chance of fashioning compromise, a chance of reorienting individuals, a chance of reaching agreements that people actually want to maintain*. So for schooling, as for the rest of life, it is good to know how to compromise with the inevitable, but it's better to know how to, and to be permitted to, compromise voluntarily.

Sixth, we need to understand that *nothing can be more destructive of community than the zero-sum game of political specification of knowledge, of majority control of content in schooling, of epistemology, of worldview*. Majority control of intellect and belief only breeds conflict, and conflict — especially the kind that pervades public schooling — is as divisive as it is unnecessary.

Finally, *we have to create an equality of individual choice for all in schooling if we wish to have cultural freedom and the possibility of community building for any of us.*

To put the whole thing in as simple a fashion as I can, we need schools to be available as a forum for community building if we are to avoid the alienation that leads to tyranny. We destroy that necessary forum and that desired community if we do not secure the freedom to opt out of a community and choose another, if we don't secure our individual rights of conscience in schooling, if we don't assure the voluntary nature of participation in schooling, if we don't institute a regime of universal and equal school choice, if we don't expand our idea of community beyond local school districts. If we do not protect both conscience and community, we shall end not only by crippling our basic freedom of intellect and spirit, but by disabling our most useful mechanism for creating the communities that sustain culture and support the education of our children.

Let us return to Goals 2000 as a re-constitution of schooling in the United States and talk about how to resist Goals 2000, not simply from a negative posture, but with an idea in mind of how schooling in fact might be reconstituted to make it better serve the rights of conscience and the building of community.

Goals 2000 is a reallocation of power over the content of schooling, away from individuals and communities. This reallocation is massive, systemic, and inconsistent with the basic principles of constitutional democracy. The constitutional principle that is most balked by Goals 2000 is this: In order for a system of majority rule to actually work effectively, and for the "just consent of the governed" to be something other than a hollow phrase, it is necessary to prevent government from manipulating the content of schooling in particular and of intellect and belief in general. Goals 2000 accelerates the marginalization of conscience and the weakening of community.

But reestablishing the primacy of local control is not an adequate response to this reallocation of power, because the freedom of belief and intellect are already so poorly protected under the regime of local control, and because the same problem that infects Goals 2000 infects the idea of schooling controlled by local majorities as well.

Now, here are some ideas for ways in which we might reconstitute education without these problems.

The first and simplest is simply to repeal Goals 2000, especially the content standards and the mechanisms that are created to enforce these standards.

The second, recognizing that local control is no better than state or national control, would prohibit government at *any* level from regulating the content of schooling except where fundamental freedoms found in the United States Constitution are implicated, such as the freedom from racial discrimination.

The third would be to provide specific, affirmative protections for individual and cultural freedoms of belief in all schooling. That is to say, to recognize not only the importance of doing away with Goals 2000 and prohibiting all government from regulating school content, but as with the Bill of Rights, to provide an affirmative statement of rights with regard to education.

The fourth would reaffirm the society's commitment to a right to an education for every child and to the provision of public funding on an equal basis for all children, *without* content regulation. This would in essence be a guarantee of freedom of school choice to all families regardless of their ability to pay. I am totally and unalterably opposed to government manipulation of the content of schooling, whether public or private, but I am in favor of distributing public funds for a right to an education equally among all students. This will sound like a contradiction to many people; that is why it is a truly revolutionary demand.

These four principles need to be established at the level of the Constitution. I'm not talking about a piece of legislation or about winning a particular case. I'm not talking about a political agreement that can be washed away easily. I'm talking about reconstituting schooling, not as Goals 2000 would have it, but as the needs of conscience and community would have it. I'm talking about a new compromise for schooling and about writing that compromise into the United States Constitution.

There's a certain political unreality in this way of thinking about school reform, but that has led me to think that what we really should be doing is creating a public discourse about these issues so that we can move toward amending the Constitution. Were we to create such an Amendment now, I'm sure it would be a disaster because, as Goals 2000 demonstrates, our consciousness of these issues is terribly distorted. I think the initial challenge therefore is to find ways of talking to each other about these issues and of making sure that everybody is at the table when this discussion is taking place. The original drafting of the Constitution in 1787 had very few of the affected parties present. As a result, grievous mistakes were made. I would not like to see that happen again.

"Once the decision was made that there shall be 'voluntary' national standards in history and other school subjects, holding a closed-door meeting to negotiate differences among the governing elites in Washington over what shall be the content of the history curriculum in the nation's K-12 classrooms appears quite normal."

— *Harold Berlak*

Culture, Imperialism, and Goals 2000

Harold Berlak

... so influential has been the discourse insisting on American specialness, altruism, and opportunity that "imperialism" as a word or ideology has turned up only rarely and recently in accounts of United States culture politics, history. But the connection between imperial politics and culture is astonishingly direct.

(Said 1994, 8)

I see the intensifying struggles over Goals 2000 as arising out of former and continuing struggles over geography. Goals 2000 is, of course, about other things: national educational standards; the role of government in the schooling process; the quality of teachers' and children's lives in school; technocratic versus human values — the list could go on. I begin with the struggle for dominance over land and resources or *imperialism*, to use its proper name, and its consequences on generations of subjugated and conquering peoples because it is a major driving force in the ongoing political, economic, and cultural struggles *within* and *among* nations and peoples, including the wars and skirmishes over schooling policies and practices in the United States. There just is no way that the history and experience of imperialism can be quarantined from the present, and there is surely no place where this is any more evident than in the struggles over Goals 2000.

Without an effort to come to terms with the arguments made by the eminent Palestinian-American scholar Edward Said about the centrality of the cultural questions, it is impossible to make sense of the political and economic forces and political alignments that produced and continue to sustain Goals 2000 — and I refer here not only to the particular piece of legislation passed and signed into law by President Clinton in March 1994, but the entire movement to enact national and statewide educational goals and standards. Debates over educational philosophies and the uses and limitations of objectives-driven classrooms and schools have been around for a very long time as have the problems facing the nation's schools. Why is it then that this movement for setting national standards, which produced not just the 1994 Act but a host of other federal and state rules and legislation, arises at this particular moment of our history? This is not an idle question. Understanding the historical and the cultural forces that produced the Goals 2000 movement is essential for those of us who are appalled and deeply disturbed by the direction our current national educational policies are now taking us and who hope to successfully derail this movement and create and project to the public a radically different vision of schools for the next century.

In the public arena the words "imperialism," "colonialism," "subjugated peoples," and "racism" inflame, offend, and often preclude civil discussion. However, though burdened with ideology and misunderstanding, these words and concepts are essential. Following Said, I define imperialism as "thinking about, settling on, and controlling land that you do not possess, that is territory lived on and owned by others," and colonialism, a chief consequence of imperialism, as the establishment and maintenance of settlements on some one else's territory (1994, 7). What Said demonstrates is that older and newer varieties of imperialism and colonialism were not — are not — simply a matter of accumulating land, resources, creating trade and wealth, but are also "about ideas, about forms, about images and imaginings" (p. 7). Among these images and imaginings are histories, myths, symbols, and forms of knowledge that prove or take as self-evident the inherent inferiority of subjugated peoples. This, the ideology of racism, rationalizes physical subjugation of the body, suppression or destruction of the culture and language of conquered peoples, and the use of subtle and not so subtle government power — including brutal force, even genocide.

Said also reminds us that our language, literature, and history books are filled with concepts and words like "subject races," "subordinate peoples," "dependency," and "expansion." He quotes, among others, the established conservative historian D. K. Fieldhouse (1965) who argues that the basis of imperial authority is "the mental attitude" of those colonized, their "acceptance of subordination — either through a positive sense of common interest with the parent-state or through the inability to conceive of any alternative" (p. 104). The implication of this argument is that there will be resistance which a conquering state minimizes by creating a set of processes and an organizational apparatus to assist in the manufacture of the appropriate "mental attitude."

Journalists, historians, social scientists throughout the Western metropolitan world as well as in "Third World" (i.e., formerly colonized) nations share the view that the era of classical or territorial imperialism ended, more or less, with the dismantling of empires and the creation of independent nations from formerly occupied territories. This process accelerated rapidly after World War II and is ongoing — witness events in South Africa, Northern Ireland, eastern Europe, and the former Soviet Union. Except perhaps for right-wing academics and polemicists, it is no longer considered polite to speak in public about the glories of empire, and the natural right of some to deny rights to others and hold dominion over them by virtue of superiorities rooted in race, gender, ethnicity, cultural heritage, or language.

While European nations, if not in the present, at some point in history celebrated and honored their respective brands of imperialism, the United States as a nation, except for the occasional revisionist, remains in near full denial that this nation is or ever was imperialist, or if so, only in the faded past. Yet it is no more possible to deny the Holocaust than it is to deny that the U.S. government vigorously pursued its "manifest destiny" over the peoples and lands of indigenous Americans; in Mexican territories in what are now Texas, California, and the Southwest; in areas in Central and Caribbean America; as well as in places half way around the world: Hawaii, the Philippines, and islands in the South Pacific. Yet belief in U.S. beneficence is so pervasive that, as the battle over the recent proposed national history standards (which I will later discuss) shows, any public figure, writer, or intellectual who dares to question this myth will almost certainly be vilified as un-American and excluded from mainline public discourse.

The historical ties between imperialism and racism are also clear (West 1993). The forced removal and enslavement of African peoples to work the sugar, cotton, and tobacco plantations and mines in the Americas was essential to the European nations' imperial designs for the "New World" (Richardson 1968). Whether we speak of the subjugation of African or indigenous peoples, repeated U.S. invasions of Central American and Caribbean lands, or the catastrophe of Vietnam, the imperial past has entered and remains in the consciousness and everyday realities of millions of people in the United States and elsewhere across the globe, both the conquerors and the conquered. Two ideas hold sway: imperial powers, the U.S. included, have the right to safeguard their interests wherever they may be, and lesser powers are lesser peoples, with a lesser culture and lesser rights, morals, and claims (Said 1994, 36). Imperialist and racist ideas do not in themselves create racist and imperialist acts, but these acts are unthinkable without them (p. 70–71). Even if we grant that American expansionism was primarily economic, it was, and still is, highly dependent on and moves with a "regime of self-aggrandizing cultural ideas and ideologies about 'Western Civilization' and of 'America' itself" (p. 289). While the vast majority of people within imperialist nations did not directly profit, their consent or acquiescence to the ideologies of racism and imperialism is necessary for the survival of imperialist governments.

I put aside the complex moral question of what are the obligations of current and former imperialist nations to peoples who were enslaved or ruthlessly oppressed. What cannot be ignored, however, are the historical and demographic facts. A chief consequence of these imperial adventures is that the children of the formerly colonized, enslaved, and subjugated peoples in many North American metropolitan centers and states already, or soon will, outnumber those whose forebears see themselves as white or of European descent. Nor is it possible to deny that all of us who reside in North America, recent arrivals as well as peoples who have lived here for generations or for as long as this continent has been populated, are affected in multiple and complex ways by racism and imperialism. The purpose of acknowledging this living legacy is not to condemn offender nations nor their leaders, past or present, but to help us understand why the Goals 2000 standards movement appears at this moment in history, and what seethes just below the surface that drives both Goals 2000 advocates and various oppositional camps across the political spectrum and cultural borders.

We live in a time a number of writers call the age of *decolonization*. Formerly subjugated peoples not only resist further extensions of imperialism and racism, but are attempting to reclaim, create, and/or recreate cultural identities. There is underway what could rightly be called cultural *re-formations*. As is evident, this process of culture destruction, reconstruction, and recreation is not benign (Hall 1992); it is often accompanied by increasing pride and deep rage (Fanon 1967; Bell 1992), especially in relation to the narratives of American exceptionality, beneficence, and cultural superiority.[1]

The sharp right turn in U.S. electoral politics is evidence of the great fears and hatreds that have been stoked by these changes. Clearly, there is an intense reaction to the growing self-consciousness of various communities who are asserting their rights to reclaim and redefine their cultural identity. Resistance takes many forms. Violent white supremacists are at one extreme. More common is the hate-mongering and scapegoating of immigrants and African, Latino, and Asian Americans by politicians, but also pernicious are the more nuanced and subtle reconstructions of imperialist ideology for the 1990s (by Allan Bloom, Arthur Schlesinger Jr., William Bennett, Lynne Cheney, and others), which demean or discount efforts of peoples to claim their cultural identities as "tribalism" or "separatist" and dismiss as a "culture of complaint" efforts of these "minorities" to recount and revisit their tragic histories.

---

[1] Mohanty, Russo, and Torres (1991) clarify the interconnections between the ideologies and practices of imperialism and the subjugation of Third World women.

One response to this collective experience of cultural and physical oppression, not surprisingly, is for formerly subjugated peoples to strive to correct distortions and/or their invisibility in the officially sanctioned story of the nation's history and their virtual exclusion from "high" culture. They also demand *public space* for telling their own stories, expressing their own ideas and ways of seeing, and for having their cultural expressions seen and heard. Fine-tuning the official (i.e., textbook) story so that it finally recognizes their existence, acknowledges their current and past oppressions, and recognizes their cultural contributions is not sufficient. The process of decolonization includes not merely recognition of past resistance to oppression, but a struggle for the power to retell and redefine the place of one's own people; that is to write one's *own* rendition of the "official" story of "Western Civilization," the development of "Western" culture and arts, and the growth of the United States as a nation. It is, in short, not only a matter of which story is to be told, but who has the power to tell it.

The power to narrate or to block other narratives from forming and emerging lies at the heart of the Goals 2000 struggles. As Said notes, living cultures have a rhetoric, a set of occasions, revered leaders, myths, narratives, and texts *and* strive to develop institutions and processes for creating, preserving, and re-creating culture in the subsequent generation of children. Schooling is central to this process, and elementary and secondary schools are among the prime locations for generating, transmitting, as well as destroying cultural stories and myths.

Goals 2000: A Genealogy

Goals 2000, the movement and legislation, is a new chapter in the continuing story of decolonization and resistance. It exemplifies how a widely shared concern for educational reform was transformed by government, business interests, and several of the larger and more influential foundations, and independent and university-based research centers into a movement to control and shape a common culture and distribute economic opportunities. Many of the controls are not obvious or overt. Indeed what marks Goals 2000 are the nuances in the joining of federal and state governmental power to the power of the NGOs (not-for-profit, non-governmental organizations) and larger corporate interests. There also appears to have been an effort to disguise the clearly compulsory nature of Goals 2000 by advocates repeatedly referring to the standards the scheme would impose as "voluntary." In the popular press, hundreds of supporting reports and papers, and in the text of the legislation itself, the term *"standards"* is used many thousands of times, and virtually each time it is used it is preceded by the word *"voluntary."*

The criticism that Goals 2000 is an effort to impose a national curriculum is usually met with the claim that the standards are voluntary. The basis for this claim is that states have an option not to participate in the national Goals 2000 process, and should they choose to participate, they have wide latitude in developing their own Goals 2000 plans. Both are true, the latter within limits. The limits are that in the end, a national Goals 2000 body must certify that each state's plan meets *national* requirements, one of which is that it includes a suitable testing or assessment system — one that meets national testing standards, which also must be approved by a national board. This requirement will not be felt at the local school site for a number of years. Professional associations, state testing agencies, and the testing industry have four years to develop standards and reliable and valid assessments, and there is a five-year moratorium on using test scores for what the testing trade calls "high-stakes" decisions, that is, for admission and placement of students in educational programs, jobs, or as requirements for promotion and graduation.

Defenders may insist that Goals 2000 is primarily about setting standards and not primarily a form of deliberate, coercive cultural control managed from the top by testing. However, all the major supporting documents, provisions, and history of the legislation itself and the stated intentions of the chief Goals 2000 advocates belie this. There are dozens of places in the reports and in supporting technical papers of the advocates that argue that a national auditing system for measuring progress in terms of the goals is key. Nationwide testing, they argue, is essential because without discipline, the entire enterprise is of little use. No one says it more forthrightly and states the case for Goals 2000 more succinctly than CEO of IBM, Louis V. Gerstner, a long-time supporter.

> We must establish clear goals and measure progress to them. We must articulate exactly what we expect from schools, teachers, principals, students and parents, and we must provide rewards and incentives to

reach them.... If the goals are not met we need to exact stiff penalties, changing the leadership and even dismissing staff members in schools that aren't performing.... All this will require revamping licensing requirements, [and the] testing and assessment of both students and staff. (Gerstner, 1994)

The need for cultural control in the form of disciplinary testing is more explicit in the writing and work of one of the chief theorists and exponents of Goals 2000, Lauren Resnick, a professor of education, former president of the American Educational Research Association, and member of the National Academy of Education. She now co-directs "The New Standards Project," which is writing performance objectives and test items for a new generation of "authentic" tests that are to be linked to performance goals.

Our goal is to build a revitalized education system using assessment as a tool for transforming instruction and learning.... Without performance standards, the meaning of content standards is subject to interpretations, which if allowed to vary would undermine efforts to set high standards for the majority of American students. (Simmons and Resnick, 1993)

The political and legislative history reveals that the politicians and professionals are aiming to shape culture. During the Bush years, a previous incarnation of Goals 2000 called Education 2000 was submitted to Congress by Lamar Alexander, President Bush's secretary of education. As governor of Tennessee, Alexander served with fellow governor Bill Clinton in producing *Time for Results* (1986), a report of the National Governors' Association. Out of this effort emerged a "National Goals Panel" that drafted six of the national educational goals codified into federal law by the 1994 Act. George Bush, as candidate for president taking his cue from Lamar Alexander crowned himself the "education president" during the 1988 campaign. In Bush's inaugural address entitled America 2000, he embraced as his own the six national educational goals drafted by the Goals Panel. In the summer of 1989, Bush convened an "Education Summit" in Charlottesville to plan next steps. With a one million dollar Congressional appropriation, a bipartisan committee of nationally prominent experts was created to "advise on the desirability and feasibility of national tests" and recommend "policies, structures, and mechanisms for setting *voluntary* standards and planning an appropriate system of tests" (italics added).

Six months later, this committee calling itself "The National Council on Education Standards and Testing" in 1992 produced and released to the public *Raising Standards for American Education*. Chief lieutenants for the undertaking within the Bush Administration were two professors: Diane Ravitch of Columbia Teachers College, a widely known, outspoken, neo-conservative historian, and Chester E. Finn, an education professor at Vanderbilt, a long-time supporter of national testing and "privatization" of schooling. To no one's surprise *Raising Standards* concluded that a system of national standards linked to national testing was "critical to the nation in three primary ways: to promote educational equity, preserve democracy, and enhance civic culture and to improve economic competitiveness" (p. 1). *Raising Standards* became and to this day remains the bible for national elementary and secondary school reform through the millennium, providing the justification, guiding principles, and blueprint for creating and maintaining a system of national standards and testing.

Membership in the task force and advisory groups that produced the *Raising Standards* reads like a who's who on the national educational scene for the last 20 years — high-profile business and education leaders, professional educationists, state education officers, well-known and up-and-coming liberal and conservative state and national officeholders, as well as representatives of several of the more influential Washington-based citizen lobbies. I take special note that among the members of the Standards Task Force was the one-time Superintendent of Public Instruction in California, Bill Honig, who as we shall see played a crucial role in shaping the national Goals 2000 blueprint.

By the fall of 1992, it appeared that Bush's Education 2000 bill was doomed or perhaps would be approved by the Democratic Congress, but without the testing provisions intact. Secretary Lamar Alexander was then reported to have urged Bush to veto the bill. Without the testing provisions, he said, Education 2000 was "worthless." Congress adjourned killing Education 2000 and putting an end to Bush's brief reign as education president, but not to the plan itself. Front-runner Democratic presidential candidate at the time, Bill Clinton, announced publicly that he, like Lamar Alexander, favored national standards coupled with testing. After Clinton became president, he negotiated a version that disarmed strong opposition from several national civil rights organizations, public interest, and the fairness-in-testing citizens' lobbies that with the help of the Black Caucus in the House had blocked Bush's bill. A compromise was reached which included provisions for funding a new national commission of experts and children's advocates to write model "opportunity-to-learn standards," which presumably would set minimum standards for children's health and welfare. The price for Republican support, however, was the inclusion of a provision that specifically bars the current and future use of "model opportunity standards" in denying access to federal funds.

Though Bush's bill was defeated, Secretary Alexander and deputies Ravitch and Finn were not deterred from their mission of creating a system of national testing. With an assist from Lynne Cheney, Bush's director of the National Endowment for the Humanities, they managed to continue on the path by funding seven projects, each composed of professors and coalitions of various experts and professionals, to draft national content standards in all the major school subjects, a necessary step for developing national testing. A grant was given to Gary Nash, professor of history and director of the National Center for History in the Schools at UCLA to develop U.S. and world history standards. As we shall see, Nash became one of the principal players in controversies surrounding Goals 2000 policies.

The alignment of tests to national standards is the central but not the only form of cultural coercion. According to the Goals 2000 blueprint, key for encouraging "voluntary" participation and discouraging non-compliance, states and localities would be denied federal funds available under other programs, Title I of The Elementary and Secondary Act for instance. Finally, and perhaps most important, the Goals 2000 national blueprint is *not* dependent on receiving direct federal support. Goals 2000 will not die even if, as is probable, the Gingrich-led Congress disables the Act by failing to appropriate funds for the national educational standards board known as NESIC (National Standards and Improvement Council) or enacting the Heritage Foundation's (1994) recommendations to the incoming Republican Congress to scrap the Act altogether except for the first ten pages, which include only the rationale and goal statements. Should this occur the Goals 2000 process which is already heavily "privatized" will only become more so — which in practice means that costs of the national Goals 2000 bureaucratic apparatus will be borne by corporate gifts and grants from the major foundations, with the states' Goals 2000 apparatus operating on state and local education funds augmented by private giving and foundation grants.

When Clinton's bill passed in March 1994, it appeared that Goals 2000 would remain in the shadows. The popular news media more or less took at face value the advocates' claims that there was a wide consensus for Goals 2000. The bill passed with bipartisan support and with sizable majorities (House: 305–121; Senate: 63–22), with the blessings of several current and former secretaries of education and labor during the Reagan-Bush and Carter years, Republican and Democratic governors, chief state education officers, and many well-known big-city school superintendents. Twenty-three national business and professional associations also publicly endorsed it. Among Goals 2000's most ardent supporters is Albert Shanker who endorsed it on behalf of the American Federation of Teachers. The rest of organized labor approved or at least appeared not to disapprove. The national director of the Children's Defense Fund, Marion Wright Edelman, while she did not endorse the bill, attended and her presence was acknowledged by President Clinton at the bill's signing ceremony. There was hardly a whisper of dissent reported in the national press about an act the *New York Times* as well as friends and foes called "sweeping," "unprecedented," and "historic." It was debated by Congress, passed and signed into law by Clinton virtually without public notice. Neither the left-leaning *Nation* nor the right-wing *National Review* spent many words on Goals 2000. At the school level teachers, principals, and students also didn't take much notice, continuing about their daily work unaffected by this new turn in national educational policy. While there were and remain a number of articulate oppositional voices, and some spirited debates among educational academics, policy makers, and upper-echelon federal and state government officials (*Harvard Education Review* 1994), dissenting voices were largely ignored by the national news media and the Congress.

Then came the firestorm. In the midst of the now infamous 1994 mid-term election campaign, news reached the public of the proposed new national history standards produced by Nash's National Center for History in the Schools at UCLA. The story of white men's anger, the electoral right turn, and Gingrich's "Contract with America" eclipsed all else, but the controversy over the proposed national history standards nevertheless received the full treatment: a hostile *Wall Street Journal* editorial, sharply worded *New York Times* op-ed exchanges by famous historians and big-name policy wonks, front covers on the newsweeklies, angry exchanges on *Nightline*, and a hate-your-neighbor fest on talk radio and TV.

Much of what was said in the exchanges is familiar, the same arguments, counter-arguments and issues aired in the decades-old debate over the *canon* — which history, whose great ideas, which books, heros, myths, and ways of knowing shall be in the required curriculum. Lynne Cheney and Diane Ravitch, who had arranged for the grant to the center that produced the standards, were outraged. Cheney said the proposed standards represent the authors' politically correct "obsessions" with McCarthyism, racism, and mistreatment of indigenous peoples to the neglect of "core" developments and major figures in U.S. history. Ravitch complained "[i]t honors the nation's diversity but ignores the nation's commonalties and unfairly stigmatizes male white Protestants." Albert Shanker weighed in with "it's leftist point-of-view history" wherein white people are often portrayed "as evil and oppressive" (*Education Week* 11/2/94). Gary Nash, who is not only director of the Center which produced the standards but current president of the Organization of American Historians, responded, saying that the public was being misled. He likened the attacks to those in the 1930s on historians Carl I. Becker and Charles Beard, which he noted were organized by military and business interests. "There are white people on every page of this [the history standards] document," (Weiner 1995) Nash countered, "When Clio's ranks are broadened new stories are told. That offends some people"(Nash 1995). These hostile exchanges, however were polite talk compared to the outright racism and sexism of the far right.

An effort was made to hold together the Washinton right-center Goals 2000 coalition. At a closed-door meeting held in Washington in January 1995, Nash and colleagues met with several of their less extreme adversaries in the history standards dispute including Ravitch, an individual representing Cheney, Al Shanker, and Gilbert Sewel, the director of the American Textbook Institute. At the end of the meeting, Nash announced at a press conference that there was agreement to omit several of the offending suggested teaching activities and to "consider" revisions in the standards. "Not every issue is resolvable," Nash said, "but I think we can go a long way toward accommodating the criticisms." There were signs, however, that the consensus would not hold. At the meeting's conclusion, Cheney's representative was reported to have said, "the standards are seriously flawed from start to finish ... and there's no commitment [by the authors] to change" (*Education Week* 1/18/95.) The hard right, which is well-organized and funded and has a populist base, will not be brought into the fold. The Robertsons, Buchanans, and Gramms want no part whatsoever of the Nash/Ravitch moderate, accommodationist, multicultural perspective or any perspective that makes an effort to incorporate into its story the subjugation of women and people of color, and they certainly would not countenance any content standards that mention the plight of the poor and oppressed or the needless pain and suffering inflicted on the nation's wartime enemies.

What is extraordinary in all this are not the substantive differences in opinion over the history lessons American children should be taught in school, but the fact that such a meeting could take place at all. Debates over the historical and cultural content and approach of the social studies school curriculum are long-standing, but what makes this particular meeting like none other is that a group of private citizens, a president of a professional association of American historians, the national president of a teachers union, a former member of the Bush administration, meeting together with a chief lobbyist for the textbook industry, all apparently "white" and of European descent, took it upon themselves to shape the *official* interpretation, *the* story of the United States and the world's history that *all* the nation's children will be expected to know in order to earn a high school diploma. Clearly, they were attempting to shape and control the nation's story and to create an enforcement apparatus to insure it is transmitted to school children. The purpose, as the previously quoted Fieldhouse (1965) has suggested is to manufacture in them "the appropriate mental attitude," which is "a positive sense of interest with the parent state" and "the inability to conceive of an alternative."

Once the decision was made that there shall be "voluntary" national standards in history and other school subjects, holding a closed-door meeting to negotiate differences among the governing elites in Washington over what shall be the content of the history curriculum in the nation's K–12 classrooms appears quite normal. Also seen as normal is the inclusion in the meeting of an official representative of the major textbook publishing companies. The publishing industry has a significant interest in standardizing course content so that the next generation of textbooks, tests, and supplementary teaching materials will qualify for state and district adoptions.

The well-orchestrated, publicized objections by the right to the proposed new history standards during the 1994 elections was also understandable They recognize that it matters deeply who controls the culture and governs what is to be included and omitted in the next generation of textbooks and achievement tests. Their impact on national, state, and local electoral politics must be taken very seriously because they not only have a popular base and are very well funded but drive the national Republican agenda and are organized for the long term. The Clinton Administration's and other chief lieutenants for Goals 2000 appeared mystified. "What you've got here is a small but well-organized group who simply misunderstands or misrepresents Goals 2000," one spokesman said. Diane Ravitch and the current Secretary of Education, Richard Riley, decried the "politicalization" of the process. "Pull back from making the public schools a political football," said Riley, "and give the [Goals 2000] process a fair chance" (*Education Week* 11/19/94). In spite of the overwhelming evidence, many Goals 2000 advocates apparently believe it remains possible to depoliticize education, a cultural process that is inherently political and inevitably connects to the racial, economic, religious, and cultural divisions in U.S. society.

Goals 2000, the California Experience

Since 1992, The U.S. Office of Education has granted more than 24 million dollars to 30 states to fund the Goals 2000 process. As of this writing, 46 states have applied for federal grants authorized under the Goals 2000 legislation for the purpose of developing state plans. Most are still drafting or reviewing their standards. (*Education Week* 4/12/95). I conclude my argument drawing upon California's experience for several reasons: it is the nation's most populous state and in many respects is a microcosm of the politics of the nation as a whole. Not only are many of its major population centers a majority "minority" and becoming more so, California's experience with Goals 2000 is the longest, dating back to 1983, 11 years before passage of the federal act and before Goals 2000 policies had acquired their name.

In 1983, Bill Honig had just been elected to California's highly influential statewide office of Superintendent of Instruction on a platform of reforming the State's ailing public schools. This was also the year of *Nation at Risk*, the Reagan-era report, which transformed school reform into a national political issue, spawning the work of many dozens of groups including the national associations of governors and chief state education officers. Honig was a leading figure in the latter organization and later served on the previously mentioned national task force that produced *Raising Standards* and the Goals 2000 legislation. His plan for California — a plan still in effect — was to use the bureaucratic powers of the state to press for change from the top. He commissioned the State Department of Education to develop and adopt new rigorous statewide academic standards or "frameworks" for each curricular area, which were to be linked directly to a new generation of tests replacing the multiple-choice tests in common use. The novelty of the plan was not the development of state curriculum frameworks, but the creation of a system of assessment aimed specifically at insuring close conformity to the frameworks. This is the policy that came to be known as Goals 2000.

I briefly recount two related stories accompanying the development of two curriculum frameworks, in 'History and Social Science' and 'Language and Literature.' Each illustrates how the cultural warfare provoked by Goals 2000 played itself out in paradoxical ways at the local and state levels, and how the Goals 2000 process became increasingly drawn into bitter and corrosive electoral politics.

The Oakland Textbook Controversy

In 1991, prime movers of Goals 2000, Diane Ravitch, Gary Nash, and Bill Honig, were party to the precursor to the recent dispute over national history standards. On its face, the battle was over whether the Oakland school district should adopt a new Houghton-Mifflin K–8 social studies textbook series. These books were authored by Gary Nash based on the then newly written "History and Social Science Framework," which had been commissioned by Honig. The Houghton-Mifflin series as it turned out was (and remains) the only one approved by the State of California as fully aligned to the new Framework. The Framework itself had been written by the National Center for History in the Schools — then co-directed and now directed by professor Nash — the same organization that several years later produced the disputed national history standards. Assisting him as the chief consultant in writing the history-social science framework was Professor Ravitch who, like Nash, had been selected by Mr. Honig.

In the Oakland textbook episode, this same triumvirate, Honig, Nash, and Ravitch, failed to grasp the underlying cultural question. They, as do many other Goals 2000 advocates, often appeared bewildered and defensive when their efforts to be more inclusive and multicultural was met with rage. In Oakland and in several other districts in California, the chief opposition came not from the extreme right wing (which is a weak political force in Oakland and most large metropolitan cities), but from many of the same groups whom Nash and Ravitch sought to integrate into their more inclusive version of U.S. and world history, "minorities," primarily African Americans, Asian Americans, and Latino Americans. These are the groups who populate and hold political power in Oakland's city government and the school board. At the time, the board of education was composed of four African Americans, two Asian American, and a white member.

After nine months of acrimonious debates, open meetings, intense organizing efforts, telephone trees, picketing, and public demonstrations organized by a coalition of public education activists and community and civil rights groups, the School Board rejected the Houghton-Mifflin books in the early morning hours of June 6, 1991, overriding the recommendations of the superintendent, curriculum coordinator, and a district-wide committee of teachers. In the final vote, all four African-Americans school board members were opposed while the votes of the remaining three members who represented the more affluent and whiter areas of the city were split.

Superintendent Honig's response to the Oakland dispute unfortunately exemplifies what Said says is one of the chief responses of governing elites to the efforts of the formerly colonized to create their own narratives of emancipation and enlightenment: repression, denial, and invocation of fears of "Lebanonization" or of creating another Yugoslavia. Honig, sounding much like Ravitch and Cheney labeled the Oakland opposition "separatists," "tribalists," and "the victimization crew," and in words which could easily be mistaken for Cheney's:

> They do not like the the the idea of common democratic principles. It gets in the way of their left point of view that this country is corrupt.... Everything is not race, gender, or class. The world cannot be seen just through these glasses. (Waugh 1990)

The opposition clearly was not, however, a collection of separatists, tribalists, and disgruntled leftists, but a temporarily assembled but nevertheless politically and intellectually sophisticated, well-organized, racially mixed, multicultural coalition composed of mostly mainstream educational, business, and religious leaders, parents, professors, and teachers. The schisms on the textbook question cut sharply across traditional right/ left political lines, with the member of the school board with arguably the most politically correct left credentials consistently defending the Nash-Ravitch line.

The "CLAS" Episode

Just as the Oakland textbook dispute foreshadowed the national history standards controversy, CLAS (California Learning Assessment System) foreshadows the disputes which will likely follow as the circle is closed, that is, as the new generation of improved or "authentic" tests are aligned to the content standards. CLAS was integral to the Honig plan of linking syllabi in every academic subject to a new form of testing. The first of the CLAS tests was in the area of reading and language and was tied to the Language and Literature Framework commissioned several years earlier by Honig and approved by the State Board of Education. At the time, the framework was widely welcomed by the mainstream press and most educational professionals as "innovative" and "pioneering" and hailed as the first framework in the nation to couple multiculturalism and a whole language approach to the teaching of reading and writing.

During the adoption process of the language framework, the California extreme right tried hard, but at the time lacked the political clout to defeat the adoption of the new language framework. Their intent, however, was clear. They wanted no part of "critical thinking" or the likes of Toni Morrison, Maxine Hong Kingston, or Malcolm X installed into the officially sanctioned California literary canon. The far right lost this initial skirmish over the language framework but targeted Honig, an up-and-coming, articulate, and relatively liberal San Francisco attorney and politician, who was being touted as a possible Democratic gubernatorial candidate. For these and other offenses to the right wing, Honig's promising political career was abruptly ended in 1993 with the assistance of California's far right attorney general who charged and won conviction of Honig on a blatant and unwise, but relatively benign, violation of the state's conflict of interest laws.

As luck would have it, 1994 was not only the year of the right wing's electoral victories and Gingrich's ascent, but of the CLAS test's first outing, and the year for reauthorizing state funds for CLAS. (Fifty-four million dollars had already been spent on development and another 23 million was requested.) The results of the first administration of a CLAS test were reported in early 1994 and widely covered in the California daily press, talk radio, and T.V. Then, the sky fell. Reasonably civilized disagreements over how to teach reading and writing and what books kids should read in. school became enmeshed with one of the ugliest California gubernatorial and senatorial election campaigns in memory, one that routinely scape-goated African-American men, women on welfare, and immigrants. It was also the year of Propositions 185 (three strikes you're out), 187 (denial of virtually all public services to non-citizens), and of a proposal for a new so-called "Civil Rights Initiative" intended to undo affirmative action. The onslaught during the election came almost entirely from the far right. Paradoxically, many of the same groups who were opposed to the Nash-Ravitch history standards generally supported the new language frame-work and remained silent on the CLAS issue, while the mainstream press generally attacked, not the failed policies that produced the controversies, but the far right's criticisms of CLAS. They also blamed the test's technical problems on the California State Department of Education and/or Educational Testing Service who was the prime contractor for the CLAS test.

While CLAS may have been been born out of the very best of intentions, to replace the much and deservedly maligned multiple choice tests, CLAS managed to have several unfortunate effects. It became an issue in an election campaign trading on hate, polarizing even further the State's electoral process. In the process, the far right's influence over public education policy was strengthened. The governor, Pete Wilson, who was reelected to office by exploiting the rising tide of anti-immigrant sentiment and get-tough-on-crime racism, accepted the right-wing position and vetoed the CLAS appropriation during the campaign, even after promises that a process would be set up for removing offensive pieces and assurances were given that many of the new open-ended test questions would be dumbed down and replaced with the old-fashioned "objective" multiple choice items. CLAS is now officially dead and is generally regarded as a very expensive mistake. While officially on the Goals 2000 path, California's policy of directly linking test to curriculum remains in shambles.

The major reason the CLAS test became easy prey is that, in spite of the effort to pose thoughtful questions to students, for example, "Write an essay in which you interpret the moments of silence or inability to speak in Maxine Hong Kingston's autobiography" (*Education Week* 7/11/94, 8), from a technical point of view the test was a mess. A panel of expert statisticians appointed to respond to widespread criticisms of the test concluded, "CLAS and similar assessments are in uncharted waters. Some difficulties are inherent in the new types of assessment, which face unprecedented problems related to test construction, sampling scoring rules, reporting, and statistical analysis.... [Each] trial run is a major learning experience" (Wagner, 1994).

The flaws the experts identified, however, are far more than a collection of difficult technical glitches capable of being repaired. CLAS reveals a key deficiency in the disintegrating epistemological foundations of educational testing *as a field of applied science*. While it is far beyond the scope of this chapter to make these arguments here, a number of "Third World," feminist, and postmodernist critics have, in effect, dismantled beyond repair the most basic precepts of the field (Haraway 1989; Rosenau 1992; Giroux and McLauren 1994; Lather 1991), including the concepts of test "validity" and "reliability" that lie at the core of the professional evaluation and testing profession's claims to scientific objectivity. The technology of the new "authentic" tests and of the old multiple choice variety is in crisis because of the inability to accommodate into its scientific logic human motivation, cultural differences, conflict, and change (Berlak 1992; Raven 1992; Madaus 1994).

The chief battles and tugs of war over Goals 2000 are simultaneously cultural, political, and economic. What Goals 2000 has managed to do very successfully is to provoke cultural warfare and open new arenas for the political struggles between the efforts of governing elites to maintain cultural and political dominance, and of the children of colonized peoples to decolonize themselves, affirm and create, and recreate their identities as peoples with shared culture, history, and linked destiny. Perhaps there is not much new or remarkable in the discovery that governing elites attempt to hang on to their economic privileges and cultural and political preeminence, nor that at this moment in history, various men and women of color (a euphemism for the formerly colonized and subjugated) peoples are actively affirming, creating, and recreating their identities.

Many writers in this volume show that there are many other ways of thinking and going about schooling and education in this the era of decolonization. There is not yet a vision for a coherent national educational policy to supplant Goals 2000, but there is no shortage of ideas, possibilities, or energy. However, unless Goals 2000 with or without federal subsidy is untracked, many of the most successful and promising efforts currently underway in many places across the country to improve schools in the interests of all children, not just for the more privileged, are endangered, as public attention is diverted and public and foundation funds continue to be unwisely wasted on a destructive and unworkable set of national and state educational policies.

References

Bell, Derrick (1992). *Faces at the Bottom of the Well.* New York: Basic Books.

Berlak, Harold (1992). The Need for a New Science of Assessment *and* Toward a New Science. In Harold Berlak, Ed. *Toward a New Science of Educational Testing & Assessment.* Albany: SUNY Press.

Education Week. September 8, 1992; August 11, 1994; October 19, 1994; November 2, 1994; January 18, 1995; and April 12, 1995.

Fanon, Franz (1967). *Black Skin, White Masks.* New York: Grove-Weidenfel.

Fieldhouse, D. K. (1965). *The Colonial Empires: A Comparative Search from the Eighteenth Century.* Reprint, London: Houndmills–Macmillan, 1991.

Gerstner, Louis V. Jr. (1994, April). Our Schools Are Failing; Do We Care? *New York Times.*

Giroux, Henry A. and Peter McLauren, Eds. (1994). *Between Borders*, New York: Routledge.

Hall, Stuart (1992). New Ethnicities. In James Donald and Ali Rattansi, Eds., *'Race', Culture & Difference*, London: Sage & Open University Press.

Haraway, Donna (1989). *Primate Visions: Gender, Race, and Nature in the World of Modern Science*, New York: Routledge.

Harvard Educational Review (1994, Spring). 64(1).

Lather, Patti (1991). *Getting Smart*, Albany: New York: Routledge.

Heritage Foundation. 1994. *Members Guide to the Issues*. Washington D.C.: Author.

Mohanty, Chandra Talpade (1991). Under Western Eyes: Feminist Scholarship and Colonial Discourses. In Chandra Talpade Mohanty, Ann Russo, and Torres Lordes (eds.), *Third World Women and the Politics of Feminism*, Bloomington: University of Indiana Press, pp 51–80.

Madaus, George F. (1994). A Technological and Historical Consideration of Equity Issues Associated with Proposals to Change the Nation's Testing Policy. *Harvard Educational Review*, 64(1).

Nash, Gary. (1995, April 21). The history children should study. *Chronicle of Higher Education*, p. A60.

National Council on Education Standards and Testing. *Raising Standards for American Education* (1992). Washington D.C.: U.S. Government Printing Office.

Raven, John (1992). A Model of Competence, Motivation, and Behavior, and a Paradigm for Assessment. In H. Berlak, Ed., *Toward a New Science of Educational Testing & Assessment*. Albany: SUNY Press.

Richardson, Patrick (1968). *Empire and Slavery*, London: Longmans.

Rosenau, Pauline Marie (1992). *Post-Modernism and the Social Sciences*. Princeton: Princeton Univresity Press.

Said, Edward (1994). *Culture and Imperialism, New York:* Vintage.

Simmons, Warren and Lauren Resnick (1993). Assessment as a Catalyst of School Reform. *Educational Leadership*, 50(5), 11–15.

Time for Results (1986). Washington D.C: National Governors' Association.

Wagner, Vernis (1994, Aug. 8). Problems Found in School Ttest. *San Francisco Examiner*, p. A–5.

Waugh, Dexter (1990, July 22). City May Not Buy New Books. *San Francisco Examiner*.

Weiner, Jon (1995, January 18). The critic who didn't actually read the national standards for history. *San Francisco Examiner*, p. A15.

West, Cornel (1993). *Prophetic Thought in Postmodern Times*, vol.1, Monroe, Maine: Common Courage Press.

"The harsh reality is that there is now official sanction and anointment for a particular curriculum perspective, a reality made poignant if not tragic given that this perspective is culturally narrow and intellectually shallow.... Apart from the ideological concerns, this legislation surely must be seen as totally devoid of any kind of semiserious educational theorizing or reasoning; to put it another way, it is written as if there is *no* tradition of educational discourse."

—*David E. Purpel*

Goals 2000, the Triumph of Vulgarity, and the Legitimation of Social Injustice

David E. Purpel

I believe that the policies, procedures, and programs composing the Goals 2000 legislation represent a significant crystallization of recent trends in educational thought, so much so that it can be used as a telling if not chilling index of a quite clear social and cultural consensus on a number of critically important professional and public issues. This legislation, its support, and the nature of the critical response to it tells us a great deal about the present state of the continuous debate on the basic direction of American society and the role of public education in the determination and shaping of the direction. In this essay, I want to comment on those aspects of the legislation that seem to have provoked the least negative response, as it is my assumption that these are the aspects that represent the greatest amount of consensus by the public and the profession. Like the dog in the Sherlock Holmes story, what is significant here is the absence of barking and howling, or more precisely, the particular rhythms and qualities of the barking and the silences.

It is quite clear that the passage of the law was not a matter of great public interest; it received little attention in the media, and it certainly was not highlighted as one of the major political battles of the Clinton administration, such as health care and welfare reform. It is premature to fully gauge mainstream professional reactions, but my impression is that it has been relatively tepid and that the criticisms tend to focus on the meagerness of the funds involved and the high degree of federal involvement in curriculum decisions. Time will tell whether this relative indifference represents a shrewd insight into what might turn out to be toothless legislation with marginal consequences or a gross miscalculation of the far-reaching consequences of landmark educational policy making. However, the debate and eventual passage of this program is a permanent record of what seems to constitute a clear current consensus (public and professional) on both what the purposes of education and what the basic curriculum orientation ought to be.

What is particularly revealing about this legislation is that it represents an effort to integrate educational policy into a clear, unambiguous, and coherent social, economic, political, and cultural agenda. This is not a program directed at education "for its own sake," it is openly and proudly presented as an instrument of a particular set of government policies. Indeed, there is little indication that those who proposed the legislation make *any* distinction between education and socioeconomic policy, although there is no ample evidence of a close analysis of the relationship between proposed curriculum policies and economic goals.

Curriculum Theory

Although the legislation does not obviously attempt to delve into serious curriculum theorizing, it does deal quite decisively, if rather heavy-handedly, with what we have come to believe is a complex and perplexing issue, namely the question about what should be taught. After all the struggles and all the painstaking and heated debates on the nature of knowledge, on what knowledge is of most worth, on whether we should strive to be child-centered or subject-centered, on whether we can integrate critical pedagogy with ecofeminism, on the place of the arts, on the balance of the body, mind, and spirit, and all the other countless and important controversies, proposals, projects, and critiques, finally the President and Congress have cut through all these knots and conundrums and have decided.

One clear winner is the ever-popular and remarkably resilient gaggle of conventional disciplines: "English, mathematics, science, foreign languages, civics and government, arts, history, and geography." Another winner is the much unloved and critically abused "mastery and competence" approach to learning, which says something about the comparative influence of Madeline Hunter and Paulo Freire on American consciousness. The losers include many of the areas that progressive and humanistic educators have emphasized over the years: interdisciplinary studies, critical thinking, constructivism, service learning, education for democracy, education for personal expression, education for social responsibility, aesthetics education, moral education, multicultural education, environmental education, physical education, health education, and sexuality education to mention a few prominent ones. This is not to say that these areas are dead and buried, but the legislation makes its priorities crystal clear, and one doesn't have to be clairvoyant to figure out how the United States Government sees the difference between the truly important and the merely interesting components of the curriculum. The harsh reality is that there is now official sanction and anointment for a particular curriculum perspective, a reality made poignant if not tragic given that this perspective is culturally narrow and intellectually shallow.

This poignancy is magnified when we consider what seems to be the utter irrelevance and futility of the sum total of the profession's efforts to sophisticate the public dialogue on these issues. After decades of articles, books, experiments, debates, investigations, and critiques and with a heritage of brilliant and imaginative pedagogical theories, we are told that the best we can do is to turn to a dreary collection of depressing clichés and anachronisms. Apart from the ideological concerns, this legislation surely must be seen as totally devoid of any kind of semiserious educational theorizing or reasoning; to put it another way, it is written as if there is *no* tradition of educational discourse. In this regard, we in the profession must confront what appears to be our humiliating and shameful failure to penetrate the consciousness of mainstream American intellectual and political thought. How do we as a profession account for the failure to at least ameliorate the effects of political cynicism and public naiveté? To what degree is the profession complicit by dint of those who pander to the powerful? To what degree is the profession incompetent by dint of its failure to establish a framework of a sophisticated public discourse of education? To what degree is the profession derelict in its responsibility to engage the public in genuine dialogue on the social, political, economic, cultural, and moral dimensions of educational policy and practice? Ultimately, as we have seen in the case of Goals 2000, educational policy is determined by those in power, but the ease by which vulgar and shallow educational thought have triumphed tells us that we must work a great deal harder and smarter to insist that such decisions be made with full knowledge of the complexities involved. In this way, we can maintain hope in the educability of the public and reenergize our sense of the purpose and importance of our work.

Socio-Economic Policy

There is not much ambiguity here. The words "productive" and "competitive" reappear with amazing regularity as if to reassure everyone that this piece of educational legislation is for real, i.e., it is specifically designed for the very real and heavily competitive world of the global economy. The political and economic contexts for the significance of the legislation had been long established and, astonishingly enough, largely accepted: We are to believe that America is in a desperate struggle for economic dominance if not survival with other, more disciplined and hard-working nations. We are in this predicament and in danger of losing even more ground, in part because of the slackness and mediocrity in our schools, as it is clear that our competitor nations are outdistancing us in intellectual achievements, particularly in the crucial areas of science, technology, and mathematics. What is urgently needed, then, is to stiffen our will, increase standards, demand more work from our students and teachers, and carefully scrutinize and monitor educational achievement. The problem is a lack of sufficiently trained cadres of hard-working, productive, technologically savvy workers, and the solution is for the schools to cull out those with promise and motivate, train, test, and produce them. The cry became "The nation is at risk: Fix the schools!"

This readily accepted myth represents policies that serve a number of purposes. First, it co-opts the public schools to accept as their primary task feeding and sustaining the interests of international capitalists who require a lot of hard-working, productive, technologically savvy workers and a great number of people who believe that this is the only right and proper purpose of education. Secondly, it distracts us into believing that our social and economic problems are rooted in our schools rather than in our social and economic policies and institutions, thereby avoiding rather messy and troubling questions on what constitutes a just and equitable system of distributing wealth and privilege. Thirdly, it provides a convenient justification to impose more control, uniformity, and orthodoxy in a culture very unsure and uneasy about dissent, difference, and pluralism; i.e., it is to say that we simply can't afford 1960s-style experimentation and counterculturalism in a period of economic crisis. In addition, the myth encourages the best friends of those who want to maintain their power — namely, fear and anxiety and their companions of suspicion and divisiveness. The message is clear: The future belongs to the willing and the talented, and for them it holds fame and fortune. Such people need only follow directions. For those who insist on slovenliness, laziness, and surliness, the future is bleak and threatening, and they are advised to get out of the way and be prepared to take their just desserts. For those who are willing but who have limited talents, the future is extremely uncertain, and such people are well advised to be obedient, work harder, lay low, be alert, and stay on guard.

It is clear that we are now immersed in a more virulent form of capitalism in which national boundaries, social contracts, and moral frameworks become increasingly irrelevant. It is a time of downsizing, bottom-line thinking, mergers, and intense competition, and it is an era when greed is masked as freedom and hustling becomes a creative activity. The effects on our community have been staggering: persistent unemployment and underemployment; an ever-widening gap between have and have-not nations; greater pollution and erosion of natural resources; increasing disparities in income; a shortage of meaningful jobs; intense pressures on families to earn a living wage; homelessness; poverty; welfare bashing; the rationing of medical care; and many other manifestations of a cruel and relentless economic order. This triumphant and unchallenged order must be seen as the driving force of not only Goals 2000 but of virtually all current official efforts at school reform, and indeed, we are well advised to examine the substance of this economic grounding rather than focusing only on the procedural and curricular dimensions of this legislation. This legislation is not primarily about advancing knowledge or expanding intellectual and creative horizons, nor is it about the pursuit of meaning and the nurturing of the soul; it is, instead, concerned with the deployment of human resources into immense struggles for economic dominance, privilege, and hegemony. Goals 2000 is not directed at individual empowerment or social democracy but is instead designed to supply the arsenal of human resources needed for the bloody economic wars being fought by transnational corporations, national economies, and financial entrepreneurs.

President Clinton summed up this point rather well in his 1994 State of the Union speech in which he endorsed public school choice and chartering, "as long as we measure every school by one high standard: Are our children learning what they need to know to compete and win in the global economy?" What a commentary on our society when the President, in a major policy address to the nation, enunciates our basic educational policy as one that reduces the purposes of education to the promotion of material success and the intensification of international economic competition.

Moral Vision

The kind of economic policy that drives the Goals 2000 program has had an enormous influence not only on material issues as I have already indicated, but also on our relationships with each other and on our basic human values. It is a time when meritocracy has shifted from being a term of accusation and dread to one of approbation and celebration, a time of a reenergized and revalidated social Darwinism. Our new postindustrial society and postmodern culture require highly skilled, tough-minded, highly sophisticated people who can and do change intellectual, cultural, and moral loyalties easily and joyfully. All bets are off, traditional loyalties and allegiances are suspect, communities and credos are all problematic, it's all flow and go. Presumably, the good news is that what will, or at least should, count is not family or social connections or previous conditions of mastery but sheer talent, and for that reason we must not discriminate by the outmoded cultural categories of race, class, and gender but by the more democratic and hip ones of cybernetic literacy, language fluency, and entrepreneurial *chutzpa*.

This consciousness is well expressed in the almost universally accepted shibboleth of "leveling the playing field," i.e., the importance of reducing socially artificial barriers to achievement. Indeed, this concept is reflected in the Goals 2000 legislation with its references to the development of "opportunity standards," defined in the act as "the criteria for, and the basis of, assessing the sufficiency or quality of the resources, practices, and conditions necessary at each level of the education system ... to provide all students with an opportunity to learn the material in voluntary national content standards or State content standards." Presumably, once we have established and controlled for the independent variables (e.g., quality and quantity of educational resources), we can get on with judging children on the critical dependent variable of achievement. The metaphor of a playing field is very likely used to evoke images of enjoyable contests among willing, fair-minded folks who relish the opportunity to display and hone their skills with other evenly matched and motivated folks. Everyone is expected to play by the rules, to try hard, to be fair, and to accept the outcome with grace. Leveling the playing field is about removing irrelevant, unfair, and preventable barriers to fair competition. So, what is wrong with this picture?

Let's take a closer look at this metaphor and examine the consequences of games played on a level playing field under the assumption that miraculously there is a political will to do this and that we are successful at achieving the goal. Such games still involve competition, contestants of enormously varied interests, abilities, and competitiveness, winners and losers, ranking, and differential rewards that in this case have enormous consequences. The spoils go to the victor, and this is to be celebrated because the victory is "fair" — i.e., based on the inherent and demonstrable superiority of the winner. The major moral tragedy here is that such a contest requires and structures losers, for indeed the game cannot be played without losers, and its primary purpose is to identify them as part of the process of distributing the wealth.

What we have here is a variation of the age-old process of powerful groups imposing a system of hierarchy and privilege and simultaneously providing a discourse of pragmatic justification and social inevitability for what is at base a cruel and callous policy of calculated legitimated inequality. Presumably the myth of equality of *opportunity* allows us to believe that both the victors and the losers deserve their fate and that the community has fulfilled its responsibilities by removing "artificial" barriers to "genuine" competition. What, in fact, the community has done is to mask a system in which human beings are required to compete even if they are averse to competing and to compete in contests even if it requires them to display skills in which they are uninterested and/or lacking. The penalty for not engaging in these compulsory contests is the same, if not worse, as coming in dead last in the games themselves. The consequences are *intended* to be very serious, namely, one's socioeconomic standing in the community, or put another way, they will affect whether you will be rich or poor, hungry or well-fed, and whether you will have a home or not.

One of the major technological problems of our society, therefore, becomes how to develop a "fair" system of affording privilege, legitimating inequality, and evading the Golden Rule. As usual, the intellectual and professional classes have been eager to stoop to the task and have developed a stunning array of sophisticated modes of judging people's worth, which goes under more euphemistic terms like measurement and assessment. Accountability and evaluation become indispensable dimensions of a cruel but fair meritocracy in which our compelling moral responsibility is shifted from creating a more just and loving community to the moral imperative of providing reliable and valid techniques to maintain an inherently unfair society. If nothing else, Goals 2000 is an epiphany to the evaluation and sorting process, an official enshrinement of valid and reliable rituals of ultimate judgment, and an iconization of testing. So much for the traditions of education for play, creativity, and growth; so much for nurturing respect and compassion for each other; so much for the notion of public education as an instrument for nourishing a democratic community with liberty and justice for all.

Goals 2000 is an apt metaphor for a cultural vision of personal achievement, materialism, individuality, survival of the fittest, ruthless competition, political realism, and detached technology. It is a vision that discourages solidarity among peoples, since people are not seen as family members but as competitors. It is a vision that is so powerful that educators find themselves having to work very hard to make convincing and persuasive arguments on the importance of caring and compassion. The fact that nourishing the impulse to care is seen as an intriguing and interesting educational innovation and that the presence of guns is now accepted as commonplace in schools is powerful testimony to the desperation and divisiveness in our culture. The response of Goals 2000 to our social and cultural crises is to define the major educational problem to be that of low productivity and to locate the solution in raising educational achievement and formalizing and institutionalizing a national policy of even more testing, sorting, discriminating, classifying, allocating, and channeling of children so that we might "compete and win in the global economy."

So What's New?

As I've already mentioned, the public response to Goals 2000 has been something less than heated and, indeed, seems to have been one of the major nonevents of 1994. I believe that this, in part, represents a "so what?" reaction to what is by now the emergent and familiar public consensus on what constitutes the essential process and purpose of education, which has now been formally ratified by the President and Congress. There has been some professional and public criticism, most of which has centered on the issues of federal control and the imposition of uniform educational standards. What is truly extraordinary in the reaction, however, is the explicit and implicit acclaim with which the public and profession have lavished on the broad goals themselves even in criticizing them as unrealistic and romantic.

A typical form of criticism begins with a disclaimer on criticizing the goals themselves and then proceeds to take the legislation to task for not providing sufficient funds for these well-intentioned goals or for not recognizing the structural problems that are barriers to achieving these lofty aspirations. Writing as guest editor of a special issue of the *Phi Delta Kappan* mostly devoted to a critical symposium on Goals 2000, Evans Clinchy describes the contributors to the symposium as "transformationists," and clearly their articles are thoughtful and insightful critiques of major elements of the legislation. However, in the very beginning of his lead article, Clinchy (1995) says that "this new national mission may at first glance appear to be *no more than a list of obviously desirable goals and generally non-controversial aims.* Indeed, the question here is not whether these ... goals are worth pursuing but whether the Clinton Administration and the Congress understand what the goals imply and thus what it will take to actually achieve them" (my emphasis). What Clinchy characterizes as "transformationist" critique for the most part turns out to be essentially grounded in serious concerns about pedagogical, curricular, and organizational issues with only occasional references to fundamental social and cultural concerns and none to economic ones. Therefore, what is not new here is the endorsement of an educational policy thoroughly folded into the dominant industrial, financial, and business interests and one that is totally integrated into the ideology of the free-market system (i.e., capitalism). Moreover, what is also constant in the reactions, both pro and con, is the implicit ratification of the existing social, political, and economic paradigm, at least by default, by the vast majority of the profession.

To the extent that there is strong criticism from the profession, my impression is that it tends to focus on the issues of an unimaginative curriculum, an overdetermined degree of testing, and on the matter of the federal imposition of educational uniformity. I have already made reference to the dreariness of the curricular orientation represented in Goals 2000, and as depressing as it may be, there is the reality that it is an orientation that has persisted and prevailed both in the schools and in the public consciousness as virtually inevitable if not incomparable. The status of the five sacred subjects (English, science, mathematics, social studies and foreign languages) has reached a level of near permanence and has remained basically unchallenged as the starting point of curricular discussions for several decades. Again, Goals 2000 does not represent an abrupt change in what constitutes the prevailing views on curriculum, but it has simply affirmed a political reality, namely, that the struggles for serious and fundamental reexamination of the curriculum have had little or no impact on broad educational policy. And surely the emphasis on testing and accountability is hardly a surprise in an era when we are supposed to cheer "authentic assessment" and "portfolios" as progressive ways of rendering to Caesar his insistence on ranking and judging children.

What does appear to be new and ominous is the rather large foot of the federal government in the door of educational regulation, notwithstanding the clearly disingenuous and promiscuous use of the term "voluntary" in the legislation. I agree with those who see this as a potentially devastating blow to our vital principles and traditions of teacher autonomy, community involvement, and student participation, and as an important aspect of an irresistible tide of centralized rigidity, uniformity, and control. The dangers here are very real and involve the possibility of the total politicization of education by the federal government, the erosion of pluralism, diversity, and experimentation, and an escalation of bureaucratic interference, harassment, meddling, and Mickey-Mousing.

As dreadful as these policies may be, they basically represent a continuation, perhaps at a somewhat more intense level, of well-established, basically uncontested, and generally accepted educational policies and practices. Through a combination of various factors and forces — e.g., the homogenization of American culture, the near uniformity in college admissions requirements, the enormous mobility of American workers and families, the existence of a de facto national curriculum (see above), accreditation and certification requirements, the textbook and testing industry, etc. — to all intents and purposes, the public schools in the United States are virtually uniform in all the most important respects, one very important exception being in the area of allocated resources. Indeed, because we as a society have wanted to be able to move from school to school easily, we have arranged an organization, curriculum, and culture of public education of easily assembled and recognizable, interchangeable parts. There surely are vigorous programs in many communities that allow for significant parental and/or teacher involvement, but they still work, for the most part, within the framework of these interchangeable parts. The enthusiasm for state-mandated accountability as a mode of imposing uniform standards is as real as it is depressing, and the striking similarity of these standards across the states should not be in the least surprising.

What's Going On Here?

For me, the main issue is not so much about clarifying the new dangers to public education that Goals 2000 poses but rather to be alert to the old dangers of public education to our vision of a just and loving community. What Goals 2000 represents, extends, magnifies, and cements is an essentially unchallenged educational paradigm that mirrors and seeks to extend a cruel and unjust cultural vision. I believe that critics are right to point out that the legislation seriously erodes the vitality of grassroots, local involvement in the public schools — surely an important dimension of a democratic society. I also agree with the critics who lament the rather crude emphasis on test results that seriously undermines efforts at stimulating critical thinking, individual expression, and human creativity. And, as I've indicated, Goals 2000 accentuates an extremely unwise and self-defeating growth in uniformity, rigidity, and overregulation. However, as important and vital as these criticisms are, they do not go nearly far enough in interpreting the social, political, and cultural significance of the meaning of this latest round of educational reform. We get more insight into the bedrock issues from the critics who correctly point out that our political leaders are very reluctant to confront the real financial and political cost of actually trying seriously to meet the goals, e.g., by failing to discuss the impact that programs directed at the virtual elimination of drugs and violence would have on federal and state budgets or by avoiding discussion of what it really takes to reduce poverty, so necessary even for the relatively modest goal of equal opportunity.

Disingenuousness, however, is not the exclusive prerogative of politicians and is very much in evidence among educators who seek to distance schooling from the social, cultural, economic, and political visions in which they are embedded. The operative present visions (educational and otherwise) actually require, structure, and ensure inequality and poverty in their insistence on hierarchy, competition, and meritocracy. Key to the understanding of why education is such a hotly debated issue is the well-understood tenet that it is a critically important mode of attaining an edge in achieving privilege in a society that embraces and legitimates an unequal distribution of wealth. It seems to me that this is *the* critical axis that our educational institutions turn on and, astonishingly enough, the least questioned and resisted. I certainly prefer that teachers and parents work at the local and school levels to improve educational programs, but not if the programs maintain and accentuate the present system of structured inequality and poverty. I also love to support imaginative, child-centered, developmentally appropriate, and thought-provoking curricula, but my concern for an education that fosters a just and loving community is far greater. Perhaps we do not have to choose between local control and justice or between a humane curriculum and equality, but we must make the connection very, very clear because the reality is that our dominant public and professional discourse is very muddy on these relationships. Actually, the politicians (as in Goals 2000) tend to be much more up-front in their insistence on connecting education to the needs of business, government, and the military. It seems that many professionals are invested in reifying education so that it can be separated from ideological concerns, operating from the myth that good education is good education, good teaching is good teaching, and good schools are good schools, regardless of the political and economic contexts.

What Should We Do?

There are, as I see it, three major problems here: (1) the triumphalism of the reactionary educational reform movement as reflected in the ho-hum reaction to the passage of the Goals 2000 project; (2) the timidity and modesty of oppositional forces as reflected in the mildness of the criticisms of Goals 2000; and (3) the sense of futility and despair as reflected in the near absence of alternative social, economic, and cultural visions to the one represented in Goals 2000. The energy that is created from the interaction of triumphalism, timidity, and despair is surely entropic and hence can only magnify our crises of poverty, inequity, and polarization. What needs to be done is, therefore, quite clear and very difficult, and that is to reinstill our visions, dreams, and hopes for creating a loving and just world and to recover our confidence in the human capacity to overcome the obstacles to them. This is not the time to be timid precisely because there is so much timidity; this is not the time to be despairing especially because there is so little hope out there; this is not the time to preserve the status quo particularly because there is so little effort to work for social and cultural transformation.

Let's put it another way: We don't need professional and intellectual classes to ratify and legitimate policies that engender and sustain social injustice, poverty, and privilege or to add to the sense of their inevitability and immutability. If there ever was a time for those who aspire to leadership and responsibility to speak out with passion and conviction on our shared vision of an end to poverty, to unnecessary human suffering, to homelessness, to humiliation, to authoritarianism, and to anything else standing in the way of a life of meaning and dignity for all people, this is surely it. There is an extraordinary vacuum in the public sphere needing to be filled with a greater understanding of the moral, social, and cultural consequences of our educational policies and with an educational vision that is grounded in a commitment to a world of peace, love, and community. As educators, our responsibility is surely not to carry out current educational policies and practices however oppressive they may be, but to uphold and nourish the cherished principles that inform our deepest dreams and highest aspirations. As responsible professionals, we are uniquely positioned to affirm the capacity of education to contribute to a consciousness of compassion and justice. However, this is a time when we need to talk less about our educational goals and more about our moral aspirations, less about our professional role as educators and more about ethical responsibilities as citizens. We need to stop accommodating to the forces of institutional control and instead renew our commitment to the spirit of joyous community. To paraphrase Rabbi Hillel, if we as a profession do not support education, who will? If we are only for our profession, what are we? If not now, when?

Reference

Clinchy, Evans (1995, January). Sustaining and Expanding the Educational Conversation. *Phi Delta Kappan*, 353–354.

"For the conditions of deep diversity to prevail, people need to have complete freedom to educate children according to conscience rather than the dictates of the marketplace. Deep diversity demands that we recognize that in ordinary life there is no one right way and that individuals as culture participants, both individually and collectively, must be free to educate their own children according to their own values."

— *Gerald Porter*

The White Man's Burden, Revisited

Gerald Porter

Take up the White Man's burden—
  Send forth the best ye breed—
Go bind your sons to exile
  To serve the captives' need;
To wait in heavy harness,
  On fluttered folk and wild—
Your new-caught, sullen peoples,
  Half-devil and half-child.
— Kipling (1898), "The White Man's Burden"[1]

Goals 2000 has ushered in a new era in education and American life. Schools have become one of the pivotal battlegrounds in an increasingly vicious culture war. To the power-hungry coalition of big business and big government, which are the same elements in American society that Will Rogers used to call the "big boys," Goals 2000 is a major

---

[1] Kipling was the poet laureate of European colonialism. The text of this poem includes both an explication of the naked motives for imperialism and the euphemistic rationalizations that were used to obscure the ugliness of stealing someone else's homeland and degrading their culture. To fully appreciate Kipling's perverse genius for complaining about the effort of dehumanizing non-European people, one should read the complete text of the poem (in Knowles 1974).

victory. These elements are robbing the people of the power and capability of becoming fully human by controlling the formation of young minds. By capturing the schools, they are robbing people of the ability to become autonomous self-determining individuals free to express their convictions according to conscience. Goals 2000 is an outgrowth of a constellation of educational ideas, such as Outcomes-Based Education (OBE), that presumes a single standard of thought and behavior is right for and should be imposed upon all people. It is a contemporary version of Max Weber's "emissary prophecy" described by Bowers (1993) as "the belief that one possesses a truth that must be shared with others, and even imposed on others in order to save them" (p. 41). Goals 2000 is the enemy of diversity and as such it is an attempt at stamping out those cultural streams that are not assimilated into the modernist Eurocentric mainstream.

By "diversity," I refer to ethnic and racial differences between people as well as any characteristic that is used to classify and separate populations, such as gender, social class, physical traits, and psychological functioning. I also refer to the diversity of ideas, which is less commonly considered but is even more important. People vary in their thinking and understanding of themselves and the world. Implicit in the notion of diversity of ideas is the recognition articulated in Brown's (1978) theory of metaphor, that how a person thinks about oneself and what one believes about the world shapes one's experience of the world. A person's sense of self becomes intimately linked to one's ideas, especially the assumptions one makes about metaphysics, ontology, and epistemology. People normally derive these root assumptions virtually unconsciously from the culture in which they grow up. But shifts in core assumptions inevitably lead to changes in a person's experience and the significance attributed to it. Maintaining an environment that fosters or at least allows for a diversity of ideas is essential because these core ideas are building blocks for the construction of personal experience, and, on the collective level, for the construction of a consensus reality.

Both of these kinds of diversity are threatened by Goals 2000. For traditionally disenfranchised minorities, Goals 2000 constitutes a new variation of the white man's burden. Originally, this term referred to the imperialistic conviction that the superior white man, having conquered the inferior colored peoples of the world, was responsible for the care and well-being of the colonized people. The white man's attitude toward the defeated races was presented by Kipling as *noblesse oblige*. But beneath the thin patronizing veneer was fundamentally an attitude of contempt and hatred that dehumanized the white man's alleged beneficiaries. No culture was regarded as equal to the European standard, which was held up as the yardstick of true civilization. To the extent that the cultures of colonized people were judged to be different, they were found wanting and inferior.

In our time, with the collapse of overt forms of European expansionism and colonialism, the white man's burden might be assumed to be merely an artifact of the past, but it is not. In one supremely important domain the white man continues to bear his burden with jealous zeal. In the world of ideas, the white man's thinking and habits of thought are the only ones that matter. The European modernist core beliefs are still the sole legitimate standard for the construction of a worldview. Any worldview founded on assumptions other than these is simply not taken seriously. This is the most damaging and insidious form of colonialism, because for the culturally different, it constitutes enslavement in a foreign and hostile worldview, a consensus reality where the involuntary minorities of western nations always come out on the bottom because they are always judged wanting.[2] However these minorities be defined or reconstituted in the next century, they are *a priori* losers in the new world order to the extent it is constructed around the modernist mindset.

Philosophers such as Sloan (1992), Pearce (1971, 1974), Griffin (1989, 1993), Berman (1981), and Bowers (1993) have analyzed the core metaphysi-

---

[2] The notion of involuntary minorities was developed by the anthropologist, John Ogbu (1983, 1987, 1988, 1991). Involuntary minorities, in contrast to voluntary minorities or immigrants, are defined by Ogbu as "people who are brought into their present society through slavery, conquest, or colonization. They usually resent the loss of their former freedom, and they perceive the social, political, and economic barriers against them as part of their undeserved oppression" (1991, 9). Examples of involuntary minorities in the United States include not only African Americans but Native Americans and most Latino groups. Voluntary or immigrant minorities are described by Ogbu as people who "have moved to their present societies because they believed that the move would lead to greater economic wellbeing, better overall opportunities, or greater political freedom" (1991, 9). Both groups encounter discrimination, but immigrants "interpret economic, political, and social barriers against them as more or less temporary problems" that can be "overcome with the passage of time, hard work, or more education" (p. 11). Immigrants tend to see the present situation as an improvement over conditions in the old country, whereas involuntary minorities compare the conditions of their second class status to "that of members of the dominant group and usually conclude that they are worse off than they ought to be for no other reason than that they belong to a subordinate and disparaged group" (p. 15).

cal and epistemological assumptions that provide the foundation of the modern mindset that have led Western societies to the brink of human and environmental disaster. At the root of this worldview is an *objectivist* position which holds that the subject and object are wholly separate and divorced, that the mind and body are essentially disconnected. Knowledge — or at least all legitimate knowledge — of the outside world is derived from sense experience and cannot come directly from intuition, inspiration, or spiritual insight. Like the prisoners in Plato's cave, we tend to live in a world of shadows where we substitute our representations of reality for reality itself, a peculiar way of seeing conditioned by the materialistic education provided by modern schooling. Socialization in modern Western society induces the separation of subject and object, and consequently, the self is experienced as progressively more disengaged from the world. As a result, the self is isolated and reduced to a mere ghost in the machine.

An inevitable consequence of the artificial separation of mind and body is the now traditional conviction that mind as discursive thought is purer and loftier than the comparatively crude and debased body (Sloan 1992; Pearce 1971, 1974). Although contemporary thought denies that the separate mind is constitutionally different from the body, it persists in thinking of the body as subservient in function and value to the higher organizing principle of mind. The emphasis in Eurocentric thought on hierarchy and evolution makes it difficult for modernists to consider that mind and body could be functionally different but qualitatively equal.

The modernist mindset has inevitably led to the arid vision of a dead, purposeless, meaningless universe that is absent of God and devoid of ultimate value or meaning. This dead and purposeless world has inevitably

---

Involuntary minorities are overrepresented among the poor but there are other outgroups within American society that are unable to exercise their fair share of power, such as women. These "minorities" are not necessarily numerical minorities, but they are subordinate to the dominant group in terms of power and have inequitable access to societal resources. At the same time, we ought not overgeneralize about any of these groups. It is clear that social class can either exacerbate or moderate the adverse effects of racial discrimination. A poor black child growing up in the inner city faces much crueler life prospects than a middle class black child growing up in an upscale suburban community. Similarly, while it is statistically true that white males as a group enjoy advantages at the expense of every outgroup in society, this is false for most white men, cruelly false for many; the advantages and privilege of being a white male are only effectively exercised by a minority of such men in the upper socioeconomic classes of society. However, many average white men identify with their privileged brothers and mistakenly perceive their interests to be the same; this perception effectively extends the influence of the privileged few.

led to untold personal misery and despair. On a societal level, it has deprived people of the perennial values of basic humanity that might have prevented the tragedies of projected and externalized self-hatred that arises when the self is cut off from meaning, such as the Holocaust not just of Jews in Europe, but in Cambodia and Uganda, and now in the former Yugoslavia. The brutal persecution and dehumanization found virtually everywhere in the world are made possible by the modern worldview's denial of the sacred and moral relativism. While modernism is not the only worldview that can lead to tragedy and human degradation, it is the primary ideological architect of such in our time.

The core problem with the modern worldview is its failure to bring its adherents happiness, a sense of meaning, wholesome interpersonal relationships, or a healthy relationship with nature and the earth itself. Our society is decomposing before our eyes because at its core it has substituted dead mechanism for the life of the soul. A society such as ours is the embodiment of the living dead; like the vampire images that resonate so strongly in our popular culture, modernist societies have retained only a dim semblance of inner life by draining the soul from living indigenous and premodern cultures.

The presumption of the white man's superiority is supported by the objectivist epistemology of modernism: If there is a single objective reality that can be known by distinguishing true facts from false beliefs, then the modern Eurocentric worldview of scientific objectivity is clearly superior to the "primitive" beliefs of indigenous and nonwhite cultures. There is one right answer to every question because there is a single reality that is either known or unknown. From here it is a short jump to the conclusion that there exists one "right" people and all the others are somehow wrong. The implicit assumptions of non-European cultures are devalued because they do not support the construction of modernist consensus reality.

The interests of African Americans and other traditionally disenfranchised minorities in the United States are already marginalized in the practices of public education and are likely to have their collective interests further marginalized by Goals 2000. The idea that government schooling is a method for reproducing Eurocentric culture and the social inequities implicit to it has been explored by theorists such as Althusser (1971) and

Apple (1978, 1979). The OBE/Goals 2000 mindset is merely an educational incarnation of the European modernist core assumptions. Goals 2000 is merely an operationalization of OBE ideas, and both are applications of the same modernism that gave us Jim Crow, apartheid, the Holocaust, and Jensenian rationalizations of standardized IQ tests; the modernist world-view can only lead to comparable injustices without profound revision of its core assumptions.

Healing the Pains of Eurocentrism

The non-European involuntary minorities of North America, such as people of African descent, pose a profound alternative to the modern mindset. African Americans and other involuntary minorities have, as a survival mechanism, retained vestiges of their traditional culture that place them at odds with the values and folkways of mainstream middle class Eurocentric modern culture. While it cannot be denied that Africa is a big continent and the cultures transported to the new world were as diverse in folkways, customs, and ethnicity as those cultures that came from Europe, certain underlying commonalities of the diverse cultures of Africa were forged together under the oppression of slavery. This pan-African sensibility differs in its underlying root assumptions from European modernism in some very significant ways. In particular, African worldviews provide a holistic alternative to the objectivist epistemology of modernism. B. A. Allen and A. W. Boykin have identified nine traditional West African cultural values that have been transmitted to contemporary African Americans:

> (a) spirituality, a vitalistic rather than mechanistic approach to life; (b) harmony, the belief that humans and nature are harmoniously conjoined; (c) movement expressiveness, an emphasis on the interweaving of movement, rhythm, percussiveness, music, and dance; (d) verve, the especial receptiveness to relatively high levels of sensate stimulation; (e) affect, an emphasis on emotions and feelings; (f) communalism, a commitment to social connectedness where social bonds transcend individual privileges; (g) expressive individualism, the cultivation of a distinctive personality and a proclivity for spontaneity in behavior; (h) orality, a preference for oral/aural modalities of communication; (i) social time perspective, an orientation in which time is treated as passing through a social space rather than a material one. (Allen and Boykin 1992, 589; see also Boykin 1983)

Perhaps the most unique African transplant to the new world that has posed a coherent challenge to modernism has been the spiritist tradition (Deren 1953; Ventura 1987a, 1987b; Davis 1985; Barbosa 1989; Hurston 1983). Throughout the Caribbean, Central and South America, and most especially Brazil and Haiti, the African spiritist tradition has been very strong and culturally influential. In the southern United States, especially in the New Orleans area, the spiritist tradition has had and continues to have a vital influence. It is clear that jazz and much of rock and roll and rhythm and blues that are so pervasive a part of the contemporary sensibility are derived from African spiritism (Ventura 1987a, 1987b; Finn 1992).

What is so subversive about spiritism to the modern mind-set? African spiritism with its animistic emphasis on dance and spirit possession challenges the Cartesian split between mind and body. Spiritism recognizes no sharp division between them and consequently, the body is not devalued as lesser or inferior. Instead, the body serves as the means to our access and experience of the spiritual forces that are identified as the basis and source of meaning in life. In the practices of African spiritism, the worshipper dances to invoke the *Loa* or spiritual forces. The music accompanying the dance is an expression of the universal rhythms and the dance serves as a physical enactment of the patterns of a deeper and more profound order. This deeper order cannot be grasped discursively as an external object. Instead, it must be subjectively experienced through the body as the instrument of the divine. The whole purpose of invocation is to blur the boundaries between the material and spiritual worlds. By enacting the rhythms of the spirit world, the dancer/worshipper becomes the spirit being whose movement she describes and is transformed by the experience. What matters is the participation in the spirit world and the abandonment of self to something greater and more meaningful than ordinary life, but which has the effect of infusing ordinary life with a sense of the transcendent. After this experience, our place in the scheme of things is not a theoretical abstraction known only discursively, but a living reality of experientially verified majesty, beauty, and purpose. The dancer abandoned to the spirit entertains none of the doubts or crises of faith that are the fruits of modernism.

To truly accept the African, her culture and fundamental mindset would open the modern West to a profound revision of its root assumptions. Ultimately, it would open Westerners to a dramatically different experience of self. Such a revision holds the promise of a desperately needed renewal of spirit and personal wholeness. I am not advocating that the West should simply adopt wholesale the worldview of traditional Africa. I am suggesting that the deep wounds suffered by the West could be healed by a genuine open-minded reconsideration of root assumptions. Open-minded means not being limited by preconceived ideas about what constitutes acceptable solutions to the problem. Traditional worldviews, while undoubtedly limited in their own ways, offer the West alternative assumptions that could enable us to construct a more humane and innately satisfying consensus reality.

The Promise of Deep Diversity

Traditionally, diversity has been seen as a factor to be minimized in the interest of facilitating national unity. Diversity was assumed to be problematic, a chaotic force introducing the destabilizing effects of entropy and disorganization into a social system. Individualism was expressed in American society quantitatively, as the freedom to participate in the open marketplace or to consume according to the dictates of personal desire. Individualism was egoism — an expression of the individual's exploitation and control over one's environment. But the individual was not encouraged to diverge qualitatively from the cultural and paradigmatic norms of society. The person was not expected to be anything more than the product of one's own conditioning and biology, and certainly not to be the instrument for the realization of some higher volitional force.

"Deep diversity" is a principle that challenges modern objectivism with the recognition that all knowledge is merely a description or a representation of experience. Deep diversity assumes that the subject is commingled with the object, that what we can know is our experience of an essentially mysterious reality. Experience should not be confused with the reality it represents but is merely that portion of reality we allow ourselves to consciously acknowledge. Reality is full of an indeterminate number of possibilities that we reduce to what our culture has taught us to believe is possible. Deep diversity recognizes that it is essential to encourage as many descriptions of reality as possible since all are necessarily incomplete. Hence, it keeps us humble by forcing us from the hubris that Blake called "Newton's sleep" (Erdman 1965, 693). Descriptions are not so much "right" or "wrong" but need to be evaluated on different criteria. The effectiveness of a description is relative to the perspective of the perceiver; in the very act of constructing a description, the describer necessarily draws on her/his values and implicit assumptions. A description might, for example, be evaluated in terms of aesthetic qualities or how convincingly it evokes in another person the experience of the initial describer (Wilson 1986; Bennett 1978; Wilber 1993).

Implicit in a depth conception of diversity is the assumption that differences express a natural and healthy condition. Deep diversity goes beyond tolerance or even concepts of mutual coexistence or interdependency. Deep diversity implies that differences between people and their ideas are indicative of a level of organization that is more fundamental than the comparatively superficial structures imposed by conventional thinking about racial/ethnic, cultural, or ideological differences. Deep diversity is an expression of the intelligence intrinsic to human life or life on earth in general that all systems of knowledge are attempting to fathom. It assumes that meaning and significance for humanity necessarily originate not in ourselves as egos, but from our participating selves rooted in a hidden and (for most of us) unrealized unity. By embracing diversity, we open ourselves to a deeper level of insight into the implicit order of human affairs.

The concept of deep diversity differs from the more conventional notion of diversity in the same way that deep ecology differs from mere ecology. In both cases, the adjective "deep" implies a dimension of interrelatedness where the greater the mutuality between elements in the system, the greater the overall integrity of the system as a whole. The promise of deep diversity to education comes from the assumption that the most essential educational goal for the child is the process of becoming and realizing in practice one's deepest, most essential self. This process has been called self-actualization, but in this context, it implies something more than the alienated self commonly cultivated by our society. The role of education in self-actualization is much more than merely developing the child's academic and social skills; it really means enabling the child to be an effective and conscious instrument for realizing the divine in the life of the body and the experiential world associated with it.

The promise of deep diversity, denied and rejected by the modernist policies of Goals 2000, is that it creates a kind of open environment where our constructions of experience are not confused with objective reality. If we do not have access to as full a range of core assumptions as possible, then individuals are deprived of the raw materials to construct their own experiential world. As an autonomous individual, one's freedom to be one's own person is the ultimate attainment. This can only be achieved in an unfettered environment where the individual can be guided by conscience to values that reflect one's unique perspective on the fundamental mystery of life. This experience must be discovered and interpreted for oneself, or the individual can accept the assumptions implicit to her/his birth culture. We as individuals are all unique and have irreproducible contributions to make to society. If we, as individuals, can find our own inner muses, our own sources of identity, beauty, and inspiration, then a life of meaning and purpose becomes possible. In the same way that qualitative differences reflect the uniqueness of individuals, different cultures are unique and irreducible (Fideler 1994).

In nature, diversity can be observed both across and within species. This may superficially appear as unnecessary multiplicity, but upon closer examination, biologists have demonstrated that the enormous diversity of behavioral and morphological characteristics within a species provides it with a greater chance of surviving unanticipated environmental threats. A misplaced sense of parsimony can easily underestimate the deeper utility of diversity (Pepper 1993). Just as biological diversity can provide the human species with survival benefits, the diversity of human ideas, especially those root assumptions that provide the foundation for people's worldviews, ensures the capacity to survive unanticipated hazards (Bowers 1993; MacLaughlin 1993). Ultimately, we want more than mere survival; we long for meaning and purpose.

For the conditions of deep diversity to prevail, people need to have complete freedom to educate children according to conscience rather than the dictates of the marketplace. Deep diversity demands that we recognize that in ordinary life there is no one right way and that individuals as culture participants, both individually and collectively, must be free to educate their own children according to their own values.

National Standards: The Suppression of Diversity

Diversity is challenged on grounds that we need universal standards. There are two frequently heard rationales justifying the need for such standards: the economic argument and the unity argument. The first claims that if all children in the country do not learn the same essential job-related skills, the nation will be overpowered by better-educated competitors from other countries. Hence, all students need to learn the same essential skills to enable America's technology-driven industries to be more competitive in the global marketplace.

This demand for universal educational standards without regard for individual or cultural differences is more of the white man's missionary zeal. The reduction of education from nurturing a soul to preparing workers to be grist for the economic mill reflects the internal colonization of the West. Ordinary middle class citizens fearful of losing their livelihood and stripped by materialistic education of any coherent notion of themselves as anything more than units of production or consumers are the contemporary equivalent of Third World peasants in an old colonial empire.

We are taught in government schools to distrust our own inner compass and look outside ourselves for direction from officially sanctioned experts. This lesson enables us to be led by the nose by any force rich enough to control the media. Then, through constant fear of losing a typically degrading and unrewarding job, people come to view their employers more as philanthropists than exploiters. But the worst intrusion is the colonization of the mind, which robs the self of its intrinsic legitimacy. Alienated from one's own inner sense of purpose or direction, the colonized person's actions betray his or her own interests and serve those of one's conquerer.

The fact is, we simply do not know whether schooling affects the economy or international competition. The theories underlying Goals 2000 are unproven (Stake 1991; Bracey 1987). These policies were motivated and tailored to gratify popular opinion. Unfortunately, popular opinion is skillfully manipulated by Rogers's "big boys" through a continuous diet of lies and half-truths.

If there is any merit to the "schooling affects global competition" argument, it is the opposite of what the OBE and Goals 2000 advocates claim. Too much rigid boiler-plate instruction strips children of the qualities really needed to make American industry competitive — imagination, creativity, playfulness, enthusiasm, compassion, and sensitivity to the needs of others. More importantly, it prevents schoolchildren from growing up into happy, healthy, contributing adults. Universal government-imposed, business-inspired standards will, in the words of John Gatto (1992), even further "dumb down" America's children and future workers.

Standard-setting and criterion-referenced standardized testing will not improve education if the goal is the child's self-actualization (Gordon 1989; Kohn 1993). Educational policies that are driven almost exclusively by economic considerations are staggeringly superficial and devoid of any recognition of the developing child's essential needs. To reduce people to merely quantitative elements devoid of qualitative significance, to be treated as interchangeable parts for the needs and purposes of industry, is wrong. Legitimate education can never become purely utilitarian. As a society, especially in the area of education, we need to affirm the qualitative elements of our lives.

Another rationale for opposing diversity with universal standards might be called the unity argument. This position holds that we must teach children a single set of values to direct their lives. Without these common values (which happen to serve the interests of big government and big business), it is argued that it will be impossible to preserve a united and harmonious society. This perspective is compelling to the extent it recognizes the rightness of having a common life, but it fails to acknowledge the wisdom of democracy, a form of government intended to accommodate diverse opinions in a common civic life. There is no need to artificially remove diversity in the interest of having a harmonious common life. There does need to be a common ground between people sharing a collective life, but that common ground cannot and should not be imposed from outside by denying people their right and ability to think for themselves as individuals or to realize their cultural ideals in the education and socialization of their children. By imposing external, economically-motivated standards on schooling, Goals 2000 reflects deep-seated doubt in the capacity of human interest, ability, and need to reflect an implicit higher organizing principle.

The bottom line of this discussion is that most people in American society suffer some form of dehumanization (Kohn 1993). This is true not only of members of groups on the standard list of victims, but even of those who are dehumanized by assuming the role of oppressor. State-sponsored public schooling has been one of the primary agents of this dehumanization and the move toward national goals and standards will further perpetuate this trend. Public schools have always organized instruction for the convenience of the institution rather than for the needs of individual children. Curriculum decomposes real life experience into contextually meaningless facts that may be logically arranged but are not at all reminiscent of how a child would naturally learn. In public schooling, how or what a child should learn is not determined by a teacher's personal attempt to nurture a child's innate aptitudes, interests, and abilities, but by the external dictates of curriculum or bureaucratically-mandated school practice. With the advance of national curriculum standards and national educational goals, these dictates are even further removed from the classroom.

The agenda of national standards, as expressed in Goals 2000, assumes that everyone needs to know the same things at the same time, and has zero tolerance for individual differences. The legislation often gives lip-service to allowing teachers and schools to educate children in the way they think best, but in practice, educators will be held hostage under the constant threat of poor student performance on high-stakes standardized tests. Teachers, if they want to hold onto their jobs, will "teach to the test." Teaching to the test exacerbates the tendency to emphasize the institutional agenda over the needs of individual children and further narrows both teaching and learning to mere formulatic utilitarianism (Porter 1989; Stake 1991; Shepard 1991; Bracey 1987; Airasian 1988). Shepard warns that using high-stakes standardized testing to enforce standards could actually undermine educational effectiveness. She writes, "It would not be far fetched to say that testing in the past decade has actually reduced the quality of instruction for many students" (1991, 238).

Goals 2000 and similar programs will most adversely impact the traditionally disenfranchised groups within American society: the involuntary minorities and poor people of all races and ethnicities. The OBE/Goals 2000 mindset seeks to covertly eradicate diversity by imposing standards of thought and behavior. It offers the implicit promise that if African Americans conform and succeed with these standards, they can enter the mainstream and enjoy all the material success this implies. This is a promise that cannot be kept; it is the white man's burden revisited.

Goals 2000 is a false promise to involuntary minorities and the poor because success is contingent upon meeting the Eurocentric modernist standard. It is impossible for many of these people to meet that standard to the extent that they are culturally alienated and self-defined as other; the criteria for success are not objective and independent of culture but are the very embodiment of the white middle class sensibility — a sensibility derived from the economically-driven modernist vision. An animistic or spiritist culture that recognizes no sharp boundary between the inner and outer life does not raise children whose differential life experiences favor the kind of decontextualized abstract reasoning rewarded on IQ and standardized achievement tests. Boykin (1983) argues that African Americans on average do more poorly in school than their white peers because of the cultural discontinuity between home and the classroom.

Historically, we know that blacks and the poor have consistently performed below mainstream whites when evaluated with standardized criteria. There is a long-established difference in IQ of roughly 15 points between whites and blacks (Flaugher 1978; Jensen 1972). However, this phenomenon does not reflect *genetic* differences between the races but differences in how people who come to define themselves as black or white come to see themselves and their place in society. The main point of this paper is that the barriers to involuntary minorities are paradigmatic and are not amenable to simple accommodations within modernist methodologies. Efforts to design a culture-fair IQ test have always failed and will probably continue to fail because the criterion used to validate such measures is biased. Gould (1981) shows that standardized tests have frequently been used by experts with a political agenda of justifying discriminatory practices. There is no reason to assume that Goals 2000 technocrats will produce different results if the same technologies and assumptions are applied again. This tactic is particularly insidious because on the surface it seems fair (decked out with all the trappings of science), but the majority of involuntary minorities and the poor will be disadvantaged by these practices.

The idea that "might makes right," an implicit assumption of the white man's burden, is apparent in the Goals 2000 reforms. Power to set standards is being consolidated in the federal government, which will use control over funding to enforce its mandates. There is no consideration for alternative points of view or goals as legitimate aspirations. The National Education Standards and Improvement Council and the National Educational Goals Panel by definition promote a model of schooling that serves the economic agenda of the power brokers. It is a short and easy step to impose the same standards on private schools through the economic lure of vouchers. In order to qualify for vouchers, a private school might need to demonstrate it provides "quality" education by conforming to the federal standards (Richman 1994; Arons 1994). This will only further extend the campaign to crush diversity in our society.

Freedom and Responsibility

What is really needed is a separation of school and state comparable to the constitutional division between church and state. Families should be free of government compulsion in the education of their children. I agree with Richman (1994), who writes that

nothing less than a frontal assault on the current system, a philosophical challenge to the premises of state education, will work. We can begin by revisioning our very conception of the purpose of education. Contrary to the educators, elected officials, and bureaucrats, our children are not a resource that the schools are mandated to develop for the good of the nation. (p. 85)

No one has better articulated the principled basis for the separation of education and the state than Rudolf Steiner, whose theory of the threefold social order defines education as a cultural activity. According to Steiner, the proper "motivating impulse" for the establishment and governance of schooling can only come from a "free and independent cultural life." Steiner wrote that the sole determinant of what children should learn is human nature, which he perceived as deeply imbued with spiritual meaning and significance. He warned, "It is neither for the state nor the economic life to say: We need someone of this sort for a particular post; therefore test the people that we need and pay heed above all that they know and can do what we want" (1985, p. 72). Education as a cultural activity needs to be implemented in a bottom-up fashion. Each constituency needs to design instruction and schooling to serve the goals and vision of its culture. The separation of education and the state would be a step toward the free and independent cultural life advocated by Steiner. It would also be a substantive gesture of respect for those in our society who are racial/ethnic minorities or those who subscribe to minority viewpoints.

In the final analysis, opposition to Goals 2000 and national educational standards is an attempt to preserve freedom. But a determination to escape the compulsion of oppressive big government does not give· us license to ignore those in our society who are in need. Rejecting big government and the social safety net that has legitimated its intrusions only deepens and expands our personal responsibility to those in need. If, in the legitimate interest of protecting our freedoms, we seek to limit the reach of government, then we must either redefine the legitimate role and boundaries for government to serve the needy or assume the responsibility directly ourselves.

The American people at this historical juncture, when confronted with great injustices, seem selectively blind and maliciously inclined to scapegoating. The outrage and contempt leveled at the poor and weak for their exaggerated abuses of the welfare system are not reasonable given the indifference to the overwhelmingly greater abuses of the rich and powerful at direct cost to the middle class. It is morally reprehensible for our society to tolerate hopelessness and grinding poverty, while it blithely condones a tiny but spoliatious minority's accumulation of inordinate wealth. The discontent of the middle class has so far been successfully manipulated to blame the poor and weak for the sins of the rich and powerful. Now is a time for moral courage, a time to stand up for what we believe is right because, if we as a people fail, the country could easily slip from a precarious democracy into an American-style fascism. If public education has attempted to steal our children's minds, then the recent move toward national standards, conceived in avarice and contempt, reaches to steal our souls.

References

Airasian, P. W. (1988). Measurement Driven Instruction: A Closer Look. *Educational Measurement: Issues and Practice*, 7(4): 6–11.

Allen, B. A., and A. W. Boykin (1992). African-American Children and the Educational Process: Alleviating Cultural Discontinuity Through Prescriptive Pedagogy. *School Psychology Review* 21(4): 586–596.

Althusser, L. (1971). *Lenin and Philosophy*. New York: Monthly Review Press.

Apple, M. W. (1978). Ideology, Reproduction, and Educational Reform. *Comparative Educational Review* 22: 367–387.

Apple, M. W. (1979). *Ideology and Curriculum*. London: Routledge & Kegan Paul.

Arons, S. (Summer 1992). Freedom of Intellect and Spirit: A Constitutional Case for Real Choice in Education. *The Threefold Review* (Special Report), 3–7.

Arons, S. (Winter/Spring 1994). The California Voucher Proposal: A Postmortem and Prelude. *The Threefold Review* 10: 23–25.

Barbosa, E. (1989, Summer). The Presence of the Gods: Afro-Brazilian Trance Rituals. *Shaman's Drum* 17: 41–49.

Bennett, J. G. (1978). *Deeper Man*. London: Turnstone Books.

Berman, M. (1981). *The Re-enchantment of the World*. Ithaca: Cornell University Press.

Bluestone, B., and B. Harrison (1982). *The Deindustrialization of America*. New York: Random House.

Bowers, C. A. (1993). *Critical Essays on Education, Modernity, and the Recovery of the Ecological Imperative*. New York: Teachers College Press.

Boykin, A. W. (1983). The Academic Performance of Afro-American Children. In J. Spence (ed.), *Achievement and Achievement Motives*, 321 -371. San Francisco: Freeman.

Bracey, G. W. (1987). Measurement-Driven Instruction: Catchy Phrase, Dangerous Practice. *Phi Delta Kappan* 68: 683–686.

Brown, R. H. (1978). *A Poetic for Sociology*. Cambridge: Cambridge University Press.

Davis, W. (1985). *The Serpent and the Rainbow*. New York: Warner Books.

Deren, M. (1953). *Divine Horsemen: The Living Gods of Haiti*. New York: MacPhear.

Erdman, D. V. (1965). *Poetry and Prose of William Blake*. Garden City, NY: Doubleday.

Fideler, D. (Autumn 1994). Aphrodite's Companions: Beauty, Love, and Pleasure in the Humanities and Daily Life. *The Alexandrian* 4(1): 4–5.

Finn, J. (1992) *The Bluesmen: The Musical Heritage of Black Men and Women in the Americas*. New York: Interlink Books.

Flaugher, R. L. (1978). The Many Definitions of Test Bias. *American Psychologist* 33: 671–679.

Gatto, J. T. (Summer 1992). How Public Are Our Schools? *The Threefold Review* (Special Report), 8–14.

Gordon, T. (1989). *Teaching Children Self-Discipline*. New York: Random House.

Gould, S. J. (1981). *Mismeasure of Man*. New York: Norton.

Griffin, D. R. (1989). *God and Religion in the Postmodern World: Essays in Postmodern Theology*. Albany: State University of New York Press.

Griffin, D. R. (1993). Introduction: Constructive Postmodern Philosophy. In D. R. Griffin, J. Cobb, M. Ford, P. Gunter, and P. Ochs (eds.), *Founders of Constructive Postmodern Philosophy*, pp. 1–42. Albany: State University of New York Press.

Hurston, Z. N. (1983). *Tell My Horse*. Berkeley: Turtle Island.

Jensen, A. R. (1972). *Genetics and Education*. New York: Harper & Row.

Knowles, F. L. (1974). *A Kipling Primer*. New York: Haskell House.

Kohn, A. (1993). *Punished by Rewards: The Trouble with Gold Stars, Incentive Plans as Praise, and Other Bribes*. New York: Houghton Mifflin.

Kosters, M. H. (1992). The Rise in Income Inequality: What It Means for a Society Like Ours. *American Enterprise* 3(6): 28–37.

MacLaughlin, A. (1993). *Regarding Nature: Industrialism and Deep Ecology*. Albany: State University of New York Press.

National Commission on Excellence in Education (1983). *A Nation At Risk: The Imperative for Educational Reform*. Washington, D.C.: U.S. Printing Office.

Ogbu, J. (1983). Minority Status and Schooling in Plural Societies. *Comparative Educational Review* 27(22): 168–190.

Ogbu, J. (1987). *Minority Education and Caste: The American System in Cross-cultural Perspective*. New York: Academic Press.

Ogbu, J. (1988). Class Stratification, Racial Stratification, and Schooling. In L. Weiss (ed.), *Class, Race, and Gender in American Education*. Albany: State University of New York Press.

Ogbu, J. (1991) Immigrant and Involuntary Minorities in Comparative Perspective. In M. Gibson and J. Ogbu (eds.), *Minority Status in Schooling: A Comparative Study of Immigrants and Involuntary Minorities*. New York: Garland.

Pearce, J. C. (1971). *Crack in the Cosmic Egg*. New York: Julian Press.

Pearce, J. C. (1974). *Exploring the Crack in the Cosmic Egg: Split Minds and Meta-realities*. New York: Julian Press.

Pepper, D. (1993). *Eco-socialism: From Deep Ecology to Social Justice*. New York: Routledge.

Porter, A. C. (1989). External Standards and Good Teaching: The Pros and Cons of Telling Teachers What to Do. *Educational Evaluation and Policy Analysis* 11(4): 343–356.

Porter, G. (Winter/Spring 1994). Harder Times for These Hard Times: Economy-Driven School Reform. *The Threefold Review* 10: 16–22.

Richman, S. (1994). *Separating School and State: How to Liberate America's Families*. Fairfax, VA: Future of Freedom Foundation.

Shepard, L. A. (1991). Will National Tests Improve Student Learning? *Phi Delta Kappan* 71: 232–239.

Sloan, D. (1992). Imagination, Education, and our Postmodern Possibilities. *ReVision* 15(2): pp. 42–53.

Smith, P. K. (1994a). Recent Patterns in Downward Income Mobility: Sinking Boats in a Rising Tide. *Social Indications Research* 31: 277–303.

Smith, P. K. (1994b). Downward Mobility: Is It a Growing Problem? *American Journal of Economics and Sociology* 53(1): 57–72.

Stake, R. E. (1991). The Teacher, Standardized Testing, and Prospects of Revolution. *Phi Delta Kappan* 71: 243–247.

Steiner, R. (1985). *The Renewal of the Social Organism*. Spring Valley, NY: Anthroposophic Press.

Ventura, M. (1987a, Spring). Hear That Long Snake Moan (Part 1). *Whole Earth Review* 54: 82–92.

Ventura, M. (1987b, Summer). Hear That Long Snake Moan (Part 2). *Whole Earth Review* 55: 28–43.

Veum, J. R. (1992). Accounting for Income Mobility Changes in the United States. *Social Science Quarterly* 73(4): 773–785.

Wilber, K. (1993). *Spectrum of Consciousness*. Wheaton, IL: Quest Books.

Wilson, R. A. (1986). *Prometheus Rising*. Phoenix: Falcon Books.

"American competitiveness in international markets does not suffer from an unprepared work force. Rather it suffers from corporations that put their own immediate profitability over the welfare of the nation and its citizens.... In fact, employers desire most punctuality, sobriety, and compliance in their employees and value least knowledge of mathematics, natural science, and foreign languages. Companies are not clamoring for high academic standards, nor are they eager to pay high wages to anyone but executives."

— *Patrick Shannon*

Mad as Hell

Patrick Shannon

In the movie "Network," Peter Finch, in character, asks viewers to stick their heads out the window and yell, "I'm mad as hell, and I'm not going to take it any longer." His anger came from watching the network's leadership drag his beloved institution, TV news, toward irrationality in the pursuit of maximizing profits. I share some of this frustration because the Goals 2000 juggernaut to produce national standards and tests seems to be swallowing its opposition whole. As a literacy teacher, I'm mad as hell at The National Council of Teachers of English (NCTE) for taking wrong step after wrong step in the pursuit of someone else's agenda, and along the way, diminishing its potential impact in schools and society. Where once NCTE showed courage and leadership on textbooks, grammar teaching, and class size, they now defer to the government and show timidity and opportunism as they perpetuate the myth of public school inadequacy in the corporate political project to maximize profits and protect privilege in America.

The issue of national standards originated from the Bush Administration's "America 2000," a document negotiated at the National Center for Education and the Economy by Hillary Rodham Clinton, former Secretary of Labor Ray Marshall, then-governors James Hunt and Thomas Kean, then-CEOs Kay Whitmore, David Kearn, and John Sculley of Kodak, Xerox, and Apple respectively, and David Rockefeller, Jr. The original work was sponsored by the Carnegie Foundation, which funded previous projects during this century resulting in Carnegie units, the Educational Testing Service, and the *A Nation Prepared* report. The National Center group began their deliberations with a questionable assumption about schooling, and they used a curious logic to arrive at the conclusion that a lack of educational standards is what is ailing our nation's economy (Weisman 1991).

According to this group at the National Center, schools are tied directly to America's economic competitiveness because the United States must create a work force that is highly skilled, flexible, and able to think for a living (Reich 1991). Business can't accomplish this for itself because of unions, ignorant workers, and the expense. However, reformed schools could prepare new workers who can shift from one productive organization to another in order to overcome the threat of low wages paid to workers in other countries. Unless schools are willing to adopt business principles of standards for students, efficiencies of organization, and accountability for teachers, Americans' lifestyles will decline as the title of the National Center's report states: *America's Choice: High Skills or Low Wages* (Commission on Work Force Skills 1990). According to this report, schools need high, tightly organized standards and testing in science and mathematics in order to adapt to the "realities" of today's world, and standards in English Language Arts to insure that everyone is able to read and write sufficiently to retrain for different organizational and production requirements when necessary.

With mounting trade imbalances, national debt, and factory closings as well as decreasing wages, employment, and leisure, it is easy for anyone to recognize that something is wrong with the United States economy (Bartlett and Steele 1992). With a virtual blackout on critical analyses of our economy (Jensen 1994), it is more difficult for many of us to understand what's causing these problems. Schooling, however, is another matter altogether (*Nation* 1992). It's not at all easy to make the case that schools are failing to deliver on their traditional goals, using any reliable or comprehensive data. In fact, most Americans believe that their local schools are, at least, pretty good (Elam, Rose, and Gallup, 1993). This finding holds across race and social class stratification, although it does vary in spots. In order to affix blame for the economy and credit for its possible improvement, the public must be taught that schools don't work in their current forms. Beginning with the *A Nation at Risk* report (National Commission on Educational Excellence 1983) and continuing through to the Educate America Act of the Clinton Administration in 1994, business leaders, government officials, and news pundits have delivered that message through all available media. Using questionable arguments about both business needs and school performance, they call for increased school efficiency, higher demands in curricula, and improvements in teachers' knowledge and dedication (Noble 1992). To induce agreement, corporations, philanthropic organizations, and state and federal departments of labor and education offer educators cash incentives through grants to buy this line of goods.

Along the way, they've even claimed the language of progressive education to position nay-sayers as defenders of the status quo in failed schools. For example, Mark Tucker from the National Center for Education and the Economy and Ray Marshall, former Secretary of Labor and current Carnegie Foundation Trustee, state, "what employers need now are workers who bring the kinds of skills that progressive educators have always said they wanted to develop in their students....The demand for a highly skilled work force is in fact a call for educators to realize what have always been their highest aspirations" (1992, p. 82). This has become the official position of the federal government during the Bush and Clinton Administrations, and its pro-business, high-tech stance and its skills rhetoric are likely to increase in intensity with the Republican control of the House of Representatives and Senate.

As compelling as this logic may seem and this rhetoric may sound, the facts suggest that the logic, assumptions, and information that underlie the standards movement in English Language Arts and other subjects are wrong. American competitiveness in international markets does not suffer from an unprepared work force. Rather it suffers from corporations that put their own immediate profitability over the welfare of the nation and its citizens (Mishel and Bernstein 1991; Weisman 1993). That is, 95 percent of American businesses organize their workplace along the lines of classic Taylorism with low skill and low-wage jobs. Even the National Center admitted as much in their *America's Choice* report. Despite the media blitz to the contrary, there are very few high-skill, high-wage jobs available in this economy (Richman 1993). In fact, employers desire most punctuality, sobriety, and compliance in their employees and value least knowledge of mathematics, natural science, and foreign languages (Noble 1992). Companies are not clamoring for high academic standards, nor are they eager to pay high wages to anyone but executives (Bok 1993).

As David Berliner (1992) and the Sandia National Laboratories (Carson, Huelskamp, and Woodall 1991) attest, schools are not the failures that business, government, and the media have painted them to be. Student scores have not fallen through the floor (in fact, they are making steady gains), funding for schooling has not kept pace with other institutions and it does make a difference in what happens in schools (in real dollars, teachers' salaries are close to what they were in the 1970s), and students do seem to be prepared, even overprepared, for the jobs that are available to them (unemployment for workers 18 to 25 years old is approaching 25 percent). The truth be told — the connection between schooling and the economy is at an all time low. Additional schooling can't promise a student a better job, steady employment, or even higher wages (Bernstein and Mishel 1992) because the economy is not able to keep these old promises regardless of school standards or student achievement (Aronowitz 1994).

Finally, the liberal belief that standards will somehow arm society's have-nots so that they can defend themselves against discrimination in schools is naive (Shannon 1995a). On the fortieth anniversary of the *Brown vs the Board of Education* of Topeka, Kansas, decision, can we really say that the law has ended or significantly reduced the savage inequalities of schooling in this country (Kozol 1992)? As Derrick Bell (1992) tells us, the Brown decision has been used creatively to ensure that these inequalities continue. Self-interest apparently can erase the potential benefits of humanitarian policy. We can't legislate morality because abstract policies and laws do not overcome deeply held biases based on lived experiences of officials, teachers, or anyone else.

If not to create a highly skilled, highly paid work force, to fix failing schools, or to legislate against racism, then what is the national standards and Goals 2000 movement all about? I see it as part of a coordinated effort by corporate America to discredit public schools in order to reduce the costs of social services in the United States, and thereby, significantly reduce the tax burden on businesses. Standards, vouchers, two-tiered certification, privatization, block grants, reductions in enrollments due to IQ qualifications and citizenship status, and total quality management are all pointed at public schools like loaded guns ready to rob them of the too few resources under which many already suffer. If school curricula are reduced to standards, if per pupil costs can be cut to a national average, if an elite, well-paid cadre of master teachers can oversee a low-paid teacher core, if parts of or most school functions can be subcontracted to private businesses, if federal funds can be reduced, lumped into discretionary grants, and allocated only to some schools, if students with low IQs, students without citizenship papers, or repeat failers of national exams can be cut from student bodies, or if schools will use "strategic planning" to direct their resources only to the most "productive units" of schooling, then the costs of schools can be significantly reduced. Coupled with welfare limits, social security benefit taxation, and workman's compensation reform, government can spend much less on social programs, and they can cut corporate, and perhaps, individual property taxes. Of course, the reduced corporate taxes are supposed to increase business investment and jobs, which will then trickle down to the rest of us, but we've been through that before, eh?

Shortly after the federal call for national standards in all academic subjects, the NCTE, a professional organization of 90,000 English teachers, elementary school teachers, and college professors, began their fall from grace. To my knowledge, and I was Director of the NCTE Commission on Reading at the time, the NCTE had not considered the possibility of developing national standards for English/Language Arts before the federal request for proposals to do so. After the government brought the subject up, however, the NCTE leadership "discovered" a consensus among its membership that favored standards. The membership was told in moderated open forums at both its Louisville (1993) and Pittsburgh (1994) annual conferences that having the federal funding as well as the membership's mandate gave the standards project both political and professional legitimacy. The NCTE leadership told us that it was imperative that we participate in developing national standards because the government and the public wanted them, someone else would do it anyway, there was money in it now and later, and these standards could be used by society's have-nots to protect themselves against schools that won't teach (Myers 1993). Further, the leadership said that the Department of Education put no contingencies on the funding. In Louisville, Miles Myers, Executive Director of NCTE reported, "we are free to write the standards as we see fit, and if the membership doesn't like the standards we can reject them." Chair of the English Standards Board Janet Emig (1993) stated, "No federal body can legislate our success or failure." The NCTE joined with the 90,000-membered International Reading Association and the Center for the Study of Reading at the University of Illinois, accepted a $3,000,000 grant from the Department of Education, established task forces at the elementary, middle, and high school levels, hired chair and task force directors at handsome salaries, and began work without a formal vote of the membership.

After a year's work, the federal government cancelled the grant, withheld almost half of the initial allotment, and kept their second installment of more than a million dollars. A government official reported the rationale for the firing as a lack of "expected progress" toward promised goals (Diegmueller 1994). At the time of the announcement, David Pearson from the Center for the Study of Reading and a director of the project was quoted as responding, "I thought we were developing these standards for kids, their parents, and their teachers" (Diegmueller 1994, 9). Cancelling a national standards grant is unprecedented among the federally funded standards projects in other disciplines. For example, although the history standards have been labeled a national disgrace by the popular media (Elson 1994), the National Center for History in Schools at UCLA received their full million and a half from the government.

The NCTE is now engaged in "a going it alone" project to write national standards for English Language Arts, a project funded by $500,000 from NCTE and the same amount from the International Reading Association (*Council Chronicle* 1994). This funding raises many questions for me, a member of both organizations for 15 years who has served on several committees as a volunteer in each organization. Where did these membership-supported groups find such large sums of money on such short notice? How are they spending this $1,000,000? How much more money does the

NCTE have available for other large projects? Why didn't the membership know that its organization is so flush that the leadership can simply write a check for half a million dollars? I never realized that our non-profit organization was so..., well, profitable. Nor did I realize that they were so foolish.

Right from the beginning, the NCTE leadership chose the road too often traveled by accepting the money, the corporate assumption about schools, and the logic that standards are the answer to our economic woes in perhaps the hopes that they could be players in school reform. Of course, they had other options. They could have asked the membership to use their considerable talents and resources to inform the public about the economy, schools, and institutional biases. However, once the leadership took the federal money, their options for resistance and action were significantly reduced. The second misstep came when the leadership failed to make a public stink about the political squeeze in which they found themselves when they submitted their preliminary standards to the government. If the government could determine that the NCTE/IRA Joint Project was not making "expected progress," then the government had expectations for the standards from the start. That is, the English Language Arts Standards were always politically motivated. Now the NCTE will write professional, not national, standards that the government has already found lacking. In short, the government finessed the NCTE leadership. Once the NCTE leadership agreed to produce standards, the government would get what it wanted either through the NCTE's production of acceptable standards or through discrediting the professional organization and standards and finding another more politicized agency to produce them. No matter how good the NCTE Standards for English Language Arts may be when finished, they are already moot. Expensive and moot. To anyone paying attention, it is clear that standards are meant to serve the corporate unreality rather than the reality of America's children. It is also clear that the standards are and will remain beyond the control of the NCTE, schools, and teachers.

If the NCTE wants to help teachers of English at all levels, the membership must decide what type of future we want for ourselves and our children. If we seek a future that values people over corporations, then we must become mad as hell about this corporate hoax, and we must expose it by using the literacies and teaching talents at our disposal. The leadership should admit that it was wrong about the government's intentions from the start and wrong about the likely consequences of writing standards — a reduced emphasis on English Language Arts, reduced resources for teachers in general, and reduced control over what and how we teach. Finally, the NCTE must show that we are not going to take it anymore by redirecting the funds allotted for standards toward grassroots efforts among the membership to demonstrate the value and effect of English Language Arts on the development of literate citizens who will participate actively in their community, state, and nation (Shannon 1995b). For example, NCTE should find ways to support and promote the work of teachers like Audrey Sturk (1992) who used Margaret Laurence's *The Stone Angel* to invite greater understanding between adolescents and the elderly in their community, Ruth Vegas (1994) who sponsored writing workshops to help kindergarten students deal with their feelings about the Persian Gulf War, or Jim Hubbard (1992) who supplied cameras and photographic expertise to homeless children and allowed them to "shoot back" at the world that neglects them. Such efforts attack personally held social biases at the immediate level of lived experiences, and they might just reclaim our teaching lives from corporate America, which now holds the NCTE and public schools in the palm of its hand.

Although we may be unsure of ourselves, confused about what to do, and worried that we don't have every detail worked out ahead of time, we must follow the advice of A. J. Muste, the famous labor, civil rights, and peace activist. We must "make up our minds and act, while our actions might make a difference."

References

Aronowitz, S. (1994). A Different Perspective on Educational Inequality. *The Review of Education/Pedagogy/Cultural Studies*, 16: 135–151.

Bartlett, D., and J. Steele (1992). *America: What Went Wrong?* Kansas City, MO: Andrews & McNeil.

Bell, D. (1992). *Faces At the Bottom of the Well: The Permanence of Racism.* New York: Basic Books.

Berliner, D. (February 1992). Educational Reform in an Era of Disinformation. Paper presented at American Association of Colleges for Teacher Education, San Antonio, TX.

Bernstein, J., and L. Mishel (1992). *Declining Wages for High School and College Graduates.* Washington DC: Economic Policy Institute.

Bok, D. (1993). *The Cost of Talent: How Executives and Professionals Are Compensated and How It Affects America.* New York: Free Press.

Carson, C., R. Huelskamp, and T. Woodall (1991). *Perspectives on Education in America.* Albuquerque, NM: Sandia National Laboratories.

Commission on Work Force Skills (1990). *America's Choice: High Skills or Low Wages.* Rochester, NY: National Center for Education and the Economy.

Council Chronicle. (June 1994). NCTE/IRA Say Standards Effort Will Continue. 3: 5, 43.

Diegmueller, K. (March 1994). English Group Loses Funding for Standards. *Education Week,* 13: 1, 9, 27.

Elam, S., L. Rose, and A. Gallup (1993). The 25th Annual Phi Delta Kappa Gallup Poll of the Public's Attitudes Toward the Public Schools. *Phi Delta Kappan,* 75: 137–158.

Elson, J. (1994). History, the Sequel. *Time,* 144: 19, 64.

Emig, J. (1993) Curriculum Standards: Federal or National? *Reading Today,* 10: 40.

Hubbard, J. (1992). *Shooting Back: A Photographic View of Life by Homeless Children.* San Francisco, CA: Chronicle Books.

Jensen, C. (1994). *Censored: The News That Didn't Make the News — And Why.* New York: Four Walls Eight Windows.

Kozol, J. (1992). *Savage Inequalities.* New York: Basic Books.

Mishel, L., and J. Bernstein. (1991) *The Myth of the Coming Labor Shortage.* Washington DC: Economic Policy Institute.

Myers, M. (1993). Work Worth Doing. *The Council Chronicle,* 2: 24.

Nation (1992). The Battle for Public Schools. 255, 266–307.

National Commission on Educational Excellence. (1983). *A Nation at Risk: The Imperative for Educational Reform.* Washington, DC: Department of Education.

Noble, D. (1992). Who Are These Guys?: Corporate Involvement in the New American Schools. *Rethinking Schools,* 6: 3, 20.

Noble, D. (1994). Let Them Eat Skills. *The Review of Education/Pedagogy/Cultural Studies,* 16: 15–29.

Reich, R. (1991). *The Work of Nations.* New York: Knopf.

Richman, L. (September 1993). When Will the Layoffs End? *Fortune,* 43: 54–56.

Shannon, P. (1995a). Can Reading Standards Really Help? *The Clearing House,* 68: 229–232.

Shannon, P. (1995b). *Text, lies & videotape*. Portsmouth, NH: Heinemann.

Sturk, A. (1992). Developing a Community of Learners Inside and Outside the Classroom. In P. Shannon (ed.), *Becoming Political: Readings and Writings in the Politics of Literacy Education*. Portsmouth, NH: Heinemann.

Tucker, M., and R. Marshall (1992). *Thinking for a Living: Education and the Wealth of Nations*. New York: Basic Books.

Vegas, R. (1994). Los Ninitos Estan muy Percupado por la Guerra: The Persian Gulf War in a whole language kindergarten in Puerto Rico. In S. Steffey & W. Hood (eds.), *If This Is Social Studies, Why Isn't It Boring?* York, ME: Stenhouse.

Weisman, J. (November 1991). Some Economists Challenging View that Schools Hurt Competitiveness. *Education Weekly*, 24: 14, 17.

Weisman, J. (1993). Skills in the Schools: Now, it's Business' Turn. *Phi Delta Kappan*, 74: 367–370.

"It does not appear to be an option for parents or a community as a whole to choose not to have their children strive to be 'first in the world in mathematics and science' or 'prepared ... for productive employment in our nation's modern economy.' The issue is not whether these are admirable goals or loathsome ones; rather the issue is who chooses for a particular family what the goals for its children should be."

– Seth Rockmuller and Katharine Houk

Holding Our Ground: Goals 2000 and Families

Seth Rockmuller and Katharine Houk

The importance of families and parental involvement is a major theme in most approaches to educational reform. What we are lacking at this time is a clear definition of what constitutes parent involvement. Certainly the phrase is broad enough to mean one thing to a public school administrator and something entirely different to a parent. From a family perspective, it is important not to let institutional reform packages such as Goals 2000 provide the decisive definition. Rather, families must maintain the freedom to choose an education for their children that suits the needs of each child and of each family.

Parent participation in education can be found all over Goals 2000. Parents must be invited to participate in the development of state and local improvement plans. They have a role in the review and monitoring of state and local plans, are given an opportunity to comment before any waivers from statutory or regulatory requirements are granted by the Secretary of Education, have primary access to and serve on the board of directors of the parent information and resource centers to be established in each state,

and are provided access to the Office of Reform Assistance and Dissemination and the National Library of Education. Perhaps the most obvious
reference to parents is in the eighth and final national education goal in the
Goals 2000: Educate America Act:

Parental Participation

(A) By the year 2000, every school will promote partnerships that will
increase parental involvement and participation in promoting the social,
emotional, and academic growth of children.

(B) The objectives for this Goal are that—

(i) every State will develop policies to assist local schools and local
educational agencies to establish programs for increasing partnerships
that respond to the varying needs of parents and the home, including
parents of children who are disadvantaged or bilingual, or parents of
children with disabilities;

(ii) every school will actively engage parents and families in a partnership
which supports the academic work of children at home and shared
educational decision making at school; and

(iii) parents and families will help to ensure that schools are adequately
supported and will hold schools and teachers to high standards of
accountability.

Both Goal 8 and its objectives are for the most part quite general and
capable of being interpreted in many ways to meet the needs of the
interpreter. It is helpful, therefore, to look at Goal 8 in the context of the
other National Educational Goals established in the legislation. While there
are many in our society who would question the wisdom or justice of
insisting that all students become contributors to our current economic
system, Goal 3 provides "...every school in America will ensure that all
students learn to use their minds well, so they may be prepared for responsible citizenship, further learning, and productive employment in our
Nation's modern economy," and Goal 5 provides that, "By the year 2000,
United States students will be first in the world in mathematics and science
achievement." Different parents have different goals for their children. One
parent may believe that his or her child's future happiness depends largely
upon that child's math and science ability or the child's capacity to fit neatly
into the expanding information and service economy. Another may believe
that the opportunity for a child to develop his or her own interests — be
they technical, artistic, athletic, empathetic, or whatever — is the appropriate goal for education and the most likely route for the child to lead a
satisfying, productive, and responsible life. Should it be the federal govern-

ment that determines the goals for our children's education or should that be the role of individual families and communities?

Whatever an individual's view may be of the value of Goals 3 and 5, it is clear that parents did not arrive at the educational decision making table at the beginning of the discussion. Rather their participation involves ways in which to implement fundamental decisions that have already been made about the education of their children. Although parent representatives are required to be included on "the broad-based State panel" which, in cooperation with the state Department of Education and the governor, is to develop a state improvement plan, the legislation requires that the plan include "strategies for meeting the National Education Goals" — the desirability of the goals is not open to question. Similarly, parents must be represented on the panel convened by each local school district wishing to receive funds under the Goals 2000 legislation to develop a local improvement plan, but again the plan must be directed toward enabling all students to meet state content standards and student performance standards, which, as indicated above, must be in line with the national education goals.

How will Goals 2000 affect parental involvement in public education? In the first place, it defines the agenda that will be discussed by shared decision making teams at the school and school district levels. Any issues about the need for content standards and student performance standards have been removed from the discussion table. If states want the funds provided by the Goals 2000 legislation (and most states certainly will), the state plans and the local plans must include such standards. Moreover, the standards must be consistent with the national goals. It does not appear to be an option for parents or a community as a whole to choose not to have their children strive to be "first in the world in mathematics and science" or "prepared … for productive employment in our Nation's modern economy." The issue is not whether these are admirable goals or loathsome ones; rather the issue is who chooses for a particular family what the goals for its children should be.

A more subtle influence of Goals 2000 and of many institutionally sponsored programs of parental involvement in public education is that they tend to limit the forum for parental involvement. While the public education system may work hard at improving itself, it can hardly be argued that it is seeking to reinvent education in any real sense or, perhaps even more to the point, that it is open to all suggestions about the myriad ways in which children learn. By providing an easy avenue for parental involvement within the system and defining the roles that parents will play, Goals 2000 and similar efforts may well dissipate some of the energy that might otherwise be directed toward more fundamental changes in the ways in which we look at the learning process.

While the Goals 2000: Educate America Act applies most directly to public education, it is unlikely that nonpublic and home education will remain unaffected. In many states, alternatives to public education must be "substantially equivalent" (or some similar phrase) to education in the public schools. Thus, public school education becomes the standard against which alternatives are measured. If states develop content and performance standards that reflect the educational approach embodied in Goals 2000, it is entirely likely that many of those states will attempt to impose those same or very similar standards on private schools and home educators. In doing so they will limit the viability and vitality of educational alternatives, and families and communities will have to struggle harder to create educational alternatives that meet their needs. Alternative educational approaches will be compared to local school district programs that will be based on state standards, which in turn will be based on federal standards. Even though those alternative programs may in fact receive no federal funds themselves, they may well feel the pressures of conformity brought to bear by the lure of federal money.

Title IV of the Goals 2000 legislation authorizes the establishment in each state of at least one Parental Information and Resource Center. The centers are to provide training, information, and support to parents of children aged birth through five years and to parents of children enrolled in elementary and secondary schools, as well as to people working with such parents. Although the centers may assist parents in obtaining information about the range of options, programs, services, and resources available to them, parents of children who are learning at home — an educational option in all 50 states — do not appear to be included among the parents to be supported, at least not in those states in which home education programs are not considered schools. An important protection of Title IV does protect parents from being compelled to participate in any parent education or developmental screening programs and provides specifically that "no program assisted under this title shall take any action that infringes in any manner on the right of a parent to direct the education of their children." Parental Information and Resource Centers may well prove to be a valuable asset to families, but in order for them to be so, it is essential that they provide information about a wide variety of approaches to learning rather than advocating any particular approach or educational setting. The danger to be avoided is that the centers provide information only about institutionalized mainstream education and ways to work within the system. If they do so, they may not only fail to empower parents but also may have the exact opposite effect of strengthening the grip of the already entrenched forces in education.

The structures established by the Goals 2000: Educate America Act suggest at least two constructive responses. One is to dive into the process, take advantage of the open door, and push the federal government, the state government, local school districts, and individual schools in directions they might not otherwise choose to go. The federal government and many state governments have determined that parental involvement is critical. They have also, at least to some extent, predetermined what that involvement should look like (it should mirror the national educational goals and standards). It may be possible, however, especially at the local level, to use the parent involvement process to raise issues and advocate for programs that the local community wants. The process may be used to help communities define their educational goals.

Perhaps most importantly, it can serve as a forum in which to develop the notion that many different approaches to education are possible and desirable and that conformity to one specific educational approach is both undesirable and counterproductive. Children differ greatly from one another in their interests and their learning styles. Families differ from each other in their hopes and aspirations for their children. To this point no one has discovered a single approach to education that meets the needs of and adequately serves all children and all families. If the federal, state, and local governments cannot assure that each child will flourish in the education they offer, they should encourage families and communities to experiment with alternatives in much the same way that the governments continue to experiment with educational theories.

After all, it's the parents who know their children best. In the final analysis, it's a question of trust. Will we as a society trust the family to look out for the best interests of its children? If we will, then parent involvement will be a meaningful exercise, and programs designed to meet the needs of children will abound. If we won't, the potential for meaningful parent involvement will be severely limited, and we will continue to be locked into our current mediocrity. Families should be given great latitude in educating their children, and the community should support them in any way it can. The role of the community in this process is essential. It is within the real world of everyday life in their communities that children learn the values of tolerance and respect for others that are at the core of our society. These are not values that can be "taught" in the school sense of that word, but they are definitely values that can be learned in day-to-day family and community life.

A second response to Goals 2000 is to opt out of the government-sponsored forum and to work within individual communities to bring together like-minded people to develop educational alternatives. The solutions need not be limited to a single one for each community. Rather, groups within the community can form around a discussion of what they want for their children and for themselves. Such discussion groups have already formed in some communities and alternative education networks. One group might decide that Goals 2000 is just what it wants; another might choose a Waldorf-inspired learning center for home-educating families; a third might want to set up a program of mentor/apprentice/intern opportunities to more fully involve the community in education and the children in the community. In the words of John Taylor Gatto, "A slow, organic process of self-awareness, self-discovery, and cooperation is what is required if any solution is to stick...." "Encourage and underwrite experimentation; trust children and families to know what is best for themselves;... look for local solutions and always accept a personal solution in place of a corporate one." (*Dumbing Us Down*, 25, 102). The possibilities are unlimited unless we allow ourselves to be limited.

And finally, that is the true danger of the Goals 2000: Educate America Act — that in the name of parent and community involvement, the federal and state governments will, in fact, limit the educational options available to families when they should be expanding them. Notwithstanding the years of effort and the billions of dollars spent, the government has yet to find the single approach to education that works for everyone or a single set of goals and standards that are universally accepted. Perhaps it's time to stop looking and instead to give those families and communities that so desire the freedom to design and develop alternatives from the ground up.

Resources for Discussion Groups on Goals 2000

Alliance for Parental Involvement in Education, P.O. Box 59, East Chatham, NY 12060-0059; 518/392-6900; allpiesr@aol.com.

Building Community Partnerships for Learning, U.S. Department of Education; a free copy is available by calling 800/USA-LEARN.

Dumbing Us Down: The Hidden Curriculum of Compulsory Schooling, John Taylor Gatto, 1992, New Society Publ, 4527 Springfield Ave., Philadelphia, PA 19143.

Education: How Can Schools and Communities Work Together to Meet the Challenge?, 1995, Study Circles Resource Center, P.O. Box 203, Pomfret, CT 06258; 203/928-2616.

For All Our Children: An Action Guide to Parents' Rights and Responsibilities in Education, Wisconsin Parents Association, P.O. Box 2502, Madison, WI 53701-2502.

Goals 2000 Community Update — A monthly newsletter from the U.S. Department of Education on efforts to implement Goals 2000 around the country; call 800/USA-LEARN to receive a free subscription.

Goals 2000: Educate America Act — To obtain a copy of the actual legislation, call the House of Representatives' Documents Room at 202/225-3456 and ask for Public Law 103-227, the Goals 2000: Educate America Act.

Government Nannies: The Cradle-to-Grave Agenda of Goals 2000 and Outcome-Based Education, Cathy Duffy, 1995, Noble Publishing Associates, P.O. Box 2250, Gresham, OR 97030; 503/667-3942.

Parenting Our Schools: A Hands-On Guide to Education Reform, Jill Bloom, 1992, Little, Brown.

"It is already a paradox for our government to demand *compulsory attendance* in any institution if we truly live in a free and democratic society. But with Goal Three we are also headed down the path of *compulsory mental management* by the education/political complex. Certainly we all want our children to know specific things, like how to do math, read, conduct research, and so on. But these things can all be learned in school *or out of school.* They can be learned in any number of scopes and sequences and they can be learned at any time in one's life."

— *Pat Farenga*

Unschooling 2000

Pat Farenga

John Holt, in 1969, wrote the following words about learning and society in his book *The Underachieving School*:

> Education is something a person gets for himself, not that which someone else gives or does to him.

> What young people need and want to get from their education is: one, a greater understanding of the world around them; two, a greater development of themselves; three, a chance to find their work, that is, a way in which they may use their own unique tastes and talents to grapple with the real problems of the world around and to serve the cause of humanity.

> Our society asks schools to do three things for and to children: one, pass on the traditions and higher values of our own culture; two, acquaint the child with the world in which he lives; three, prepare the child for employment and, if possible, success. All of these tasks have traditionally been done by the society, the community itself. None of them is done well by schools. None of them can or ought to be done by the schools solely or exclusively. One reason the schools are in trouble is that they have been given too many functions that are not properly or exclusively theirs.

> Schools should be resources, but not the only resource, from which children, but not only children, can take what they need and want to carry on the business of their own education. Schools should be places where people go to find out the things they want to find out and develop the skills they want to develop. The child who is educating himself, and if he doesn't no one else will, should be free, like the adult, to decide when and how much and in what way he wants to make use of whatever resources

the schools can offer him. There are an infinite number of roads to education; each learner should and must be free to choose, to find, to make his own.

Children want and need and deserve and should be given, as soon as they want it, a chance to be useful in society. It is an offense to humanity to deny a child, or anyone of any age, who wants to do useful work the opportunity to do it. The distinction, indeed opposition, we have made between education and work is arbitrary, unreal, and unhealthy.

Unless we have faith in the child's eagerness and ability to grow and learn, we cannot help and can only harm his education. (Holt 1969, 4–5)

About ten years after writing this, Holt founded *Growing Without Schooling*, a magazine and network for adults and children living and learning together at home and in their communities, for it became apparent to him that individuals and families, not schools, were the ones who most wanted change in the direction Holt was describing in 1969. Holt coined the word "unschooling" in the late seventies to counter perceptions people bring to the word "homeschooling," namely turning one's home into a miniature school. Unschooling — the practice of allowing children as much freedom to control their own learning as we can comfortably bear as their teachers — rejects compulsory attendance, forced learning, fixed curriculum, grades, and standardized assessments. Children who are nurtured and raised like this do get into college, do find work worth doing, and do become good citizens. There is a significant research base for these claims (Van Galen and Pittman 1991), but more importantly there are thousands of families over the past two decades whose stories and examples continue to feed the growth of homeschooling in general, and unschooling in particular.[1] Unschooled does not mean uneducated: as Holt implied in the quote above, schooling is not the same as education.

Goals 2000, our national blueprint for education into the next millennium, is an attempt to reform education in ways that run counter to Holt's vision of education. By emphasizing the debatable technical aspects of professional education, such as calls for specific exit outcomes and holding kids back until they reach them, and more intensive certification and ranking not only of students but of teachers and schools, Goals 2000 perpetuates the notion of schools as sorting machines for the winners (graduates and honors students) and losers (dropouts and poor students)

---

[1] *Growing Without Schooling* magazine, founded by John Holt in 1977, now has 18 years of such stories.

in society rather than the concept of education envisioned by Holt where schools are communal resources where people "can take what they need and want to carry on the business of their own education."

The first goal of Goals 2000 is: *All children will start school ready to learn*. This demand is the start of many false assumptions about the nature of learning that Goals 2000 makes. Children aren't *ready* to learn by the time they are school-age, they have been learning all the time before then. Indeed biology informs us that children are learning even *in utero*. A young child learning to speak is engaged in the most difficult learning task a human being faces, and the vast majority of children excel at this task without formal instruction. Indeed, observing how children learn so much, so easily, and so joyfully, before they reach compulsory school age is a primary reason people decide to homeschool: why stop doing what is so evidently working for their children? But Goal One illustrates the education establishment's deep authoritarianism: what one learns outside of school simply doesn't count. The only learning that matters is the learning schools make students do. So, there's nothing new in this goal, it's just a restatement of the old school dodge: if you succeed in school, it's because of school; if you fail, it's because of you. For most students, if they get an "A" on the test it is assumed they were *taught* well; if they fail the test, parents, teachers, and administrators will almost inevitably blame the student for not *learning* well, and rarely, if ever, question whether the failure is due to the teacher not teaching well. Here is a recent, and hopeful, reflection of this phenomenon:

> Ten years ago, Professor Mook says, he would have told a failing student: "I did everything I could. Maybe you're just not cut out for this." Now the wispy-haried, round-faced physics professor says that response is weak, if not dishonest.
>
> He speaks of a "realization, on my part, that in a sense I'd been swindling a lot of students." They come to him, as "customers," and say "teach me physics." He and other professors hand the students textbooks based on an education gained from similar textbooks, Mook says, and "if they don't get it, we fail them."
>
> … Mook contends: "different people learn in different ways." By working very closely with students on the brink of failing his course, he tries to prepare "a smorgasbord" of ways physics concepts can be grasped, greatly increasing a student's chances of passing. A student's success or failure, Mook asserts, should be "a shared responsibility." (*Christian Science Monitor*, Dec. 12, 1994, 12)

The second goal is: *The high school graduation rate will increase to at least 90 percent.* There have been countless efforts over the years to raise graduation rates and lower dropout rates and the results are always the same: educators teach to the test, or lower the standards. In either case, the nature of learning is focused and reduced from learning out of interest, curiosity, and self-improvement to merely passing, to satisfying requirements, to getting a piece of paper. Certainly our graduation rates can increase, and now that they have become a national goal I have no doubt the rates *will* increase, but getting a certified diploma is no guarantee that one is a qualified learner. There are court cases where the parents of high school graduates have sued school districts because their children received diplomas without being able to read or write competently; the parents lost. Focusing on the numbers, as this goal and several others do, shows how schools have reduced teaching and learning to a technocratic process that simply measures inputs and outputs. Many school reformers claim that without numbers such as graduation rates, we will not be able to know what is actually working in education. The problem is, they are measuring the process, the system, not the substance, of learning. Ivan Illich pointed out more than 20 years ago in *Deschooling Society* that schools confuse for us the process of schooling with the substance of learning so we think that by taking classes we have actually learned something. Graduation rates do not tell us whether the student studied hard or slept through classes: they are both counted as graduates.

The third goal is quite sweeping and is actually one that will probably affect us all the most: *American students will leave grades four, eight, and twelve having demonstrated competency in challenging subject matter, including English, mathematics, science, history, and geography; and every school in America will ensure that all students learn to use their minds well, so they may be prepared for responsible citizenship, further learning, and productive employment in our modern economy.*

This is a flat out call for national curricula and testing reflecting the growing interest among educators and policy makers in specifying definitive "outcomes" of the educational process. They are finally concerned about the actual substance of learning, but their efforts to control it are being met, understandably, by fierce resistance in several states where Outcome-Based Education has been implemented.

Most objections to OBE programs are based on the components that mandate achieving specific attitudes and values, particularly when they are in conflict with other attitudes and values held by families. This is a primary source of opposition to OBE from religious conservatives who claim that OBE deemphasizes traditional academics ("Politically correct values replace 3 R's" is a headline about OBE from the *American Family Association Journal*) and has many outcomes that are tied to "non-academic feelings, emotions, and personal evaluations." (*AFA Journal*, April 1994, 18)

A leading OBE proponent, Robert Marzano, acknowledges the significant philosophical differences between people in American society but still insists that a central institution of schooling can educate all children.

> I now see them [Ultra-fundamentalists] as fundamentally different from me in some of the basic assumptions that underlie their worldview. The assumptions on which their worldview is based are as unprovable as the assumptions on which my worldview (and that of most educators) is based.
>
> What do we do when groups with different worldviews collide? It appears that we either fight … or communicate. I, for one, reject the first alternative. Instead, I hope that as intelligent people we can begin a dialogue toward the ultimate goal of an educational system that works for all. (Marzano 1994, 10–11)

However, it is difficult to see how these worldviews can be reconciled in one educational system that "works for all," since that system is based on coercive, centralized control over children's learning experiences. Various conservative groups have picked up the banner to fight OBE, Goals 2000, and similar statewide initiatives, but they are only willing to criticize schools to a point, since they hope schools will return to some previous level of excellence. I think these critics miss the forest for the trees: much of this criticism of OBE is true of any form of compulsory learning. The deeper problem with OBE and all attempts to control children's learning, such as Goals 2000, is identified by homeschooling activists Larry and Susan Kaseman:

> By requiring that children acquire specific knowledge, skills, and attitudes, OBE would add compulsory education to the current requirement for compulsory school attendance. Children would not only be required to attend school but would also be required to demonstrate that they had

acquired specific knowledge, skills, and attitudes. This would be a very big and very serious change. Compulsory education is incompatible with a free society. (1993, 18)

It is already a paradox for our government to demand *compulsory attendance* in any institution if we truly live in a free and democratic society. But with Goal Three we are also headed down the path of *compulsory mental management* by the education/political complex. Certainly we all want our children to know specific things, like how to do math, read, conduct research, and so on. But these things can all be learned in school *or out of school*. They can be learned in any number of scopes and sequences and they can be learned at any time in one's life. The variety of experiences and techniques for teaching and learning as described by Steiner and Dewey, Montessori and Neill, Early Childhood and Adult Education, Mastery Learning and Multiple Intelligences — are testaments to our human capacity to learn in numerous ways. Such a multitude of educational experiences fly in the face of any mandate by educators and politicians to make us all learn the same thing, at the same time, at the same location.

Interestingly, some contemporary reforms resemble concepts and practices that unschoolers have used and championed for years: emphasizing self-directed learning, project learning, interdisciplinary learning, learning in real-world situations, using portfolios and demonstrations of competency in lieu of standardized evaluations. But in an authoritarian institutional setting, these practices take on a vastly different character. Rather than use techniques like self-directed learning and real-life experiences to liberate and facilitate learning as unschoolers do, educators are using them to further manipulate and define learning. For instance, the Wisconsin Department of Public Instruction recommends this activity for use in grades 3 to 5. It is called "Fish Tank."

First, the curriculum indicates which of the ten Wisconsin learner outcomes are being addressed by this task. In this case it is:

Outcome 4, which is "Achieve desired results by interpreting and executing instructions, plans, models, and diagrams."

Outcome 5 is "Recognize and devise systems and describe their interdependence."

The next section describes Main Knowledge and Processes Required.

Subject base: mathematics and science

Problem solving, reasoning, communicating, computing whole numbers, understanding fractions and decimals, measuring, and reading for a purpose.

Sample Task should require high levels of knowledge and a variety of thinking processes and communication skills.

The class will be getting a 30-gallon aquarium. The class will have $25 to spend on fish. The students will plan which fish to buy by using the "Choosing Fish for your Aquarium" brochure to help them choose the fish. The brochure explains the size of the fish, how much they cost, and their needs.

Students choose as many different kinds of fish as they can, and then they write a letter to the principal explaining the fish chosen. In the letter, they

1. Tell the principal how many of each kind of fish to buy;

2. Give the reasons why the students chose those fish; and

3. show that they are not overspending and that the fish will not be too crowded in the aquarium.

Materials needed

A brochure that contains information on fish size, needs, cost, and habits.

Estimated Time Required for Task: One period (WI Learner Goals, Outcomes Assessments, 8)

This is the sort of experience that unschoolers frequently encounter when their children develop a strong interest, such as in fish. Unschooled children might even follow the same steps as outlined above, except instead of writing to the principal they would talk or write about the issues with their parents. But there are crucial differences between using the Fish Tank in school and using it in unschooling. In school the Fish Tank lesson takes place in an institutional setting on a specific day, not in the flow of real life. It will last an estimated one class period and requires all students to be equally motivated at the same time to do the same task. Despite its similarity to what unschoolers can do, it is fundamentally different since it lacks what teacher/author Herb Kohl terms "the role of assent in education." Simply put, Kohl is referring to the issue exemplified in the adage, "you can lead a horse to water, but you can't make it drink." You can mandate requirements from above, but you can't mandate learning. We need to stop confusing the two. The Fish Tank may excite and interest some students, but it certainly won't interest them all. What if a child has no interest in fish or is actually opposed to the collection of fish in tanks? What if the child senses no ownership of the project and decides to merely go through the motions, realizing the idea, the aquarium, and the fish belong to the school and not to him/her or the class? What if a child's interest is so strong it goes beyond the one period allotted for the project? Certainly a talented teacher might be able to work with such children, but will they have time when there are so many other goals to be achieved, so many children to evaluate? These are not new questions or problems that arise because of Outcome Based Education, Goals 2000, or the Wisconsin Learner's Assessment program, *these are the perennial problems teachers and schools face regardless of the reforms they create as long as they teach captive learners.*

The second half of this education goal, *every school in America will ensure that all students learn to use their minds well, so they may be prepared for responsible citizenship, further learning, and productive employment in our modern economy,* is so vague as to be meaningless, but also so vague that it can be frightening. Who determines what is the right way for a student to use their mind? How does one prove "responsible citizenship, further learning, and productive employment in our modern economy?" Given the new developments and constant surprises of life, who can determine with any accuracy the skills and knowledge our six-year-olds will need in the year 2010? The rightful place for deciding how to use one's mind, what to learn, and what work is worth doing is with the learner here and now, not the government or a Blue Ribbon Commission of business leaders.

One hoped-for result of Goals 2000 is to make education uniformly accountable in America by making all schools that accept funding tied to Goals 2000 meet the same content standards. This timetable approach makes sense when one manages production lines, but humans are not machines on an assembly line. Our organic development and mental maturity follows a course from birth to death, not from 6 to 16, the most common ages for compulsory school attendance. Our abilities to renew ourselves mentally, physically, and spiritually, to change the direction of our lives, or learn new skills and attitudes do not end when we graduate high school. However, Goal Three indicates that these things don't matter, that "demonstrated competency" and advancement in subjects determined by national school officials during one's youth is more important to being a good citizen and productive employee than an ability to engage life fully. Indeed, the push for demonstrating competency and forcing learning by certain ages does work: our 9-year-olds read very well when compared to children in other countries. But there is a price we pay for forcing education in this subject: after age 13 our children read less for fun (12th out of 15 countries surveyed by Educational Testing Service) and they read fewer books, newspapers, and magazines in 1990 than in 1984 (ETS Policy Information Center 1992). It would seem that forced learning produces severe counter-productive effects. Further, as the acceptance of unschoolers and other alternatively educated people into colleges and workplaces throughout the world shows, compulsory education in any form is not necessary for becoming a good citizen, life-long learner, and productive employee.

Old-fashioned tests are not better than new-fangled "assessments:" both are riddled with problems. Striking proof of this is the fact that teachers themselves adamantly refuse to have their teaching abilities tested, claiming that a test could never show what they actually know and can communicate to a class; but why then is such a blatant double-standard held for our children and their learning?[2] Be it called OBE or Basic Skills Tests, the intent of both is to reduce people to types of measurable quantities. All such testing are reductions, distortions, single perspectives of our multidimensional lives yet they are often solely used to make important decisions about our children. Asking schools to go back to their traditional roots is not the answer. Certainly OBE and its manifestation as Goals 2000 is a dangerous modern development, but it didn't come out of thin air. Its roots are in the very system it seeks to reform, which is why it is relatively easy for the system to take this transplant.

OBE and traditional school methods are both attempts at predicting success according to academic standards set by the school, the government, and now, big business, to remediate or expel the failures and to control a child's future employment opportunities through the use of school credentials. If that last statement seems outrageous, consider the newly created National Skill Standards Board. According to the government's literature, the National Skill Standards Board will "serve as a catalyst in stimulating the development and adoption of a voluntary national system of occupational skill standards and certification that will serve as a cornerstone of the

---

[2] John Holt often noted that the only difference between a good student and a bad student is that the good student is careful not to forget what he studied until *after* the test.

national strategy to enhance work force skills…" This board ties into the "School-to-Work Opportunities Act" that "support State and local efforts to build a school-to-work transition system that will help youth acquire the knowledge, skills, abilities and labor market information they need to make a smooth transition from school to career-oriented work and to further education and training. Students in these programs will be expected to meet the same academic standards States establish under Goals 2000 and will earn *portable, industry-recognized skill certificates* that are benchmarked to high-quality standards such as the skill standards that will be established under Goals 2000" (U.S. Dept. of Education 1994).

For the first time in American history, we have laid out before us a method for social control and employment that is set in motion by one's performance as a youth in a system one is forced to attend. If we are truly living in a free society, how can a Skills Standards Board that limits the jobs one can apply for even be talked about, let alone be enacted? Studies and practical experience show that most people will change jobs and careers several times in the course of their lives; why are we then limiting job prospects for adults based on their ability to earn particular skill certificates as youths? On-the-job training, personal networking and development, public libraries and seminars, independent study or other freely chosen education courses, apprenticeships, internships, volunteering — these are among the ways that people learn and find jobs in our society. Limiting job prospects by linking employment to skill certificates is a giant step in the wrong direction: we should be encouraging and publicizing our existing and more democratic methods of learning and finding work.

Further, there is no evidence at all that shows even a modest connection between school performance and later job performance and yet we are proceeding as if there is. A significant study by Dr. Lauren Resnick of the University of Pittsburgh in 1987, entitled, *Learning: In School and Out*, concluded that the vast majority of skills taught in school *are not* transferable to the real world. In short, she found that what schools almost always use to justify their existence — the generality and the power of transfer of their curricula to real-life situations — is bogus. "Growing evidence … points to the possibility that very little can be transported directly from school to out-of-school use," concludes Dr. Resnick (1987, 16; also see Berg 1971).

As most people realize after a few years in the work force, not all, or even most, learning that is used by people in their daily lives is taught and learned in schools. Educators need to stop catering to the false show of knowledge testing perpetuates and instead show the public that their tax dollars can achieve similar results by allowing learning to occur organically, out of the experiences of one's life, and let people decide how much to utilize school services to achieve personal goals, such as getting skills for a better job or learning about Shakespeare. There are thousands of alternative schools and unschoolers who do not use fixed curricula, grades, forced attendance, and standardized assessments and their students get into college and find work worth doing without special difficulty. Certainly not everyone will want their children to be taught in an "unschooled" fashion, but Goals 2000, and Goal Three in particular, is making it more difficult for people to use unschooling or other methods and goals for their educations.

I'm not against tests one freely chooses to take. I can easily imagine situations where families might want their kids to be tested, I can even imagine a child wanting to take a certain test — for instance to see how strong he is. But the results should be the sole property of the family or child and should not be used by anyone else without their permission. I can understand why one would want to know if they'd be able to answer random questions about a subject, to see where they placed in relation to others on the same test; after all, that's the allure of games like *Jeopardy* and *Trivial Pursuit*. But one's failure in such tests should be a lesson in self-correction, an opportunity to acknowledge and address both strengths and weaknesses, not a loss of opportunity, loss of advancement, or loss of self-esteem. I don't buy the argument that taking tests necessarily builds character or teaches one how to handle failure; we all have to learn to handle plenty of disappointments and failures throughout our lives regardless of whether we were "A" students or failed to reach particular "Exit outcomes." As long as testing is used to create winners and losers for the meritocracy of school, there will be fear of tests among students. As long as there is fear of tests and tests remain the final arbiters of advancement in most schools (whether the tests are outcome-based or traditional), then children will fear learning. OBE, Mastery Learning, Back to Basics, New

Math, Cultural Literacy: let's call a spade a spade and condemn all forms of compulsory learning and compulsory evaluation in school!

The fourth goal is: *The Nation's teaching force will have access to programs for the continued improvement of their professional skills and the opportunity to acquire the knowledge and skills needed to instruct and prepare all American students for the next century.* This ties in directly with the national teaching certificate developed by the National Board of Professional Teaching Standards. Keith Geiger, President of the NEA proclaimed, "We finally have our chance to be accorded the professionalism that doctors, lawyers, and architects have enjoyed for years." But Geiger overlooks an important point. Americans are free to choose their doctors, lawyers, and architects and free to refuse their treatment, advice, and designs. Except for school teachers, no professional has a clientele compelled by law to use them for years on end. As the Scarecrow learned from The Wizard of Oz, knowledge, professionalism, and respect come not from a piece of paper but from how one acts in life. There are many well-respected teachers in private and parochial schools, not to mention at our colleges and universities, who have never been state or federally certified and it would be difficult to claim that they are not accorded professional status. Further, there is nothing about interacting with children, taking them seriously, carefully observing them, or being sympathetic to them in any of the federal education goals or in any of the state outcomes I've seen so far. Certified teachers are to instruct and prepare children according to the latest research findings and parents are supposed to support and go along with these efforts. That's it. The schooling process of certification and research is not the cure-all to bad teaching or bad learning our educators believe it is because schooling is not the same as education. School is not the only place, nor necessarily the best place, for children to learn or for teachers to teach.

The fifth goal, *U.S. students will be first in the world in science and mathematics achievement,* shows the competitive talk that now fills the business-oriented climate of modern education reform. The problem is, our kids are not material on an assembly line where we can inject, via instruction, math and science. One would be hard-pressed to show that Edison's or Einstein's achievements had a direct correlation to their schooling. Einstein has written, "It is, in fact, nothing short of a miracle that the modern methods of instruction have not yet entirely strangled the holy curiosity of inquiry; for this delicate little plant, aside from stimulation, stands mainly in need of freedom; without this it goes to wrack and ruin without fail."

Further, to imply that learning math and science is better than learning something else is pure nonsense. Math and science are part of all subject areas and lose much of their meaning and significance to all but the specialist when we peel them away from geography, history, and other studies of the world. Secondly, everyone thinks their specialty is more important to learn than someone else's, so whoever's speciality is nearest the center of power when decisions to emphasize certain subjects are made gains favor with the decision makers.

Grace Llewellyn, author of the *Teenage Liberation Handbook* wrote these words about our increasing curricular emphasis on math and science in 1991, but they are more important even today. She wrote:

> Don't be brainwashed by the Bush administration's misguided emphasis on science and math education. Their goal is that American schools will produce an average population that knows more science and math than any other country's average population. This goal is based on a danger-ous, narrow sense of economic competition; it is much more likely to lead to an imbalanced, neurotic society than to any life-sustaining technologi-cal breakthroughs. I decided to bother to mention this because Your Government will be spending lots of money in the next few years to push school students to believe that science and math are gods that can fix anything. They're not. Furthermore, even if you are a big-time science or math fan, school is not where it's at. (1991)

By the way, the national standards for math and science were the first ones to be completed for Goals 2000.

The sixth goal, *every adult American will be literate and will possess the knowledge and skills necessary to compete in a global economy and exercise the rights and responsibilities of citizenship*, is more political than it is educational. Making literacy a requirement for citizenship is a new one for me, one I'm glad my great-grandparents didn't have to face when they stepped on American soil. Will this lead to literacy police or to "outings" of illiterate adults? Further, making the bold but vague claim that we need particular *knowledge and skills necessary to compete in a global economy and exercise the rights and responsibilities of citizenship* leaves itself open to all sorts of inter-pretive nightmares. Are the skills and knowledge identified by the states and supported through Goals 2000 at the federal level really the only, or best, skills and knowledge we can think of as being necessary to be a citizen? Were *you* asked what skills and knowledge *your* children need to exercise their rights and responsibilities of citizenship?

The seventh goal is:, *Every school in America will be free of drugs and violence and will offer a disciplined environment conducive to learning.* This is a direct appeal to the law and order side of us all, and of course, who wants drugs and violence in school or anywhere else? But, again, the perceived needs of schools are being put before the actual needs of students. What we are given here are prescriptions for what should not be part of school, but we are given nothing for children who do not fit in or refuse to learn in school and have no other place to go. Drugs and violence are often their only other outlet. Indeed the alienation caused by schooling exacerbates these problems: competition for popularity, grades, and soon for skill certificates, makes students who do poorly in such races feel inferior and dumb. They may find drugs and violence to be the only areas they can compete well in! There are of course deeper social issues as well that drive our youth to drugs and violence, but there can be no denying that school plays a part in alienating some kids from learning and society (see Kozol 1967; Dennison 1969; Gatto 1992).

There is nothing in Goals 2000 to help children deal with drugs and violence, just talk about keeping these things out of school. Further, why is a "disciplined" environment the only, or best, one that is conducive to learning? What do they mean by disciplined? Is a Montessori class a disciplined learning environment? A field day at the Museum of Science? John Holt said he was fired from the schools he taught at primarily because most of his colleagues felt he didn't exercise proper classroom discipline, though few claimed his students weren't learning.

The final goal, *every school will promote partnerships that will increase parental involvement and participation in promoting the social, emotional, and academic growth of children,* is one that actually indicates a positive direction for school reform as Goals 2000 envisions it. Parental involvement and participation in our children's education, as far as school seems to be concerned, often means enforcing what schools tell kids to do and asking us to fund more of it. However in some states, such as Washington and

California, schools and homeschoolers are working together. David Guterson, in his book *Family Matters* (1992), describes how some of these programs work for the benefit of all parties. The parents get the type of support from the school that they want, and the school gets the funds for carrying the homeschoolers on their rolls. As in any partnership, the degree of participation of both parties needs to be quite clear; some of the Independent Study Programs (ISPs) these districts have set up allow for nothing more than doing the public school curriculum at home. However there are some people who are quite happy with doing public school at home and that's fine. Families should use whatever approach to education they want, they should be able to mix and match approaches to different children, and they will learn from their children what is and isn't working. John Holt liked to point out that homeschoolers are self-selecting and self-correcting; I can't say it better. As long as ISPs remain a choice and not the only option for homeschoolers in a school district, I think they are the future of school and homeschool cooperation. Of course, if the school is the partner who holds all the power in this relationship then this eighth goal is much more dangerous than beneficial. For instance, if schools argue that only nationally certified people should be allowed to teach, instruct, and supervise children during school hours then this goal is meaningless.

Finally, if Goals 2000 and all the previous school reform efforts have been off-base, where is the base? Where should we be putting our tax dollars and time to help children become responsible citizens? The answer is one we face everyday as unschoolers: the base of true reform is in our relationships with children. All of Goals 2000, and the vast majority of parenting books, are about what adults should do to children: what kids should know, when they should know it, tricks to make them learn what we want them to learn. The alternative is to start thinking about how we can help children make something of themselves.

There's a lot of talk about making the school year longer because the school calendar is an outdated tool. I think they have it wrong. School, as we have known it, is an outdated institution. Our education system needs to be drastically changed in order to create routes other than school to help children become responsible citizens in our democracy. That unschoolers can accomplish this successfully demonstrates a choice for those who can not afford costly private schools; who do not like or perform well in schools; who seek options to the traditional, school-oriented family schedule; who want other routes for credentials. Unschooling can be for those who see a need to entirely circumvent the meritocracy of schools in order to work and learn at what they feel is worth doing and for those who prefer to address their social problems directly by working for social change now rather than spending their years being schooled about society's ills or, worse yet, being kept ignorant of them.

Goals 2000 completely misses the mark since it treats school as the only place where learning takes place. But schooling is not the same as learning. Real education reform is taking place one family at a time as each family decides to take their children seriously, strengthen and build their relationships with them, and help them learn at home and in their community. Schools can be part of this growing revolution about where and how learning takes place, but as long as bureaucratic remedies like Goals 2000 are being forced on schools it is hardly likely.

References

Berg, Ivar (1971). *The Great Training Robbery*. Boston: Beacon.

Dennison, George (1969). *The Lives of Children: The Story of the First Street School*. New York: Vintage.

ETS (Educational Testing Service) Policy Information Center (1992). *America's Smallest School: The Family*. Princeton, NJ: Author.

Gatto, John Taylor (1992). *Dumbing Us Down: The Hidden Curriculum of Compulsory Schooling*. Philadelphia: New Society Publishers.

Holt, John (1969). *The Underachieving School*. New York: Pitman.

Illich, Ivan (1971). *Deschooling Society*. New York: Harper & Row.

Kaseman, Larry and Susan (1993). "Saying No to Compulsory Education." *Home Education Magazine*. July-August, 1993. p. 18.

Kozol, Jonathan (1967). *Death at an Early Age*. New York: Bantam.

Llewelyn, Grace (1991). *Teenage Liberation Handbook*. Eugene, OR: Lowry House.

Marzano, Robert (1994). "When 2 World Views Collide."*Educational Leadership* December 1993/January 1994, 51(4): 6–11.

Resnick, Lauren (1987). "Learning: In School and Out." *Educational Researcher*, 16(9): 13–20.

U.S. Department of Education (1994). *Goals 2000: Educate America Act: Supporting Systemic Education Reform Nationwide*. Washington, D.C.: Author.

Van Galen, Jane, and Mary Ann Pittman (1991). *Homeschooling: Political, Pedagogical, and Historical Perspectives*. Norwood, NJ: Ablex.

"Why are 'public' schools forced on everyone from the age of five to eighteen and denied to everyone else? If we truly understand the importance of education, if we truly want an educated populace, if we truly want kids (and adults) to appreciate the joys and benefits of education, what we now call public schools should in fact be community learning centers, open to everyone who wants to partake of knowledge — or share it."

— *Linda Dobson*

Thoughts from a Free Mom

Linda Dobson

I've spent a lot of years now informing strangers that our children are educated at home. I've often considered typing a response form to hand each one, so universal and predictable are their reactions and questions. Dialogue, however, remains important — and enlightening.

In very short order, the strangers become fellow citizens intent on considering the welfare of our nation's children. Their comments and questions reflect four rough levels of previous connection to this grassroots phenomenon called homeschooling:

- They hear about it on TV, radio, magazines, or newspapers — "That's interesting." "Is it legal?"

- They think about it in relation to their own families — "What about socialization?" "How does the school system treat you?" "Do they get a diploma?" "I don't think I'm smart/patient/ organized/self-motivated enough."

- They consider and reject it, in theory or practice, primarily having measured it against existing cultural conditions — "Wait until they get into the *real* world!" "How will they be able to compete?" "Oh, I'd love to but I couldn't give up all we're working for."

- They look past homeschooling's difference and recognize its key strength — "I wish someone had given me that kind of freedom."

This observation of freedom and freedom's implications is, I regret, apparent only to a woefully small minority. Generally, these are the folks who think and act alternatively in one or more aspects of other societal institutions, such as politics, economics, religion, or medical care. It seems it takes the *experience* of freedom, in any one of its myriad manifestations, before we understand it, before we realize that steps along freedom's path occur one by one.

The idea of freedom in education, indeed, freedom in any of our firmly rooted institutions, looms inconceivable to most of us. I think I know why. At least I know why in relation to my own experience: Spending most of our formative years within an institution means training our brains, literally, to a very specific way of life — the institutional way. Minds thus trained are hard-pressed to think any other way.

With primary and, in many cases, total concentration on only the intellectual aspect of who we are as "we, the people," our spirits go unattended. Ignored, the spirit either withers or follows the head. Whichever happens, spirit, the invisible but larger part of the icebergs that we are, never becomes an important part of life, certainly not more important than the institutions the mind has been trained to thoughtlessly obey.

I went to public school and have since spent a lot of time reflecting on my training. Now I've taken responsibility for our three children's education for ten years. Our oldest child (16½ years old) spent last semester getting his feet wet at a community college along with volunteering at a state interpretive center where, for the past three years, he's spent one day a week helping and submerged in learning shoulder-to-shoulder with adults of all ages, backgrounds, politics, and perspectives. Their input is supplemented tenfold by the visitors with whom he comes in contact. He also volunteers for our fire department and when he was 15 experienced his first fire at the home of a neighbor he knows well. As a member of the fire department, he receives hands-on training in everything from radio communications to pump operation to standard operating procedures.

Regarding his future, he still hasn't decided between professional fireman, dispatcher, or naturalist, and I'm sure the list of possibilities will lengthen before a final decision comes. Our oldest child has, however, decided he's done with our "traditional" homeschooling. He told me it's time to move on. He didn't have a prom or a senior trip; this choice just fit into the flow of what was — and will continue to be — his learning life, rather than representing the end of anything. There was no graduation shindig, nor a diploma.

Some think it's horrible he doesn't have that piece of paper as a ticket to the next institution. The school system hasn't stamped him with approval! That's true. But the person who knows our son best has. He deemed himself worthy. This is educational freedom. I know what you're thinking. Many of the teens you know aren't capable of deciding for themselves when they're finished with school. (I know I wasn't at that age.) Many of them, you fear, would quit at 14 and hang around street corners. You're probably right. But that's less a reflection of them and more of their "education" that didn't include, therefore didn't prepare them for, freedom. When I hold my own public education up as the stick by which to measure the difference between my son's education and mine; when I meditate on what masquerades as free and democratic in education, my son's education flies off the high end of the freedom ruler.

I have to interject that I'm not talking about superficial, trivial knowledge as an education. I played the school game well, impressed those who needed to be, got very good grades, and always exceeded what were others' educational goals for me. I could beat my son in a game of *Jeopardy* any day. I'm saying he got much, much more of what education for a democratic society should be: To know one's self and trust one's own judgment, to uncover the courage within and stretch, unfettered, toward increased independence, to remain joyful in the never-ending journey of learning.

But without freedom to explore, experiment, and experience outright failure without humiliation, how can we know ourselves and trust our judgment? If those who pass the laws that would control our education don't recognize we need excavation tools, like time, space, and opportunity, how can we dig courage — or anything else — out from within? Unless, like a seed containing the promise of life, we are free to unfold in accordance with an internal schedule only we understand, how can we remain joyful in the never-ending journey of learning? Certainly the answer is not legislation, particularly legislation cloaked in volunteerism to get around the basic fact that the Constitution didn't turn control of the schools over to the federal government.

As a homeschooling mom, outlining educational goals was a simple act: Self-knowledge and trust; the ability to move, unencumbered, toward independence; and preservation of the inner drive to learn. With only these in mind and heart, we proceeded through life. All those little pieces that schools worry so much about are trivial in relation to reaching these goals, and the reading, writing, and arithmetic simply fall into place along the life journey, albeit not always at the time a national goals panel would deem appropriate. (When you think about it, what good are memorized times tables if an eight-year-old has no place besides a test paper on which to apply them? There are so many things out there in the world that *do* matter to an eight-year-old! It's a wonderful age at which to learn about dinosaurs, produce plays about the Middle Ages, find out how to make slime, start a bug collection, and read *Tom Sawyer*.) I don't see *anything* about what matters to children of any age in the Goals 2000: Educate America Act. I see only what matters to people so grounded in the institution of school that they've lost sight of true education, to folks so focused on those little pieces that they can't see the forest for the trees.

In *The Death of Common Sense: How Law Is Suffocating America*, Philip K. Howard sums up the consequences of relying on legislation to solve problems: "Rigidity of legal dictates precludes the exercise of judgment at the time and place of the activity" (Howard 1994, 21). Homeschooling works for us, as for thousands of others, because our decision to shoulder responsibility for our children's education gives us the freedom those oppressed by regulations don't have. We *can* make judgments about education "at the time and place of the activity." Math book not working? Get another one! Child tired because Dad's in the hospital? Spend the afternoon — with Dad — reading *Treasure Island*. It's a beautiful spring day? Take that long trip to the Revolutionary War fort. Child fascinated after seeing an impressive coin collection? Take a week — a whole month — and study the history of coins individually and collectively.

Freedom's benefits include space for flexibility and creativity, making the job of educating children a whole lot easier for me than for public school teachers like New York's Joyce Mendelsohn. She considers filling out paperwork the most difficult part of her job. "One of the forms is a detailed lesson plan in which teachers must lay out in advance what they're going to teach that day. Ms. Mendelsohn believes it is clearly counterproductive… but she also knows nobody looks at it. She knows because she frequently filled in the boxes with words like *Mickey Mouse*" (Howard 1994, 71). Enough said.

Let's move beyond the fact that increased federal regulation of education squelches the freedom necessary to apply informed judgment "at the time and place of the activity." Let's turn our attention to *whom* Goals 2000 presents the primary responsibility for education. As just one example, take Section 504 of Title V — National Skill Standards Board, the portion of Goals 2000 with an eye toward the nation's future work force. Here the procedures are set forth for identification of "broad clusters of major occupations that involve one or more than one industry in the United States and that share characteristics that are appropriate for the development of common skill standards." The clusters won't be set up until the Board engages in "extensive public consultation." It really sounds as if everyone will have a chance to contribute until you read that public comment will be solicited "through publication in the Federal Register." (Is this the most efficient way to gain parental input? The answer is obvious. As sad a commentary as it is, an ad in *Playboy* would reach a broader cross section of Americans.)

In the cover letter President Bill Clinton sent to Congress along with Goals 2000, he makes it very clear who he thinks should shoulder educational responsibility. He claims Goals 2000 provides "the basis for a new partnership between the Federal Government, States, parents, business, labor, schools, communities, and students." Since schools have been working to meet *their* needs, government, business, and labor are already dictatorial "partners" in education. A *new and improved* partnership would eliminate government, business, and labor and consist only of parents, schools, communities and students. Parents with justifiable concerns, teachers with knowledge of the front lines, and students capable of expressing their needs and desires could be assured of having a voice and making a difference at this level. Here are the only arms in which responsibility for education should rest. It's the only level at which individuals, not institutions, can repair families enough to once again provide the building blocks of aware, safe, and responsive communities (Dobson 1995, 148–149).

Of course, a true picture of public education and Goals 2000 wouldn't be complete without addressing that vital element, money. Neither government nor the general public exercise much judgment here, in large part, according to Myron Lieberman, because "taxpayers do not have the vaguest idea of how much they are paying from their own funds for public education. Inevitably, the thinking is that 'the government pays' — and for 'free public education' at that!" (Lieberman 1993, 95). I've seen reports estimating we spend as much as $1 billion a day on public education. According to some estimates, Lieberman claims, 85% of the costs of public schools are spent for salaries and fringe benefits of school district personnel. It's only fair that I share what my family's educational goals cost us. It's impossible to keep exact track because the cost does include lots of gas and wear and tear on the car with frequent excursions to the library, volunteer jobs, and field trips. Grandma and Grandpa contribute a lot, too, in the form of useful Christmas and birthday gifts. Beyond these, I'd estimate costs between $300-$500 yearly — for three kids. Flexibility and creativity work just as well for budgets as they do for daily lessons.

Our relatively minimum investment reaps great returns. Our 11-year-old son is well on his way to achieving our educational goals, benefiting as he has from the trust and flexibility that have increased in him *and* his parents over the years. But since there's no standardized test to measure these goals, let's look at the quantifiable incidentals, the "little pieces" of his real-life education. Results of his fifth grade Stanford Achievement Test just arrived. In the total reading, listening, and mathematics scores (these being the only sections administered by our local school district), he averaged in the 94th percentile with grade equivalents in reading comprehension, listening comprehension, concepts of numbers, and math applications reported at a post-high school level. Since he didn't take the science portion of the Stanford, he took a practice GED science test, instead. (He thinks tests are a lot of fun.) This he passed comfortably.

Our greatest concern in homeschooling today is not grades, goals, laws, money, or squabbles as to where the blame for illiteracy, violence, and drugs should lie. Our greatest concern looms in the background like approaching storm clouds that could ruin everything we've built. Our greatest concern is losing the freedom to continue what we're doing because the United States Congress felt compelled to further control education in an effort to correct the illiteracy, violence, and drug problems, to further "protect" the children enveloped by families and communities tossing about in an economic climate that requires all their time, energy, and attention.

"This and no other is the root from which a tyrant springs; when he first appears, he is a protector," Plato told folks a long time ago. Goals 2000 is a most tyrannical act against our children. Yesterday our forefathers ignored Thomas Jefferson's warning that "It is better to tolerate the rare instance of a parent refusing to let his child be educated than to shock the common feelings and ideas by forcible asportation and education of the infant against the will of the father" (Rothbard 1972, 42). Today we are ignoring Goals 2000's not-so-subtle attempt to replace compulsory attendance with compulsory education, effectively eradicating whatever educational freedom remains in public schools.

Politicians haven't yet seen that the act of training young minds in institutional thinking creates the very problems they expect Goals 2000 to solve. There is no excuse for educators or parents, though. You need only apply minimal common sense to realize that institutionalization, particularly at increasingly younger and younger ages, weighs heavily on young spirits curious and eager about their environment (Dobson 1995, 149). Today, in politically correct circles, we call this weight psychological illness, apparent in a frighteningly huge number of people seeking counseling and/or taking drugs for the symptoms. Yesterday, our forefathers called it oppression. Whatever we call it, oppression or psychological illness, we're crushing an awful lot of spirits in the name of — what? Reading? Writing? Arithmetic? With the weight of Goals 2000, we are setting up an entire generation for revolution, based not on an enlightened plan for democratic reform, but on hopelessness, anger, and despair.

Goals 2000 is too great a leap toward compulsory education and its side effects and away from basic principles in the care and nurturing of young children. And, to borrow Mr. Jefferson's words again, "A departure from principle in one instance becomes a precedent for a second, that second for a third, and so on, until the bulk of society is reduced to mere automatons of misery, to have no sensibilities left but for sinning and suffering." Sure sounds like today's news reports to me.

At the risk of sounding too simplistic, I'd like to suggest that we daily live with a model that could, according to words in the Goals 2000: Educate America Act, "fundamentally [change] the entire system of public education through comprehensive, coherent, and coordinated improvement in order to increase student learning." The first step toward achieving this positive change is the hardest of all: We must sweep our egos out of the way. When we began home education, we followed the only path we knew — your basic "school at home" approach. Like many other home educators describing their experiences, this led rapidly to a sort of burnout, a "why am I doing this?" conclusion. I went into a funk, eventually neglecting to keep records, study the latest resource catalogs, read the myriad teachers' magazines, or plan the next day's activities.

No one was more surprised than I to see the kids effortlessly pick up the slack. They just did what naturally came to them. I observed. Late evening reviews of the days' events revealed a broad array of accomplishments and subjects visited. I was dispensable! Of course, my ego was bruised. But I quickly got over it watching three hungry, young minds take their fill and happily approach the buffet table again and again. The funk disappeared and, instead of returning as "teacher," I joyfully extended my role as parent to educational guide. Linda, teacher and task master, turned into Linda, provider of materials and direction. Education thrived when I got out of the way. Nature took over.

This is probably why the goals of Goals 2000 strike me as assuming, pompous, and, yes, an utter waste of paper, time, and money in addition to being destructive. We give ourselves too much credit when we assume kids need to be reigned in and showered with our superior intelligence and its resulting methods. When our egos take up less space on center stage, there's a lot more room for our kids' spirits to stretch and dance in the light, creating an education that glows with personal significance. Isn't this what Samuel Adams was talking about in 1772 when he said, "The natural liberty of man is to be free from any superior power on Earth, and not to be under the will or legislative authority of man, but only to have the law of nature for his rule"?

Goals 2000 is like rearranging the deck chairs while the mighty ship rapidly slips beneath the waves of an increasingly complex world. But can the educational approach, so successful in individual homes, be duplicated on a larger scale? Yes. If we really want to "fundamentally change the entire system of public education through comprehensive, coherent, and coordinated improvement…," we can take the next step, which requires rewriting some widely held yet false definitions, among them those three little words, *free public education.*

Instead of viewing education as something we do to and/or for our youth, always with an eye on the nation's economic future instead of the children's educational present, we can return to its original meaning, "to bring out that which is within." When this definition guides us, our educational methods will change, for it's a lot easier to "get out of the way" when hubris doesn't enter the picture in the first place. We can't control that which is within individuals, we can only nurture it. An interesting side benefit of this approach is that what we typically term "moral behavior" emerges as part of the "flowering" of the individual, rendering goal seven of Goals 2000 — safe, disciplined, and alcohol- and drug-free schools — not only self-evident but unnecessary to legislate.

On to the term "free." Only one change necessary here; take the compulsion out of school attendance. How can our children possibly find independence and decision making comfortable or worthwhile if, from the age of five and, many times, younger, they are herded by legal and cultural *force* to endure conditions that, at least at the younger ages, go against their very natures, abilities, and capacities? It is human nature to resist that which restricts our liberty, and compulsory school attendance is no exception. Take away compulsion, and the first three of Goals 2000's goals take care of themselves. Of course kids will start school ready to learn. They won't walk through the door until they *are* ready. Of course kids will complete school. We tend to finish that which we *want* to do. Students will achieve, in part because of our new definition of education, and in part because those who guide their own journey choose the means by which they travel and recognize their vested interest in its outcome.

Last, we look at the word "public," which carries with it our current notion of public school as America's great equalizer, the opportunity for all to have a crack at the American Dream, usually expressed in increased ability to purchase things. *The American Heritage Dictionary of the English Language,* though, gives five definitions for public, all of which hold potential for a broader perspective on the term and lead us to a different use of our one billion dollars per day:

- Of, concerning, or affecting the community or the people

- Maintained for or used by the people or community

- Participated in or attended by the people or community

- Connected with or acting on behalf of the people, community, or government, rather than private matters or interests

- Open to the knowledge or judgment of all.

Why are "public" schools forced on everyone ages five to eighteen and denied to everyone else? If we truly understand the importance of education, if we truly want an educated populace, if we truly want kids (and adults) to appreciate the joys and benefits of education, what we now call public schools should in fact be community learning centers, open to everyone who wants to partake of knowledge — or share it. This concept is, in fact, growing rapidly around the country, particularly in homeschooling circles where loose-knit communities pool talent, energy, and time for the good of all.

In an effort to expand the idea beyond homeschooling boundaries, let's place a fictional character in both public school and learning center environments. As things exist today, a young man who sees no relevance between school and real life drops out. (While dropouts are still disproportionately black and poor, the rate among the middle and upper class is escalating, so for our scenario it doesn't matter if he lives in a ghetto or a wealthy suburb, if his skin is black, white, or purple, or if his daddy sits on a judge's bench or in a prison cell.) Let's say this fellow turns 24 and realizes he's made a big mistake. He may not be Einstein, but he can figure out that a service job paying $6 an hour (approximately $960 per month *before* taxes) isn't going to buy him a decent home, decent food, or decent transportation.

We've set up the educational system so he can't go back to high school. It's impractical and embarrassing. We tell him to get his GED, yet he knows as well as we do that this piece of paper all too often labels its bearer "loser." At $6 an hour, he can't save enough money to pay the ever-escalating tuition of even a small community college and continue to eat. Those drugs on the corner look like a better way. They look like the only way. The young man can't resist. With his newfound financial rewards, his first purchase is a gun to protect his commodity. Within months, we add $30,000 a year to our tax burden so his mind and spirit can rot in prison. It is here he gets the education that will last him a lifetime.

Now let's put the same young man in a society that practices truly free, truly public education. Let's assume that even though compulsion was removed, he still thought he was too cool to attend classes. The same realization that he's made a mistake hits him, but this time he knows he can walk into the learning center because his 35-year-old neighbor and 65-year-old aunt are doing it. No questions asked, just sign up for what you want.

He decides to take the reading course, not only because he needs it but because his 12-year-old cousin is in the class and can help him get through it. While at the center, he finds the notices on the learning exchange bulletin board. The co-op garden at the edge of the city needs a strong back in exchange for some fresh vegetables at summer's end. He decides to make the longest-term investment of his life.

He checks the apprenticeship board, too, and among the many requests is one for a sorter at a recycling center where he can also observe its day-to-day management and administration. It's only one day a week, so he can fit it in alongside his $6 an hour job and his evening class. The recycling center welcomes him. Pretty soon he's supervising a couple of new volunteers and filling out daily reports. The learning center's course on business administration looks more and more conquerable, particularly now that his reading skills are improving. Within months of his arrival, the recycling center becomes self-sustaining. Since the county doesn't have to handle the recyclables anymore, we deduct $30,000 a year from its tax budget. It is here our young man is getting the education that will last him a lifetime. Optimistic? Yes. Doable? Definitely. Already, concerned parents are gathering the necessary resources, financial and human, and making it work. Private schools and public libraries find the concept of learning center is merely an extension of the businesses they're already in.

With learning centers, we knock out the need for goals 4 through 6 and 8 of Goals 2000. We will likely redefine the role of teacher and (dare I say it?) welcome the accumulated knowledge of all sorts of "experts," including retirees who would relish the opportunity to share what they know and perhaps even stay healthier due to their involvement in such a stimulating environment. And we will always need education guides, men and women dedicated to introducing people young and old to new concepts, new ideas, new horizons. Learning centers could easily fulfill the role of providing "access to programs for the continued improvement of [teachers'] professional skills and the opportunity to acquire the knowledge and skills needed to instruct and prepare all American students for the next century," as outlined in goal four. Computer systems could easily link learning centers together so they may share the opportunities available for both leading and taking classes that may exist in neighboring cities and towns.

Now, imagine real mathematicians and scientists leading us to goal five! Children whose curiosity and imaginations haven't been dried up by dull textbooks fly to these subjects like moths to flame. Give them the materials and time to investigate, manipulate, and play (yes, play!) with numbers and scientific concepts, and the discovery of patterns and connectedness inherent in both subjects will carry them to higher and higher levels of understanding — and interest.

The ability of learning centers to reach goal six, adult literacy and lifelong learning, should be apparent from our fictional story. Truly public education will remove the stigma of illiteracy and previous failures and provide the tools necessary to correct our own mistakes. The public will then be able to intelligently figure out if and how they want to use their new-found skills to "compete in a global economy."

We've reached goal eight, parental participation. The ultimate parental participation is mom and dad standing alongside daughter as they discover the wonders of the universe together in the learning center's class on astronomy. Or join a book discussion group together. Or start a stamp collection together. Or... well, you get the idea. Freedom is the foundation on which true parental participation can stand.

Our national education budget already contains enough greenbacks to get things rolling quickly. Using our $1 billion a day estimate, we can divvy that up between 365,000 learning centers operating on a $1 million per year budget. That works out to about one learning center for every 685 American men, women, and children. This may sound like chump change compared to modern school budgets, but $1 million goes a long way where administration stays minimal, volunteers contribute, and materials are shared via the interlibrary loan systems.

A cozier atmosphere could be created if we set our sights on 730,000 centers spending $500,000 each year. With a more definitive community aura at this level, local businesses would find it in their best interest to donate human and financial resources and offer apprenticeships to area residents. As things stand now, according to a 1990 survey of 200 major U.S. corporations, 22% teach reading, 41% teach writing, and 31% teach computation to their employees (Lieberman 1993, 123). An equivalent contribution to the neighborhood learning center wouldn't cost an additional dime, and would create an honest-to-goodness, win-win situation for all involved.

Believe it or not, families don't need schools or government to act as intermediary between parents and children *if* families are free to "respond to the varying needs of parents and the home" by themselves. With recognition of "varying needs" should come the common sense recognition that there are varying ways in which to fill them. Indeed, homeschoolers have discovered that the ways are as diverse as each family. Only freedom to interject individual judgment can ensure the method and means satisfy unique situations. Legislation like Goals 2000 gets in the way, a dangerous obstacle to the liberty necessary to create the happiness and health we all want for our children.

It all boils down to whether those who support the status quo *really* want, as they say they do, to "fundamentally change the entire system of public education." With Goals 2000 acting as the cement that tightens up the existing system, these words ring hollow in this free mom's ears.

"Were we directed from Washington when to sow, and when to reap," said Thomas Jefferson in 1821, "we should soon want bread."

Our children are starving.

References

Dobson, L. (1995). *The Art of Education: Reclaiming Your Family, Community and Self.* Tonasket, WA: Home Education Press.

Howard, P. K. (1994). *The Death of Common Sense: How Law is Suffocating America.* New York: Random House.

Lieberman, M. (1993). *Public Education: An Autopsy.* Cambridge: Harvard University Press.

Rothbard, M. N. (1972). *Education, Free and Compulsory.* Wichita: Center for Independent Education.

"While Emerson is telling us to trust each unique child to find his or her own best ways to grow — 'It is not for you to choose what he shall know, what he shall do' — politicians and business people are saying that it is possible to externally shape all children to fit a common mold — to fit the needs of the state. Emerson is telling us that people are in charge of their own minds and wills. In 39 simple words, Emerson is reminding all people everywhere of human dignity, freedom, and the right of self-determination."

— *Lynn Stoddard*

The Secret of Education

Lynn Stoddard

"The secret of education lies in respecting the pupil." These words by Ralph Waldo Emerson, from his essay "Education," seized my mind and wouldn't let go. As a teacher and administrator of nearly 40 years in public education, I had long been searching to find the meaning of education. When I came upon Emerson's words I was excited by the possibility that I was about to discover what I had long been seeking.

Respect the pupil? What could be more logical and fundamental? But, hold on a minute, I thought. If it is that simple, it can't be true. I had been taught, and had come to believe, that education is a very complex process. Philosophers, educators, psychologists, and other scholars have been trying, for many years, to unravel the mysteries of education. Yet, there I was, reading words that seemed to glow and stand out from the page to command my attention. The secret was about to be revealed! Emerson went on to tell what he meant by respect: *"It is not for you to choose what he shall know, what he shall do. It is chosen and foreordained, and he only holds the key to his own secret"* (Emerson 1965, 430).

Now, more than four years since I first encountered Emerson's secret of education, I am still enthralled by the words. I continue to mull them over in my mind, trying to understand them, and wonder why those who control public education spend a great amount of time trying to decide what students should *know and be able to do* ... and then work very hard to hold teachers accountable for making sure students know and are able to do what has been predetermined. Why do we have a system of public education that goes against Emerson's admonition?

In this essay I will try to show why American public education has yet to discover Emerson's secret and then I will give a preview of what could happen if we were to respect the pupil as he suggested. I will discuss reasons why we have a system of education that is disrespectful of students and tell why I believe it is imperative that we develop a system based on respect.

Bureaucratic Systems of Education

It is the nature of government-managed systems of education for elected noneducators, mostly lawyers and business people, to determine what students should know and be able to do and expect teachers to impose it on students. This is the basis of compulsory education as reflected in compulsory attendance laws and externally imposed learning. Unfortunately, the harder we try, and the more sophisticated we become in applying pressure, the more rebellion emerges in the form of dropouts, crime, drugs, teenage pregnancies and suicides.

In a recent feature section of *Education Week*, the editors describe the mind-set of many politicians and business leaders:

> It all seemed so straightforward. Experts in the various disciplines would develop national standards for *what students should know and be able to do* at key points in their schooling; a federal council of distinguished citizens would review and certify the standards as worthy of emulation; states and school districts would voluntarily adopt them; teachers would teach them; and students would achieve them.... Content standards were to be the foundation on which educators would build excellence and equity in the nation's schools. (Editorial 1995; emphasis added)

Another author, Karen Diegmueller, writes, "The work of designing standards began with content standards. Essentially, these describe *what students should know and be able to do* in a given subject area by the time they complete the 4th, 8th, and 12th grades" (Diegmueller 1995; emphasis added).

In bureaucratic systems of education, *standards* and *standardization* have become the watchwords of the business. I have read the phrase "*what all students should know and be able to do"* many times. It is repeated over and over as curriculum designers make their plans. This mind-set has been increasing in intensity over many years: The way to improve education is to set high academic standards and impose curriculum on students from the top down and outside in.

It is inherent in the nature of bureaucratic systems of education for legislators and boards of education to impose their will on teachers, who, in turn, impose the curriculum on children. In this kind of a system, children serve the needs of teachers, who serve administrators, who serve the needs of elected officials, while parents watch from the sidelines. Students and teachers are held accountable with standardized achievement tests or with portfolios and other performance-based means. In a bureaucratic system, it is the duty of everyone to serve those who are above them in the hierarchy. Those at the top, those who control the money, dictate from a position of great power. Fortunately, or unfortunately, depending on which side you are on, it doesn't work the way it is supposed to work. The nagging, persistent enigma is that students, and many teachers, will not cooperate. They have minds of their own. Each child *"holds the key to his own secret."* Children stubbornly refuse to be molded and shaped in the politicians' image!

The idea of imposing uniformity on students may have come from the assembly-line factories of American industry where quality control was imposed by top management on the workers. Interestingly, Edwards Deming, at the end of World War II, tried to show American businessmen how to improve their products by erasing the hierarchy and showing respect to the workers in factories. He tried to show managers that the workers at the point of construction would have good ideas about how to improve their products. Deming was rejected in this country when he showed managers that they, themselves, were the main source of a company's problems (Holt 1993). He went to Japan, where the people embraced his philosophy, and went on to produce the best cars, electronics, and optics in the world.

It may not set well with managers in education to tell them that they are the main source of education's problems, but that is what I intend to show, hopefully in a kind way. I do not question the sincerity and dedication of elected representatives. They mean well. Unfortunately, they are following a pattern that has been set by generations of officeholders before them, a pattern that is set in concrete and from which it is very difficult to extricate themselves. The pattern is for politicians to dictate what all students will know and be able to do.

The problem is that it is impossible to do what educators are expected to do — make students all alike. Is it any wonder that students rebel or do not cooperate when they are treated with such disrespect? Why is it so important that all students know and be able to do the same things? Does our economy thrive on uniformity? Teachers are demoralized when they are expected to do impossible things, especially when they know that those who are running the system may know very little about teaching. What would happen if medical doctors, lawyers, mechanics, plumbers, and electricians were compelled by outsiders to do things that were impossible? Actually teachers and students are so used to being treated disrespectfully that they do not even know it is happening — it's tradition! Even those who are being disrespectful are not aware of being impolite. It's been going on too long.

In reality we must place the blame where it lies, with all of us, in society as a whole. The root of the problem may lie within our culture's materialistic focus. We have generations of people that have been raised to place a higher value on having material possessions than on the development of human potential. We are more concerned with *having* than *being*. As a result of this attitude, our schools are, by and large, dedicated to making students become productive contributors to the economy. To do this, it is necessary that each student acquires a certain set of skills and body of knowledge. Hence we are constantly trying to develop curriculum and find better and better ways to inject it into the minds and muscles of young people so they can become good producers and consumers of material things.

Here, I would like to use an illustration that I hope will not offend those who belong to one of my favorite professional organizations, the Association for Supervision and Curriculum Development (ASCD). This organization is one of the oldest and most respected organizations in education and has contributed a great service to educators all over the world, myself included, yet its title illustrates the cultural mind-set that grips people everywhere. Think about it: ASCD is an association for super-vision and *curriculum* development. The title implies that ASCD is an organization of people who have the intelligence — the "super-vision" — to construct curriculum, what students should know and be able to do. According to its name, ASCD is not an association for *human development*. It is an association for *curriculum development*.

Curriculum is the main tool used by elected officials to impose their will on those who are below them in the educational hierarchy. Curriculum is enforced with standardized achievement testing, letter-grade report cards, common high school graduation requirements, and grade-point averages. Curriculum forces students to serve the needs of teachers who serve administrators, who, in turn, serve the needs of the bureaucracy. Ironically, in this arrangement, there are very few, except perhaps maverick teachers, who serve the needs of students. We are only fooling ourselves if we think the needs of students are the same as the needs politicians have for them. Each child has a unique set of needs — to grow according to his/her own pattern and develop intelligences, gifts, and talents that are unlike that of any other person.

If we were to adopt the philosophy of Ralph Waldo Emerson, the hierarchy would be reversed. Students would be at the top of the hierarchy with everyone below serving them. Teachers and parents would unite to serve the needs of individual children, administrators would serve the needs of teachers, and elected officials would serve those who put them in office. What a radical idea!

The philosophy of Emerson and that of those who control education in this country are diametrically opposed to each other. While Emerson is telling us to trust each unique child to find his or her own best ways to grow — "*It is not for you to choose what he shall know, what he shall do*" — politicians and business people are saying that it is possible to externally shape all children to fit a common mold — to fit the needs of the state. Emerson is telling us that people are in charge of their own minds and wills. In 39 simple words, Emerson is reminding all people everywhere of human dignity, freedom, and the right of self-determination. He is telling us that no person has the right to decide for another what s/he will know and do. In sharp contrast, bureaucrats are telling teachers to see that every child learns a predetermined body of knowledge and is able to perform a basic set of skills, whether s/he wants to or not — or can in the time allowed.

When the needs of the state are conveyed as curriculum, our society tends to view curriculum in the wrong way — as a goal in and of itself rather than a means of *reaching* goals. My experience with teachers and parents shows that they do not know and cannot verbalize goals of education. When I ask parents or teachers in a group to name their school, district, or state goals of education, I am usually greeted with blank stares. If someone does respond, it's to name a subject of the curriculum, such as reading, writing, or arithmetic as a goal.

A Respectful System: Education for Diversity

The original, Latin meaning of educate (*educere*) is to lead or draw forth. If each child holds the key to his own secret, as Emerson suggests, we must abandon the top-down, outside-in approach in favor of helping children uncover and refine the precious ore that lies buried inside. I believe Emerson is telling us to develop a system of education that honors and nurtures diversity. Such a system would be, in most ways, just the opposite of what we have now. Instead of telling children what they must know and be able to do, we would be in the business of developing human potential. We would nurture the development and productive use of each child's unique talents and gifts.

Above all, we must stop worshipping curriculum. Setting higher standards and describing what all students should know and be able to do is not the way to improve education. Indeed, to continue on this path is the sure way to destroy our society. The more we try to standardize children, the more we encourage violence, crime, drugs, and other problems. When we try to stuff children into a common mold, we destroy feelings of self-worth on a grand scale. This leads to large numbers of students who drop out of the system and choose to become burdens to society. It is the highest form of disrespect to expect all children to know and be able to do the same things.

Does this mean that subject matter content is not important? Certainly not. If we decide to nurture diversity, subject matter content will be more important than ever, although in a very different way. Content will be viewed as means instead of goal — a means of nurturing unique talents and gifts. Here it helps to make a distinction between *school*-based subject areas (curriculum) and disciplines of knowledge. School-based subject areas, such as math, history, geography, and chemistry, are institutionally based representations of disciplines of knowledge. They represent a selection, often by someone who does not work within the field, of what that person believes should be known about the particular discipline. These representations usually portray a small slice of a discipline of knowledge. On the other hand, a discipline of knowledge includes everything that is known about a field of knowledge, often merging into other fields (Beane 1995). A discipline of knowledge is fluid and constantly growing — in contrast to curriculum, which is fixed and decaying from the moment of creation.

When we understand the difference between curriculum (what someone decides students should know and be able to do — a static, stagnant thing) and disciplines of knowledge, it is easier to use content in the right way — as a means of reaching higher goals. The goals we want are human development goals, not curriculum development ones. This requires access to vast reservoirs of knowledge that are everlastingly overflowing their banks to mix with other reservoirs. That is why curriculum developers are always a step behind and students are disinterested — because they know the subject at hand is old stuff.

It is easier for me to illustrate these higher, human development goals and their relationship to content if I describe my experience at two elementary schools where I served as principal. We arrived at human development goals through a process that changed the way we, henceforth, were to perceive and use content.

One year, in a preschool workshop, the teachers decided to meet with each child's parent(s), one-on-one, to get acquainted and build partnerships for the school year. In preparation for these meetings, the parents were asked to come prepared to answer three questions about each child:

1. What would you like the school to help you accomplish for your child this year?

2. What are this child's special interests, needs, talents, and gifts that we should keep in mind?

3. How can we work together?

The use of these questions in meetings with parents marked the beginning of a student-centered approach to education. For us it was the beginning of a student needs-driven system as opposed to the traditional curriculum-driven system that we had been in the habit of using. To help parents answer the first question, we developed a list of goals for parents to prioritize and tell where the responsibility for accomplishing each goal should lie. The form is shown on the following page.

Through the one-on-one meetings with each child's parent(s) and the use of the three questions, we examined the purpose of education *for each individual child*. This is a critical difference that I want to emphasize. You can plan curriculum for groups, but this is a process that doesn't work — it is essential for us to see that we can only design education around the needs of individuals (Stoddard 1992, 1995).

When we compiled the results of the surveys, we were surprised to learn that subject matter content was not the top priority of parents for the education of their children. The top three priorities of the parents at Hill Field School, and at several other schools where we later went through the same process, were:

1. Self-esteem and student individuality (individual talents, interests, skills, and abilities).

2. The student values learning and work.

3. Respect for others and communication.

In addition to our surprise that subject matter content was not the top priority of parents was the finding that parents felt these priorities could best be accomplished by the school and home working together.

Over a period of several years of going through this same process with several schools and groups of parents, we concluded that the ultimate purpose of education is to *develop great human beings who are valuable contributors to society*. The three top priorities of parents in each school community were always the same. These priorities eventually evolved into

Parents Priorities

for the education of _____

for the _____ school year

Responsibility, Where?
(check appropriate column)

(Complete left column first)
Priority 1, 2, 3, etc.
(most important to least important)

	All home	Mostly home, partly school	Mostly school, partly home	All school	Best done by school & home, working together
The Student Values Learning — Is curious, accepts challenges, becomes absorbed, enjoys learning.					
The Student Values Work — Takes initiative, is self-motivated, follows directions, plans and organizes, assumes responsibility, follows through, evaluates work.					
Self-Esteem — Is aware of strengths and weaknesses, feels valuable and unique, feels comfortable when alone as well as in a group, trusts with discretion.					
Respects Environment — Respects and maintains personal and public property, enjoys and protects nature.					
Respects Others — Respects the rights, feelings, attitudes, cultures, and occupations of others: works cooperatively and enjoys other people.					
Reading — Enjoys reading, is acquiring new skills.					
Written Communication — Is acquiring new writing and spelling skills, enjoys creative writing.					
Oral Communication — Listens and understands, can follow directions, enjoys and participates in group discussions.					
Mathematics — Enjoys mathematics; is acquiring new skills and concepts and is able to apply them.					
Physical Health and Development — Eats, sleeps, and dresses properly, practices personal hygiene, is developing new physical skills and strength.					
Appreciation of the Arts — Enjoys literature, music, visual and performing art.					
Student Individuality — The student is developing individual talents, interests, skills, and abilities.					
Responsible Citizenship — The student is developing appreciation for and understanding of the workings of a democracy.					
Other (describe):					

_____

_____

From *Redesigning Education: A Guide for Developing Human Greatness* © 1992 Zephyr Press, Tucson, AZ. Reprinted with permission.

human development goals that became the three dimensions of human greatness:

- Identity: Individual talents and gifts, confidence, self-esteem, fitness.

- Inquiry: Curiosity, hunger for knowledge, and personal inquiry.

- Interaction: Communication, cooperation, kindness, love, and respect.

These goals are human development goals. They do not rely on curriculum development for their attainment. The three I's allowed the teachers to begin declaring their independence from curriculum. We found that this was a monumental step in the process. It takes great courage to declare oneself free from well-intentioned legislators and school board members who are prescribing what all children must know and do. However it was a necessary step that was made possible by parents who enjoyed their new role as full, equal partners with teachers in helping their children grow in greatness. The support was so strong that the schools were able to begin breaking the shackles of a lockstep curriculum for every child and begin to rely more on disciplines of knowledge instead of curriculum to meet the needs of individuals. In other words, the teachers and parents began to divorce themselves from a total reliance on textbooks, workbooks, ditto sheets, and the like and started to use the materials that are found in libraries.

Curriculum Versus Disciplines of Knowledge

The distinction between curriculum and disciplines of knowledge is most easily understood when we consider the location of the printed materials. Curriculum is most generally found in things like textbooks, workbooks, and basic readers, while disciplines of knowledge are usually found in libraries in the form of newspapers, magazines, recordings, diskettes, and a great variety of books on many subjects. One exciting thing for me, in working with the two sets of parents and teachers, was the reduction of the use of worksheets that were run off on the school copy machine — before the invention of modern duplicators we used to call it the "purple plague."

With the change of philosophy came a radical change in the use of the school library. As a repository of disciplines of knowledge, the library became, literally, the heart of the school, and was always full of students doing research on many topics — following their own interests. The difference between students doing assigned research and those doing personal inquiry was also very striking. On the one hand, a half-hearted effort, and on the other, an eager, zestful, joyful searching.

With this change came a need for the library to obtain more resource materials. As a result, I was able to shift some of the budget for textbooks to the library to buy a variety of hands-on materials. We even developed a "realia" center where students could check out microscopes, binoculars, and objects to examine and investigate. I started to dream of what school media centers would be like if all the money that is wasted on textbooks could be spent on library materials.

As I look back on what happened, I believe we were in the process of discovering Emerson's secret of education. The first goal, identity, reflected Emerson's wisdom that each child holds the key to his own secret. Gardner's theory of multiple intelligences supports Emerson's view that each child is unique and holds a mental image of self that is unlike any other. Each child has a special niche to fill in society and can make a contribution with a set of talents and gifts that is different from that of any other person. The second goal, inquiry, supports the first and reflects Emerson's admonition that *"it is not for you to choose what he shall know, what he shall do, it is chosen and foreordained."* To me this means that *every person is in charge of his/her own mind* and learns through personal inquiry. This condition is supported by the latest research on how the human brain works (Caine, Caine, and Crowell 1994). No one can decide for another what that person will know or do because learning is a voluntary process. Each person decides for him/herself what information will be processed and how it connects with the information that is already in mental storage — a condition that is different for every person, due to the fact that no two people have had exactly the same set of experiences.

The third goal, interaction, as we defined it, adds the final and moral dimension to greatness. It is the dimension through which people make a contribution to society through service and activation of one's unique talents and gifts.

With these human development goals, the teachers and parents at Hill Field and Whitesides Elementary Schools were able to do some things that had never been done before. First and, I believe, most important of all, is that these goals allowed parents and teachers to unite as full, equal partners and develop a relationship that is not possible when curriculum is the main focus. Because the three dimensions of human greatness are the responsibility of both the school and the home, teachers and parents each did what they do best to help youngsters grow in greatness.

The second important result of having human development goals is that content, the disciplines of knowledge, could be put in proper perspective, as a means of reaching goals — as a servant instead of master. To develop the first and second goals, identity and inquiry, required us to accept the notion that subject matter content should be different for each student. This allowed students to use unique intelligences to follow their interests and "learn with the brakes off" (Hart 1983). This is in contrast to curriculum-driven education that limits learning to a fixed body of knowledge and requires students to learn through only the modalities officially sanctioned by the state: linguistic, logical-mathematical.

Another important result of education for greatness — of having human development goals instead of curriculum goals — was that students acquired much more than facts or inert knowledge. Students were able to learn much more content than before but in a way that became permanently useful; they developed understanding and wisdom. In contrast to traditional education, where students learn for the purpose of passing tests and forget the material as soon as the test is over, the students at Whitesides and Hill Field processed information for the purpose of integrating it into their lives.

The third outcome of the human greatness approach was focus. Inasmuch as it was comparatively easy to keep the three I's constantly in the minds of parents, teachers, and students, there was a flurry of creative invention of strategies for accomplishing the goals. The Great Brain Project was created for nurturing all three dimensions of greatness, the Shining

Stars Talent Development Project for developing unique gifts and talents (Identity), and the School Post Office for encouraging interaction; and these are just a few of the many other content-independent strategies that were developed.

The Great Brain Project was an especially exciting strategy for nurturing human greatness. Each student was invited to select a topic and study it in depth to become a "great brain" — a "specialist," "expert," "mastermind," or "genius," depending on how far each student wanted to pursue his or her chosen topic before going on to another one. It became the opportunity of parents to become full partners with the school to help their children become "great brains" in self-selected topics.

At the conclusion of each child's study of a topic, s/he prepared a special great brain presentation to share what was learned and answer questions posed by an audience composed of invited relatives, friends, and classmates. It was common for children to use their own artwork, music, and other visual/auditory aids to demonstrate their knowledge to proud parents and others in the audience. We felt it was just as valid for a child to share a great variety of knowledge accomplishments as it is for a child to share musical accomplishment in a musical recital. When recognition for accomplishment was given with "great brain" badges, certificates, and photos in the Great Brain Hall of Fame, it provided an important boost to a child's feelings of self-worth.

With each child's "great brain" presentation, it was easy to see that important, integrated learning had occurred. No one had to be shown a standardized achievement test to prove that the child had changed. Because of increased self-worth there was a dramatic decrease in discipline problems all over the school. The same thing happened when children became "shining stars" as they developed and performed a great variety of talents in class, grade-level, and whole-school talent shows. I am convinced that when students are given encouragement and help to follow their own interests and develop in their own ways, they learn much faster and better than when they are suffering under a state-imposed curriculum — when they must submit to a fixed and static body of knowledge that actually puts a lid on accomplishment. National standards are the final straw that would break the backs of many children and stunt their growth.

In summary, I would like to say that Emerson's secret involves working in harmony with human nature, not against it as we do with state-imposed learning. We found at Hill Field and Whitesides Schools that students have a built-in desire to learn and grow. The number-one need of all human beings is for identity. They want to count for something and become special contributors to society. They are intensely curious and want to acquire knowledge and wisdom. They have an inherent desire to communicate, cooperate, and have warm relationships with others. When we tell children what they should know and be able to do, as we do with government-imposed curriculum and standards, we often smother the very qualities that would make the acquisition of content possible — while at the same time alienating the human spirit.

On the other hand, when we respect children and their teachers, a door is opened for a transformation of education to occur. Even though the teachers, students, and parents at Whitesides and Hill Field were working within a bureaucratic system, they began a process for negating the crippling effects of curriculum-based education. The Utah core-curriculum had not yet been imposed on us. I am sure that we could not have accomplished what we did if we had been expected to teach the same curriculum to every child. It would have been even more constrictive under a federal government mandate such as the one proposed by recent governors and presidents. Instead of teachers, parents, and students suffering under the oppression of top-down coercion, there was much joy as parents, teachers, and students united in a creative, new educational endeavor. I believe we were on the threshold of discovering Emerson's secret of education and learning how to respect the pupil.

I believe Emerson was trying to tell us to honor and nurture human diversity — to respect each unique person. This vision is diametrically opposite to the notion of education for uniformity. True respect for individuals requires a fundamental change in the way schools are managed and do business.

References

Beane, J. A. (1995, January). Curriculum Integration and the Disciplines of Knowledge. *Phi Delta Kappan.*

Caine, G., R. N. Caine, and S. Crowell (1994). *MindShifts.* Tucson: Zephyr Press.

Diegmueller, K. (1995). Running Out of Steam. *Education Week* 14:29, April 12, 1995, Special Report, pp. 4–8.

Editorial (1995). Struggling for Standards. *Education Week* 14:29, April 12, 1995, Special Report, p. 3.

Emerson, R. W. (1965). *Selected Writings of Ralph Waldo Emerson.* Edited by William H. Gilman. New York: New American Library.

Hart, L. A. (1983). *Human Brain and Human Learning.* New York: Longman.

Holt, M. (1993, January). The Educational Consequences of W. Edwards Deming. *Phi Delta Kappan.*

Stoddard, L. (1992). *Redesigning Education: A Guide for Developing Human Greatness.* Tucson: Zephyr Press.

Stoddard, L. (1995). *Growing Greatness: Six Amazing Attitudes of Extraordinary Teachers and Parents.* Tucson: Zephyr Press.

"The art of holistic education involves responding authentically — that is, from wholeness and balance — to the children, to the subject matter, and to the social/cultural milieu of the living situation without having to follow a theory or method that rigidly dictates what one must or must not do, let alone a curriculum dictated by government bureaucrats. *This* is freedom in education."

— *Ron Miller*

A Holistic Philosophy of Educational Freedom

Ron Miller

The issue of freedom stands out as one of the central philosophical concerns of alternative, progressive, humanistic and holistic educators over the past 200 years. Indeed, it could be argued that the quest for freedom is the quintessential element of most dissident educational theories. This is certainly the case in the development of my own thinking about holistic education: I came to holism by way of Henry David Thoreau, Carl Rogers (1969) and libertarians such as Nathaniel Branden (1969) and Paul Goodman (1964), all of whom championed the individual's struggle toward wholeness against the constraints of an unfree society. I later found that virtually all dissident educators — from Rousseau and Pestalozzi to Montessori and Margaret Naumberg to A. S. Neill and John Holt — also strongly emphasized the importance of allowing each young person freedom to develop according to his or her own unique nature, a freedom denied by conventional schooling and other institutions of modern society.

This essay is a revised version of "Freedom in a Holistic Context" originally published in *Holistic Education Review* vol. 8, no. 3 (Fall 1995) and is reprinted by permission of Holistic Education Press.

A Conceptual Overview

Alternative educators' insistence on freedom represents a vitally important dissent from the tendencies of modern culture toward bureaucracy, standardization, and the reduction of the individual to an anonymous political and economic entity. The technocratic worldview embodied in the powerful corporate state poses a direct and serious threat to human values rooted in any organic or spiritual sense of meaning, wholeness, and connectedness to the natural world (Sloan 1994; Mander 1991; Rifkin 1991; Roszak 1973; Cajete 1994). For over two centuries, the lonely voices of various mystics, romantics, and transcendentalists have been warning that modern humanity must break free of this worldview or risk cultural and ecological destruction. Yet today, we see the corporate state extending its influence even further over the culture through political interference in education such as Goals 2000 and its program of national curriculum standards, universal testing and rigorous accountability. If we are to reclaim essential human values that are denied by a reductionist and technocratic culture, then clearly, the need for freedom in education is not only vital, but desperate.

Freedom, however, is a complex notion. It involves philosophical, political, moral, psychological, and spiritual dimensions that take the issue far beyond a simple dichotomy between the individual and the state; if we are not to fall into the same epistemological trap that produced our technocratic worldview in the first place, we will need a *holistic* understanding of freedom that takes these dimensions into account. Holism is an alternative, critical worldview that sees all phenomena, all existence, as intrinsically interrelated. Whether drawing from concepts being advanced in "new science" (e.g., David Bohm's "implicate order" and holographic models of the brain proposed by neuroscientists) or ancient teachings of the "perennial philosophy" (such as Buddhist cosmology), one of the major principles of holistic thinking is that all ideas, concepts, and phenomena are *contextual* (Clark 1988). That is, nothing is complete or absolute in itself, nothing has meaning in isolation, but requires a larger context in which it is related to other phenomena and ideas (R. Miller 1991, Fall). Consequently, even the notion of freedom is not complete or absolute as such but must be understood in its various dimensions or contexts.

A first step toward such an understanding would be to consider (as various philosophers have done) the difference between "freedom from" and "freedom for." Viewing the individual as an autonomous entity, many dissident educators and libertarian thinkers have sought to free the person *from* the stifling demands of schooling, society, and the state. Once disentangled from these demands, it is argued that the individual will flourish; the free individual will be psychologically healthy, creative, and economically productive and will sustain community life through voluntary social relationships. This position is the core assumption of libertarian thought, and it is reflected in the ideology of radical alternative schools such as Summerhill and the Sudbury Valley School. Daniel Greenberg, a founder of Sudbury Valley and its major spokesman, emphasizes this point. The school, he writes,

> is based on the notion that free individuals with a highly developed sense of themselves will be the best guarantors of a peaceful, cooperative society of people with a deep sense of mutual responsibility toward each other's welfare (Greenberg 1994, 63).

The cooperative community life that has evolved at Sudbury Valley and other alternative schools bears out this claim. People who are free from oppression and coercion do seem to engage naturally in cooperative endeavors, at least in intimate community settings that value such relationships.

However, I believe that from a holistic perspective, the notion of "freedom from," by itself, does not address the deeper sources of modern technocratic culture. Libertarians' emphasis on free individuals is unfortunately rooted in an atomistic epistemology bequeathed to the modern world by thinkers such as Thomas Hobbes, John Locke, and Adam Smith. This view defines persons as calculating materialists engaged in ongoing competition and negotiation with each other for economic goods (G. Smith 1992, 27–34), and as holistic education theorist John P. Miller demonstrates clearly, it is a worldview based upon an assumption of *separation*: of person from society, of people from each other, of humanity from the natural world, of the personal ego from the higher Self or spiritual essence (J. Miller 1988, 1993a). Despite his interest in cooperation, Greenberg states this atomistic epistemology explicitly:

> The very essence of the human condition is the apartness of each person, the individuality of each human being, his uniqueness, his inherent worth — that, above all, is what religions have meant by man created in the image of God (p. 59).

There are two very different claims being made here, and it is critical, from a holistic perspective, that we not confuse them. The recognition of each person's "inherent worth" is, indeed, an important aspect of alternative and holistic educational thought, but this notion does not require us to accept an atomistic epistemology stressing the essential "apartness" of human beings. A holistic epistemology, as I will describe shortly, points toward an essential, inherent *connectedness* between persons, and between person and world — a concept holism derives from the "perennial philosophy" or "primordial tradition" underlying most religious understandings of the world (H. Smith 1989). This tradition strongly calls upon the individual to cultivate a compassionate identification with Creation; from such a perspective, it is quite off the mark to equate the "image of God" with the individualistic striving for self-preservation that is celebrated by modernist epistemology in an image of human nature aptly called "economic man." Greenberg himself shows where an assumption of separateness leads:

> The world hits us with a primeval chaos of great masses of information, and we must somehow do something with it in order to be able to survive, by dealing with the world in a way that will make it fulfill our needs (p. 81).

To deal with "chaos" — that is, the absence of any meaning given by inherent connectedness — Greenberg describes how the individual needs to invent *"Modes of Dealing with Reality*, which are our own private systems of sorting, organizing, categorizing, symbolizing, and relating the inputs so that we can use them..." (p. 81, italics and capitals in original).

There are two crucial problems with this epistemology: By seeing knowledge as essentially "private," it discounts the complex relationship between individual and culture and supports the notion that freedom *from* all social imposition is not only possible, but ideal. Second, this atomistic view sanctions an exploitative, greed-driven economic system whose primary purpose is to "make [the world] fulfill our needs." This, in fact, was precisely Locke's and Adam Smith's ideological agenda, and it is politically, morally, and spiritually opposite to the holistic call for a more balanced and respectful relationship between human desires and the other inhabitants of the "biotic community" on earth (Orr 1994, 16).

Therefore, the idea of "freedom from" does not, by itself, provide a basis for a holistic understanding of freedom. It is only when we consider "freedom for" that we can come to a more sophisticated understanding of the nature of the human being than the modernist, materialist image of economic man. *For what purposes* should the person enjoy freedom? What are the highest or most essential expressions of the free human being? The libertarian would argue that we have no right to answer these questions for anyone but ourselves, that freedom itself will supply the answers, appropriate to each person's private dreams and destiny. This is an important point, if we are to avoid the sort of social engineering in which intellectuals and educators who claim to have discovered the truth about human existence often engage. But the libertarian/conservative "free market" view fails to consider the moral and spiritual consequences of the grossly competitive and materialist culture of the modern age. In this culture, we are strenuously conditioned *not* to ask questions about our true inner nature, nor about our interrelationship with the world we inhabit. While the perennial philosophy does encourage us to look for ourselves, it emphasizes that the deeper we look, the more our interconnectedness will be revealed to us. When we truly discover our essential being, we shall never again be able to think of ourselves, nor treat each other and the earth, as economic atoms. What might freedom mean then?

Holistic theorists have been approaching this question from two different but related perspectives: the ecological/cultural and the spiritual/epistemological. In the last three or four years, there has emerged a provocative literature on education for a postmodern, ecologically sustainable society. David Orr (1992, 1994), Gregory Smith (1992), C. A. Bowers (1993), and Gregory Cajete (1994), among others, have examined the cultural roots of the global environmental crisis, and all agree that the modernist overemphasis on individualism and personal freedom has shattered the communal, historical, and ecological obligations that traditional cultures universally place on their members — obligations that ensure cultural and ecological sustainability. *A global society of autonomous, competing, consuming economic atoms cannot survive because the earth's biosphere cannot indefinitely support it.* Personal freedom cannot be an absolute value but must be situated in a cultural context that recognizes the limits of economic development.

From a modernist point of view, these limits are seen as constraining to the individual (hence the ferocious backlash against the environmental movement), but from an indigenous (Cajete 1994) or postmodern perspective, such limits are experienced as an integral part of the person's identity as a member of the "biotic community." A major goal of holistic education is to develop the person's sense of relationship to the natural world, such that the individual is free *for* participating wholeheartedly in celebration of the wonder and mystery of life.

This is where the ecological/cultural theorists converge with the spiritual/epistemological thinkers. Bowers, especially, explores the relationship between ecology and epistemology, and in Cajete's Native American view, ecology and spirituality are intimately related. Additional insight comes from the holistic epistemology being worked out by education theorists such as Douglas Sloan (1994), Parker Palmer (1993), William Doll (1993), and Donald Oliver and Kathleen Gershman (1989). As they see it, the human being is not situated solely in a material world apprehended empirically (through "private systems of sorting, organizing, categorizing, symbolizing"), but in a purposeful, spiritual cosmos that can be experienced directly through insight, intuition, and meditative discipline. This holistic perspective is drawn from the thinking of Plato, Emerson, Rudolf Steiner, Alfred North Whitehead, Teilhard de Chardin, Gregory Bateson, David Bohm, Matthew Fox, and important religious figures such as Jesus and Buddha (see J. Miller 1988; 1994). Not all holistic thinkers employ religious language (some draw directly from science or from Whitehead's "process cosmology," for example), but ultimately both theistic and nontheistic holism involve a sense of awe and reverence toward the complex wholeness and unfathomable mystery of Creation.

Reverence engenders modesty, which calls for self-restraint. Freedom, according to a spiritual epistemology, is always engaged in a mutually nourishing relationship with its apparent opposite — discipline. In fact, according to this view, genuine freedom (freedom for the deepest expression of our humanity) is only achieved *through* discipline. There is a clear pattern, for example, in the history of alternative education movements, with libertarian dissidents emphasizing children's freedom and spiritually grounded pedagogies (best exemplified by the Montessori and Waldorf approaches) insisting that young people attain true freedom only through some definite educational structure (R. Miller 1992, 129).

Spiritual epistemology distinguishes between the personal ego — the social/psychological persona that is little more than a bundle of desires and fears — and the true self or divine spark that lies deeper within the personality (Del Prete 1990), which Montessori poetically called the "spiritual embryo." In order to break through the ego to discover this true self, the individual must be free from artificial restraints and social expectations, but at the same time, he or she must learn to temper personal wants and dislikes — that is, surrender a certain measure of freedom to moral and meditative discipline. Once the divine spark has been tapped and selfish desires are no longer one's primary motivation, *then* the person's "inherent worth" is truly revealed, and the individual has earned "a degree of freedom which rarely exists" in society, as Thoreau put it (in Metzger and Harding 1962, 37); his fellow transcendentalist Emerson even declared that "the appearance of character" — that is, the awakening of divinity within — "makes the State unnecessary" (Emerson 1965, 357).

Thus, a spiritual holism leads to a radically libertarian conclusion, but it is based on a conception of freedom other than the "freedom from" notion promulgated by materialist ideology. Rudolf Steiner's social vision, the "threefold" society, called for an entirely free cultural and intellectual life — that is, a system of education and a culture of art, science, and humanities entirely uncontrolled by either the economic or political spheres of society. There would, ideally, be no government schools. But before the followers of Adam Smith and Milton Friedman rush to embrace this plan, they should be reminded that freedom, for Steiner and other spiritual libertarians, is not a self-interested grasping for security by atomistic egos but a spiritual activity that arises from deep within the human soul; freedom does not set individuals apart from each other in pursuit of economic goods but unites them in the common task of the spiritual evolution of humanity. (Maria Montessori comments somewhere that "The world was not created for us to enjoy, but we were created in order to evolve the cosmos.") The key factor, as in the ecological understandings of holism, is *relationship*. A spiritual epistemology, as Parker Palmer (1993) describes so well, calls for a compassionate, participatory way of knowing and acting in the world, engaging the whole self rather than just the calculating ego. Education's task is to draw forth and cultivate this whole, connected self.

A third, and very important, body of literature has developed over the past decade that wonderfully weaves together the two holistic strands of ecology/culture and spirituality/epistemology: this is the feminist, or simply the feminine, perspective. It would seem that atomistic individualism is a characteristically male obsession[1] (Ayn Rand being a notable exception), and now that women are taking their rightful place in the arena of philosophical discourse and cultural critique, they are strongly articulating a perspective that emphasizes caring, nurturing, and the sustaining embrace of family and community (Ruddick 1989; Noddings 1984, 1992; Belenky, et. al., 1986; Sapon-Shevin 1990; Martin 1992; Wood 1991). This perspective is deeply enriched by feminist historical and cultural critiques (e.g., Merchant 1980; Griffin 1978), feminist theology (e.g., the work of Carol Christ and Rosemary Radford Reuther), and by female theorists who portray intimate connections between ecology and spirituality (Spretnak, 1982, 1991; Starhawk 1982; Plant 1989; Macy 1991; McFague 1987). Charlene Spretnak captures the essence of ecospiritual feminism in these words:

> If we believe, and experientially *know* through various practices such as meditation and holistic ritual, that neither our sisters and brothers nor the rest of nature is 'the other,' we will not violate their being, nor our own (in Plant 1989, 128).

Once again, the essential point is the cultivation of *relationships* between persons and between human beings and the rest of nature. In relationship, there is no dominating urge for "freedom-from" because the individual is willingly engaged with other persons and, indeed, identifies one's own interests with those of others. Certainly, feminist writers seek freedom from the patriarchal culture that has denied their experience and silenced their voice for centuries, but personal freedom, in the sense of an atomistic individualism, is not their primary goal. As the male holistic writers on ecology and spirituality have discovered, the freedom *for* being

---

[1] Why this is so is itself a complex issue, probably involving numerous biological, psychodynamic, and cultural factors, on which I shall not even begin to speculate.

most fully human necessarily involves connections and mutual obligations, which in turn require us to temper the demands of the individual ego.

Educational freedom, then, involves far more than freeing the child *from* an oppressive society. Although this is a necessary first step, especially if we are to defeat the destructive reductionism of Goals 2000, it is not enough. As the transcendentalists pointed out, the American Revolution has not been completed yet — indeed, on a moral and spiritual level, it has hardly begun. Who is this free being? Toward what ends, what possibilities, ought he or she to strive?

Freedom in Education

I am arguing that from a holistic perspective, educational freedom is always situated in a particular context involving the particular temperaments and developmental levels of the persons involved, the particular educational task at hand, and the particular social, economic, and cultural realities being experienced. A holistic educational environment is not fixed around a single notion of "freedom" but remains flexible and responsive to its changing situational context. I shall illustrate this point with the following account of conversations I have recently had with two very different kinds of alternative educators.

I was observing a second-grade Waldorf class, and as always, was struck by the beauty, care, and nurturing sense of order that characterize a Waldorf environment. The teacher was leading children through a series of activities that clearly were thoughtfully designed to tap into their multiple intelligences and diverse learning styles as well as the love of rhythm and colorful image that Rudolf Steiner, the founder of Waldorf education, believed children of this age to share universally. They were superb educational activities, I thought — but after a while I began to realize that the children had no freedom of choice; they were required to participate in these lessons, which followed each other one after another after another with virtually no interval. As I had noticed during other observations of Waldorf classrooms, the teacher was completely in command of this environment and the children seemed to have virtually no freedom to choose their own activities, speak with each other, or dwell in their own private thoughts. Afterward, I asked the teacher whether the Waldorf approach needed to be so thoroughly adult-controlled. I wondered whether the adult could supply a beautiful environment that would call to the child's nature, and then leave the child free to explore it. (I had in mind my own experience as a Montessori educator, though recognizing that a Waldorf "prepared environment" would emphasize imaginative and aesthetic elements more than the cognitive and empirical experience provided by the Montessori materials.)

"I was a public school teacher before I took Waldorf training," she replied, "and I used a progressive, open-classroom approach such as what you're describing. But I have come to see that children truly thrive when they are given the kind of guidance and support they receive here." Waldorf education would not work, she told me, without the strong guiding presence of the teacher.

Several weeks later, in a town not far away, I visited a lively little school modeled after the Sudbury Valley School, in which children are literally free to choose their own activities throughout the day. During the morning I spent there, I watched a group of children play Monopoly for well over two hours, another few playing with trucks and blocks, and others reading, playing computer games, or talking with friends. There was an (optional) school meeting, which was attended by five children. Later, I had a chance to interview the teachers, and asked whether there might be any positive value to having adults share their experience and knowledge with children in a structured way. Their answer was a mirror image of the Waldorf teacher's:

"We all began as public school teachers," they said, "and we believed in the open-classroom, integrated day approach. We started this school on that model, but after a while we began to feel that there was a subtle sort of coercion in planning learning activities for children rather than letting them pursue their own interests. Once we asked ourselves whether we truly trusted children's ability to make sense of the world, we knew we had to let go of our desire to control their learning."

The Waldorf educator sees unbounded freedom for young children as premature, as violating their innate developmental needs. The Waldorf approach is grounded in the understanding that the growing child possesses an unfolding spiritual identity, which needs to be guided carefully by adults who have themselves developed spiritually. Steiner insisted that in order to develop a genuine autonomous self in adulthood, the child up to age seven needs to imitate the adults in his or her environment, while the seven- to fourteen-year-old needs to have a definite adult authority figure to respect and emulate. On the other hand, the free school educators argue convincingly that a child who is trusted enough to govern his or her own life develops a secure sense of self-respect and self-discipline that are essential qualities for maintaining a democratic society based on individual rights. In a handout I obtained at the libertarian school I visited, one of the school's founders claimed that *all* other educational approaches are rooted in mistrust for "the miracle of [children's] ability to learn" (Werner-Gavrin n.d.). All forms of progressive education (including presumably Waldorf and Montessori) are categorized as the "velvet glove" approach — with the adult's "iron fist" (control over what, how, and when children learn) merely concealed by a veneer of kind words and fun activities. This is an extreme statement (too extreme, as I will argue in a moment), but it does highlight the importance of personal freedom.

It would be very interesting if we could obtain clear empirical validation either for Steiner's view — which was supposedly derived from his mystical insight into "spiritual worlds" — or for the libertarian position, which is so closely tied to an adult ideological agenda. It does seem that graduates of Waldorf education in fact develop an especially rich inner life, a deeper sensitivity and feeling for the wonder, beauty, and mystery of the world, because their souls' capacity for wonder and connection has been so carefully tended. On the other hand, partisans of free schools frequently claim that their graduates lead happy, meaningful, productive, self-directed lives, which is a great deal more than we can say for the average graduate of conventional schools, and not exactly what Steiner predicted for children given such freedom. Is it fair to wonder whether Steiner's warning against premature freedom rests on his own bias (or cultural/historical context) as much as on some absolute spiritual truth?

The holistic perspective is suspicious of claims of absolute truth and would acknowledge the paradox that there are important pedagogical truths in both the Waldorf emphasis on careful guidance and the libertarian insistence on freedom. While guidance and structure are necessary aspects of cultivating the soul, a child's life should not *entirely* be bound by discipline. In a child's life — in any person's life — there is a time for discipline, and a time for freedom. After several visits to Waldorf schools as a prospective parent, I finally decided not to enroll my children there, however nourishing the activities, because I value the experience of freedom and children's opportunities to pursue their own questions and interests.[2]

In a compelling discussion of the need for psychological balance, Bernie Neville (1989) considered the pantheon of Olympic gods as universal archetypes and concluded that all have an important place in the human psyche and hence in education. To perpetrate Apollonian rationality or a Promethean quest for power at the expense of Dionysian or Erotic joy is surely wrong — as the romantics and educational dissenters have told us over the years. But so too, said Neville, is it imbalanced to cultivate Dionysian freedom without rational discipline or the authority of the Zeus or Senex ("old man") archetype. The denial of any archetypal energies, he argued, leads to a distorted caricature of human development. (It is noteworthy that he sees Psyche — a feminine archetype — as the symbol of wholeness.)

To dismiss all adult intervention, then, as "mistrust" of the child's innate powers or to lump together a wide range of pedagogical approaches under the sinister rubric "velvet glove" is to remain stuck in an atomistic conception of human nature — the autonomous individual versus the coercive authority of society. The child's ability and desire to learn *is* miraculous, as libertarian educators such as John Holt (1989) have always insisted. But this does not mean that learning takes place in a social, cultural, ecological, and spiritual vacuum (R. Miller 1991, Spring). Holt and others like to point out how children learn to speak without adult instruction, but if learning were as completely autonomous as they suggest, there would be no cases of "feral" children who are unable to speak because they had no adult humans who responded to them at the critical time of language development. Steiner, Montessori, Vygotsky, Dewey, and other advocates

---

[2] I did not find any school in my area that satisfied my expectations of holistic education and have since helped launch a new alternative school which will, I hope, embody the principles I have been advocating for the past decade. For information, contact The Bellwether School and Family Resource Center, 120 South Brownell Rd., Williston, Vermont 05495.

of the "velvet glove" approach recognized, as atomistic individualists do not, that learning is not merely a private activity but an interactive one.

The miracle of human learning is that it is a highly complex process through which the person establishes relationships with the world. Relationship requires mutuality, dialogue, and responsibility as the essential complements of freedom. A libertarian education certainly turns out self-reliant people who value their rights (and respect those of other individuals); but, if the holistic perspective suggested by theorists in ecology, spirituality, and feminism is correct, there are vital dimensions of human experience that remain uncultivated, perhaps untouched except in sporadic and haphazard ways, when young people receive from their elders nothing but unadulterated doses of freedom. The art of holistic education involves responding authentically — that is, from wholeness and balance — to the children, to the subject matter, and to the social/cultural milieu of the living situation without having to follow a theory or method that rigidly dictates what one must or must not do, let alone a curriculum dictated by government bureaucrats. *This* is freedom in education.

The educational moment is defined by a child's (or a group of children's) emotional, psychological, and intellectual readiness, by an event (such as a war or solar eclipse) that compels attention, by a topic of special interest sparked by someone's personal experience or urgent question, and by what is taking place in the community outside the school door. An education that responds to these factors — a holistic education — needs to be informed by a wide range of experience and theoretical understanding: by developmental insight, by the pedagogical ingenuity of progressive and other open classroom educators, by a keen sensitivity to children's inner lives as well as their academic behavior, and by a social and ecological conscience. Such an educational approach cannot be condensed into a specific method; it is the cultivation within the teacher of qualities such as authenticity, empathy, mindful presence, and responsiveness to each unfolding moment. What these qualities look like in practice has been described first hand both in recent literature (e.g., Ayers 1993; Logan 1993; Kessler 1991; J. Miller 1993b, 1994; Palmer 1993) and in earlier accounts such as George Dennison's *The Lives of Children* (1969) and Carl Rogers's *Freedom to Learn* (1969) — classic works that both led me to holistic education in the first place. I am convinced that Steiner and Montessori also advocated this existentially responsive approach to teaching, before their creative innovations became hardened into near-religious dogma.

All of these master teachers have certainly been concerned with freedom in education because this authentic responsiveness is impossible in a situation dictated by political, economic, or ideological mandates. Yet they have all recognized that structure, discipline, and the wisdom of maturity are essential elements of a humane, compassionate, and liberating education as well. The interconnection between freedom and structure has implications, not only for pedagogy but for the vitality of democratic life in the larger society. The philosophical and pedagogical issues we are considering here have significant ideological implications. Does the desire for freedom translate automatically into a social system of atomistic free market capitalism? The holistic perspective points to other possibilities. If the notion of freedom takes on new meanings in different contexts, so too does the exalted concept of democracy.

Education and Democracy

Dissenting educators have often been deeply concerned with the role of schools in building a viable democratic society; probably none have expressed these concerns as consistently as have the progressive educators. The leading theorists of progressive education — Dewey, Parker, Counts, Kilpatrick, Bode, Brameld, Washburne, Kallen, and others — discussed at great length the connection between democracy in the school setting and democracy in society at large. In strong language, they argued that conventional classroom routines, with teachers controlling the curriculum as well as students' activities, represented an elitist, hierarchical, even "aristocratic" social order. They asserted that young people could not be expected to appreciate, much less engage in, a participatory democracy if during their formative years they were subjected to a rigid authoritarian system. Progressive educators often describe schools as "democratic public spheres" — as one of the few places where people may deliberately practice cooperation, respect for diversity, and nonviolent conflict resolution. In democratic schools, children are free to do independent research and practice democratic rituals such as town meetings, and educators may engage their students in critical questioning of society's various ills. It is not surprising that the movement was viciously attacked during the conservative crusade of the 1950s (R. Miller 1992).

However, progressive education diverged into two complementary but ultimately separate factions, which are historically known as the "child-centered" and "social reconstructionist" wings. The former emerged during the 1920s (another conservative era) when progressive educators felt that social reform was impossible; social reconstructionism was a response to the Depression, when social reform appeared to many to be a vital necessity. Later generations of progressive educators have also tended to fall into one or the other of these camps: Many of the "progressive" private day schools and boarding schools that tend to serve affluent families and many of the "free" schools that emerged after the 1960s concentrate on freedom of thought and action within the school setting; on the other hand, the critical pedagogy movement and activist educators aligned with "progressive" liberal politics have emphasized the role that schools should play in a larger social movement for economic and racial equity, justice, and nonviolence — in other words, social reconstruction.

There has always been a tension between these two perspectives. Reconstructionists like George Counts (1932) and Jonathan Kozol (1972) have been sharply critical of child-centered educators for avoiding larger social and cultural problems, while many alternative and humanistic educators have viewed political activism as tainting children's natural learning processes with adults' ideological agendas (Reitman [1992] offers a coherent statement of this position from a progressive perspective.) From a holistic point of view, however, a viable democratic society requires both personal freedom *and* social responsibility; education for a democratic society means allowing children freedom to develop according to their own unique (and ultimately spiritual) destinies and to follow their own personal interests *as well as* challenging them to engage their social and political milieu critically (Purpel and Miller 1991).

Dewey's theory of democracy had, in fact, sought to integrate personal development with social reconstruction, but the progressive agenda broke down into rival factions because Dewey and his followers did not understand freedom in a large enough context. They defined the human

being as essentially a social animal and saw the critical problems of education and democracy in terms of socialization. Consequently, the more
"tough minded" among them (to use a phrase William James coined in
another context) became concerned with fighting oppressive forces in
society, while the more "tender minded" have avoided this difficult battle
and concentrated on freeing persons individually from oppressive socialization. The "tough minded" reconstructionist argues that collective action
is necessary to overcome the selfish individualism underlying an exploitative economic system, while the "tender-minded," child-centered progressives, true to their romantic and transcendentalist heritage, fear that collec-
tivism tends to endanger personal individuality.

From a holistic perspective, both positions contain valid insights, and
their polarization is unfortunate and unnecessary. Both the reconstructionist and child-centered views rest on a simplistic dichotomy between person
and society that ignores the much more complex pattern of cultural and
ecological interconnections linking them (Bowers 1993). When we situate
human existence in ecological and spiritual contexts as well as the social,
the human being is seen not merely as a social animal but as a seeker and
maker of meaning who inhabits a complex "ecology of mind" (Gregory
Bateson's phrase). As the perennial philosophy has taught us, there is in this
interconnectedness a mutual relationship between person and society that
involves freedom as well as commitment to values and ideals larger than
oneself. Personal freedom in a holistic cultural context does not lead to
atomistic self-indulgence but to an awakened sense of connectedness with
all of life. The individual becomes free *for* collective action in the service of
justice and compassion. Social reconstruction, then, would not merely
involve partisan political struggle, but the moral and spiritual development
of the persons who make up society, which is not only a proper educational
task, but the defining task of holistic education (Purpel 1989).

The campaign for national educational goals and standards threatens
to uproot democratic values from the very heart of the educational process.
If we would aim for the kind of democracy that Emerson and Thoreau
envisioned, in which the most vital energies and highest possibilities of
human beings are encouraged to flourish, then education must be a process
of human engagement that awakens and nourishes our wholeness. This

will require a great measure of freedom, a great deal of guidance and discipline, and above all, a great commitment to respond authentically in each moment of educational encounter. Clearly, as educators become more heavily burdened by political and economic agendas imposed by hierarchical institutions, they become less and less able to respond authentically at any moment of the teaching and learning relationship. It is absolutely vital that they reclaim the freedom to do so.

References

Ayers, William (1993). *To Teach: The Journey of a Teacher*. New York: Teachers College Press.

Belenky, Mary F., Blythe M. Clinchy, Nancy R. Goldberger, and Jill M. Tarule (1986). *Women's Ways of Knowing*. New York: Basic Books.

Bowers, C. A. (1993). *Education, Cultural Myths, and the Ecological Crisis: Toward Deep Changes*. Albany: SUNY Press.

Branden, Nathaniel (1969). *The Psychology of Self-Esteem*. Los Angeles: Nash.

Cajete, Gregory (1994). *Look to the Mountain: An Ecology of Indigenous Education*. Durango, CO: Kivaki Press.

Clark, Edward T. (1988). The Search for a New Educational Paradigm: The Implications of New Assumptions About Thinking and Learning. *Holistic Education Review* 1, no. 1 (Spring): 18–30.

Counts, George S. (1932). *Dare the School Build a New Social Order?* New York: John Day.

Del Prete, Thomas (1990). *Thomas Merton and the Education of the Whole Person*. Birmingham, AL: Religious Education Press.

Dennison, George (1969). *The Lives of Children: The Story of the First Street School*. New York: Random House.

Doll, William E. (1993). *A Post-Modern Perspective on Curriculum*. New York: Teachers College Press.

Emerson, Ralph W. (1965). *Selected Writings*. Edited by William H. Gilman. New York: New American Library.

Goodman, Paul (1964). *Compulsory Mis-Education and the Community of Scholars*. New York: Vintage/Random House.

Greenberg, Daniel (1994). *Worlds in Creation*. Framingham, MA: Sudbury Valley School Press.

Griffin, Susan (1978). *Women and Nature*. New York: Harper and Row.

Holt, John (1989). *Learning All the Time*. Reading, MA: Addison Wesley.

Kessler, Shelley (1991). The Teaching Presence. *Holistic Education Review* 4, no. 4 (Winter): 4-15.

Kozol, Jonathan (1972). *Free Schools*. Boston: Houghton Mifflin.

Logan, Judy (1993). *Teaching Stories*. Plymouth, MN: Minnesota Inclusiveness Program.

Macy, Joanna (1991). *World as Lover, World as Self*. Berkeley: Parallax Press.

Mander, Jerry (1991). *In the Absence of the Sacred: The Failure of Technology & the Survival of the Indian Nations*. San Francisco: Sierra Club Books.

Martin, Jane Roland (1992). *The Schoolhome: Rethinking Schools for Today's Families*. Cambridge: Harvard University Press.

McFague, Sallie (1987). *Models of God: Theology for an Ecological, Nuclear Age*. Philadelphia: Fortress.

Merchant, Carolyn (1980). *The Death of Nature: Women, Ecology and the Scientific Revolution*. San Francisco: Harper & Row.

Metzger, Milton, and Walter Harding (1962). *A Thoreau Profile*. Concord, MA: Thoreau Foundation.

Miller, John P. (1988). *The Holistic Curriculum*. Toronto: Ontario Institute for Studies in Education Press.

Miller, John P. (1993a). Worldviews, Educational Orientations, and Holistic Education. In *The Renewal of Meaning in Education: Responses to the Cultural and Ecological Crisis of our Times*, ed. Ron Miller. Brandon, VT: Holistic Education Press.

Miller, John P. (1993b). *The Holistic Teacher*. Toronto: Ontario Institute for Studies in Education Press.

Miller, John P. (1994). *The Contemplative Practitioner: Meditation in Education and the Professions*. Westport, CT: Bergin & Garvey/Greenwood.

Miller, Ron (1991). Review of *Learning All the Time* (John Holt) and *Child's Work* (Nancy Wallace). *Holistic Education Review* 4, no. 1. (Spring): 62–65.

Miller, Ron (1991). Holism and Meaning: Foundations for a Coherent Holistic Theory. *Holistic Education Review* 4, no. 3 (Fall): 23–32.

Miller, Ron (1992). *What Are Schools For? Holistic Education in American Culture* (2nd. edition). Brandon, VT: Holistic Education Press.

Neville, Bernie (1989). *Educating Psyche: Emotion, Imagination and the Unconscious in Learning*. Blackburn, Australia: Collins Dove.

Noddings, Nel (1984). *Caring: A Feminine Approach to Ethics and Moral Education*. Berkeley: University of California Press.

Noddings, Nel (1992). *The Challenge to Care in Schools: An Alternative Approach to Education*. New York: Teachers College Press.

Oliver, Donald W., and Kathleen Gershman (1989). *Education, Modernity, and Fractured Meaning: Toward a Process Theory of Teaching and Learning*. Albany: SUNY Press.

Orr, David W. (1992). *Ecological Literacy*. Albany: SUNY Press.

Orr, David W. (1994). *Earth in Mind: On Education, Environment, and the Human Prospect*. Washington, D.C.: Island Press.

Palmer, Parker (1993). *To Know as We Are Known: Education as a Spiritual Journey*. San Francisco: Harper San Francisco.

Plant, Judith, ed. (1989). *Healing the Wounds: The Promise of Ecofeminism*. Philadelphia: New Society Publishers.

Purpel, David (1989). *The Moral and Spiritual Crisis in Education: A Curriculum for Justice and Compassion in Education*. Westport, CT: Bergin & Garvey/Greenwood.

Purpel, David, and Ron Miller (1991). How Whole is Holistic Education? *Holistic Education Review* 4, no. 2, (Summer): 33–36.

Reitman, Sanford W. (1992). *The Educational Messiah Complex: American Faith in the Culturally Redemptive Power of Schooling*. Sacramento: Caddo Gap Press.

Rifkin, Jeremy (1991). *Biosphere Politics: A Cultural Odyssey from the Middle Ages to the New Age*. San Francisco: Harper San Francisco.

Rogers, Carl (1969). *Freedom to Learn*. Columbus: Charles E. Merrill.

Roszak, Theodore (1973). *Where the Wasteland Ends: Politics and Transcendence in Postindustrial Society*. Garden City, NY: Anchor/Doubleday.

Ruddick, Sara (1989). *Maternal Thinking: Towards a Politics of Peace*. Boston: Beacon Press.

Sapon-Shevin, Mara (1990). Schools as Communities of Love and Caring. *Holistic Education Review* 3, no. 2 (Summer): 22–24.

Sloan, Douglas (1994). *Insight-Imagination: The Emancipation of Thought and the Modern World*. Brandon, VT: Resource Center for Redesigning Education.

Smith, Gregory A. (1992). *Education and the Environment: Learning to Live With Limits*. Albany: SUNY Press.

Smith, Huston (1989). *Beyond the Post-Modern Mind*. Wheaton, IL: Quest Books.

Spretnak, Charlene (1982). *The Politics of Women's Spirituality: Essays on the Rise of Spiritual Power Within the Feminist Movement*. Garden City, NY: Anchor/Doubleday.

Spretnak, Charlene (1991). *States of Grace: The Recovery of Meaning in the Postmodern Age*. San Francisco: Harper San Francisco.

Starhawk (1982). *Dreaming the Dark: Magic, Sex and Politics*. Boston: Beacon Press.

Werner-Gavrin, Marc (n.d.). Trust, Control and Education. Unpublished paper.

Wood, Chip (1991). Maternal Teaching: Revolution of Kindness. *Holistic Education Review* 4, no. 2 (Summer): 3–10.

Additional Resources

Books

Arons, Stephen. *Compelling Belief: The Culture of American Schooling*. New York: McGraw Hill, 1983.

✔ Bethel, Dayle M. (ed.). *Compulsory Schooling and Human Learning: The Moral Failure of Public Education in America and Japan*. San Francisco: Caddo Gap Press, 1994.

✔ Bigelow, Bill, Linda Christensen, Stan Karp, Barbara Miner & Bob Peterson (eds.). *Rethinking Our Classrooms: Teaching for Equity and Justice*. Milwaukee: Rethinking Schools, 1994.

✔ Bowers, C. A. *Educating for an Ecologically Sustainable Culture: Rethinking Moral Education, Creativity, Intelligence, and Other Modern Orthodoxies*. Albany, NY: SUNY Press, 1995.

Gatto, John Taylor. *Dumbing Us Down: The Hidden Curriculum of Compulsory Schooling*. Philadelphia: New Society Publishers, 1992.

Note: All of the titles preceded by a check mark (✔) are available from the Resource Center for Redesigning Education, P.O. Box 298, Brandon, Vermont 05733-0298. (1-800-639-4122). A catalog of extensive reviews of hard-to-find books and videos in education is available without charge.

✔ Howe, Harold. *Thinking About Our Kids: An Agenda for American Education.* New York: Free Press, 1993.

✔ Levine, David, Robert Lowe, Bob Peterson, and Rita Tenorio (eds.). *Rethinking Schools: An Agenda for Change.* New York: New Press, 1995.

✔ Miller, Ron (ed.) *The Renewal of Meaning in Education: Responses to the Cultural and Ecological Crisis of our Times.* Brandon, VT: Holistic Education Press, 1993.

✔ Moffett, James. *The Universal Schoolhouse: Spiritual Awakening Through Education.* San Francisco: Jossey-Bass. 1994.

✔ Noddings, Nel. *The Challenge to Care in Schools: An Alternative Approach to Education.* New York: Teachers College Press, 1992.

✔ Purpel, David. *The Moral & Spiritual Crisis in Education: A Curriculum for Justice & Compassion in Education.* New York: Bergin & Garvey, 1989.

✔ Purpel, David and Svi Shapiro. *Beyond Liberation & Excellence: Reconstructing the Public Discourse on Education.* Westport, CT: Bergin & Garvey, 1995.

✔ Reitman, Sanford W. *The Educational Messiah Complex: American Faith in the Culturally Redemptive Power of Schooling.* Sacramento: Caddo Gap Press, 1992.

Renyi, Judith. *Going Public: Schooling for a Diverse Democracy.* New York: New Press, 1993.

Richards, Mary C. *Toward Wholeness: Rudolf Steiner Education in America.* Middletown, CT: Wesleyan University Press, 1980.

Shannon, Patrick. *Broken Promises: Reading Instruction in Twentieth-Century America.* New York: Bergin & Garvey, 1989.

✔ Sloan, Douglas. *Insight-Imagination: The Emancipation of Thought and the Modern World.* Brandon, VT: Resource Center for Redesigning Education, 1994.

✔ Stoddard, Lynn. *Growing Greatness: Six Amazing Attitudes of Extraordinary Teachers and Parents.* Tucson: Zephyr Press, 1995.

✔ Wood, George H. *Schools that Work: America's Most Innovative Public Education Programs.* New York: Dutton, 1992.

Organizations and Publications

Alliance for Parental Involvement in Education
P.O. Box 59, East Chatham, NY 12060-0059
(518) 392-6900

AEROGRAM Newsletter
Alternative Education Resource Organization
417 Roslyn Road, Roslyn Heights, NY 11577
(516) 621-2195

Global Alliance for Transforming Education
P.O. Box 21, Grafton, VT 05146
(802) 843-2382

Holistic Education Review
P.O. Box 328, Brandon, VT 05733-0328
(800) 639-4122

Holt Associates
2269 Massachusetts Ave., Cambridge, MA 02140
(617) 864-3100

Home Education Magazine

P.O. Box 1083, Tonasket, WA 98855

(509) 486-1351

National Coalition of Alternative Community Schools

P.O. Box 15036, Santa Fe, NM 87504

(505) 474-4312

Separation of School and State Alliance

4578 N. First, #310, Fresno, CA 93726

(209) 292-1776

SKOLE: The Journal of Alternative Education

72 Philip St., Albany, NY 12202

(518) 432-1578

The Threefold Review

Social Renewal Foundation

P.O. Box 6, Philmont, NY 12565

(518) 672-5605

Contributors

Stephen Arons is an attorney and Professor of Legal Studies at the University of Massachusetts at Amherst. He has been studying, litigating, teaching, and writing about issues of intellectual and cultural freedom in schooling for twenty-five years. His latest book, which deals with conscience and community in public schooling, is due from the University of Massachusetts Press in 1996.

Harold Berlak is an evaluation consultant, researcher, and educational activist living in Oakland, California. He is also an editor and author of numerous articles and three books that deal with educational policy, evaluation, curriculum, and pedagogy. His most recent book is *Toward a New Science of Educational Testing and Assessment* (SUNY Press, 1992).

Linda Dobson loves to learn, learns to live, and lives to love at home and in the community with her children/teachers Erika and Adam. (Chuck's the one who "graduated.") Eager to share what she discovers, she has authored dozens of magazine and journal articles on home education as well as continuing workshops and talks. Linda is News Watch columnist for *Home Education Magazine*, presenting in-depth coverage and commentary on national media reports on the topic, and is author of *The Art of Education: Reclaiming Your Family, Community and Self* (1995, Home Education Press, Tonasket, WA).

Pat Farenga started work at Holt Associates/*Growing Without Schooling* (GWS) in 1981, working and learning with the late teacher and author John Holt, and he continues Holt's work today, acting as president of Holt Associates and publisher of GWS. He writes and speaks often about homeschooling and learning outside of schools and has appeared on national TV and other media. He homeschools his three girls (9, 6, 2) with his wife, Day, who is office manager at Holt/GWS — an office where children of all ages are welcome to observe, read, play, or participate.

Katharine Houk is the executive director of the Alliance for Parental Involvement in Education and a co-founder and council member of The Alternative Learning Center. She and her husband Seth Rockmuller live in Chatham, New York, with two of their three children (ages 13, 16, and 25), and they have for many years been involved in public, private, and home education — both professionally and within their own family.

Jeffrey Kane is Dean of Adelphi University's School of Education. He serves as the Executive Editor of *Holistic Education Review* (P.O. Box 328, Brandon, VT 05733). His writings in education journals and books are focused on the intuitive foundations of knowledge and on the nature of educational freedom. His works include *Beyond Empiricism: Michael Polanyi Reconsidered* and *In Fear of Freedom: Public Education and Democracy in America*. Dr. Kane lives on Long Island with his wife Janet and their three children, Gabriel, Emily, and Jesse.

Gary Lamb is President of the Social Renewal Foundation, Inc., which administers a privately funded voucher program, Hope Through Education, in the Albany, New York, area. It enables low income families to send their children to private schools. He is the co-editor of *The Threefold Review*, based on the social ideas of Rudolf Steiner, that views the social organism not as a unitary state, but "consisting of three spheres, each requiring its own distinct basis — cultural life, political life, and the economy."

Ronald Milito has a D.Ed. in biophysics, is a trained human anatomist, and has been a teacher and researcher for twenty years. He has taught middle school, high school,and university level courses in human anatomy and physiology, mathematics, chemistry, physics, biology, and health science. His main interests include the epistemology of Rudolf Steiner, Goethean science, and the history of science. He writes out of insights gained from Waldorf education on issues such as homework, testing, grading, and government control of education. He is currently engaged in writing a book on threefold patterns in human anatomy and physiology.

Ron Miller is an independent scholar and activist in alternative and holistic education. He founded the journal *Holistic Education Review* in 1988 and the book review publication *Great Ideas in Education* in 1993. His previous books include *What Are Schools For? Holistic Education in American*

Culture, and two volumes he edited: *New Directions in Education* and *The Renewal of Meaning in Education: Responses to the Cultural and Ecological Crisis of Our Times*. He helped organize The Bellwether School and Family Resource Center, which opened near Burlington, Vermont, in September 1995.

James Moffett is a national consultant, workshop leader, lecturer, and author in language education and total learning environments. He has taught at Phillips Exeter Academy and served on the faculties of Harvard, the University of California, Berkeley, San Diego State, and Middlebury College's Bread Loaf School of English. He is the author of several books including, most recently, *Storm in the Mountains* (1988), *Harmonic Learning* (1992), and *The Universal Schoolhouse* (1994).

Nel Noddings is Lee L. Jacks Professor of Child Education at Stanford. Her area of special interest is philosophy of education and, within that, ethics, moral education, and mathematics education. Her latest book is *Educating for Intelligent Belief and Unbelief*.

Gerald Porter, Ph.D., has variously worked as a psychologist and policy analyst in several New York State government agencies where he developed some expertise on issues related to the so-called at-risk and minority populations. In 1991, he joined the faculty of the School Psychology Program in the School of Education at the University at Albany, SUNY. His research and publications focus on the issues of diversity, nonordinary human experience, spirituality, and moral reasoning within the context of both education and psychotherapy.

David Purpel is Professor of Education at the University of North Carolina, Greensboro. He has written in the field of curriculum, teacher education, and moral education and is the author of *The Moral and Spiritual Crisis in Education* (1989) and (with Svi Shapiro) *Beyond Excellence and Liberation* (1995). His teaching and writing focus on the relationships among society, culture, and education, with particular interest in issues of social justice.

Seth Rockmuller is an attorney concentrating in education law and serves as the president of the Alliance for Parental Involvement in Education, a nonprofit organization that provides information and resources about the many educational options available to families.

Patrick Shannon is a former preschool and primary grade teacher who now teaches at Penn State University in the College of Education. He is a Trustee of the Research Foundation for the National Council of Teachers of English and of the State College Friends School. His most recent books are *Becoming Political: Readings and Writings in the Politics of Literacy Education* (Heinemann, 1992), *Basal Readers: A Second Look* (with Ken Goodman) (Richard C. Owen, 1994), and *Text, Lies & Videotape: Stories about Learning, Literacy and Life* (Heinemann, 1995). He is working on a book about the struggle over the definition of childhood in the United States and what that means for literacy education.

Lynn Stoddard is a retired elementary school teacher (10 years) and principal (26 years) who now spends much of his time trying to influence major changes in public education through his writings and workshops. He has written two books, *Redesigning Education* and *Growing Greatness*, and several articles for educational journals. For the past five years he has served on the steering committee of the Global Alliance for Transforming Education (GATE) and is looking for new avenues to promote an unorthodox vision. Lynn and his wife live in Utah surrounded by nine of their twelve children and most of their thirty-four grandchildren.